Personal Connections in the Digital Age

2nd edition

Digital Media and Society Series

Nancy Baym, *Personal Connections in the Digital Age 2nd edition*
Jean Burgess and Joshua Green, *YouTube*
Mark Deuze, *Media Work*
Andrew Dubber, *Radio in the Digital Age*
Charles Ess, *Digital Media Ethics 2nd edition*
Jordan Frith, *Smartphones as Locative Media*
Alexander Halavais, *Search Engine Society*
Martin Hand, *Ubiquitous Photography*
Robert Hassan, *The Information Society*
Tim Jordan, *Hacking*
Graeme Kirkpatrick, *Computer Games and the Social Imaginary*
Leah Lievrouw, *Alternative and Activist New Media*
Rich Ling and Jonathan Donner, *Mobile Communication*
Donald Matheson and Stuart Allan, *Digital War Reporting*
Dhiraj Murthy, *Twitter*
Jill Walker Rettberg, *Blogging 2nd edition*
Patrik Wikström, *The Music Industry 2nd edition*
Zizi A. Papacharissi, *A Private Sphere: Democracy in a Digital Age*

Personal Connections in the Digital Age

2nd edition

Nancy K. Baym

polity

Copyright © Nancy K. Baym 2015

The right of Nancy K. Baym to be identified as Author of this Work has been asserted in accordance with the UK Copyright, Designs and Patents Act 1988.

First published in 2015 by Polity Press

Reprinted 2016, 2017 (twice), 2018, 2019, 2020 (twice)

Polity Press
65 Bridge Street
Cambridge CB2 1UR, UK

Polity Press
350 Main Street
Malden, MA 02148, USA

ISBN-13: 978-0-7456-7033-1
ISBN-13: 978-0-7456-7034-8(pb)

A catalogue record for this book is available from the British Library.

Library of Congress Cataloging-in-Publication Data

Baym, Nancy K.
    Personal connections in the digital age / Nancy K. Baym.
      pages cm
    Revised edition of the author's Personal connections in the digital age, published in 2010.
    Includes bibliographical references and index.
    ISBN 978-0-7456-7033-1 (hardback : alk. paper) – ISBN 978-0-7456-7034-8 (paperback : alk. paper) 1. Interpersonal relations. 2. Interpersonal relations--Technological innovations. 3. Internet--Social aspects. 4. Cell phones--Social aspects. I. Title.
    HM1106.B38 2015
    302.23–dc23
                  2014042519

Typeset in 10.25/13 FF Scala by
Servis Filmsetting Limited, Stockport, Cheshire
Printed and bound by CPI Group (UK) Ltd, Croydon, CR0 4YY

The publisher has used its best endeavours to ensure that the URLs for external websites referred to in this book are correct and active at the time of going to press. However, the publisher has no responsibility for the websites and can make no guarantee that a site will remain live or that the content is or will remain appropriate.

Every effort has been made to trace all copyright holders, but if any have been inadvertently overlooked the publisher will be pleased to include any necessary credits in any subsequent reprint or edition.

For further information on Polity, visit our website:
politybooks.com

Contents

Illustrations		vii
Acknowledgements		viii
1	**New forms of personal connection**	1
	New media, new boundaries	2
	Plan of the book	6
	Seven key concepts	6
	Digital media	13
	Who uses new digital media?	19
2	**Making new media make sense**	24
	Technological determinism	27
	Social construction of technology	44
	Social shaping of technology	51
	Domestication of technology	52
3	**Communication in digital spaces**	57
	Mediation as impoverishment	58
	Putting social cues into digital communication	67
	Digital language as a mixed modality	71
	Contextual influences on online communication	74
	Summary	79
4	**Communities and networks**	81
	Online community	82
	Networks	100
	Engagement with place-based community	102
	Summary	110

5 New relationships, new selves?   112
   New relationships online   113
   Identity   118
   Identity cues   123
   Summary   140

6 Digital media in everyday relationships   142
   Building relationships with people we meet online   143
   Mediated relational maintenance   151
   Uncertain norms   168
   Summary   172

Conclusion: the myth of cyberspace   174

   References   180
   Index of names   212
   General index   218

Illustrations

2.1 "The pace of modern life"; Randall Munroe;   *page* 30–31
    © Randall Monroe (xkcd.com)
2.2 "Hold the line a minute dear . . ."; Barbara Shermund,
    1927; © Barbara Shermund / Condé Nast   35
2.3 "We met online"; David Sipress, 2004; © David Sipress /
    Condé Nast   36
2.4 "On the Internet, nobody knows you're a dog"; Peter
    Steiner, 1993; © Peter Steiner / Condé Nast   37
2.5 "How the hell does Facebook know I'm a dog?"; Rob
    Cottingham, 2010; © Rob Cottingham /
    RobCottingham.ca/cartoon   39
2.6 Leonard Dove, 1962; © Leonard Dove / Condé Nast   42
2.7 "Simple answers"; Randall Munroe; © Randall Munroe
    (xkcd.com)   45
6.1 Joel Orff, 2006   144

Acknowledgements

Thanks to my editor Andrea Drugan, and everyone at Polity who's helped. Thanks to those who gave feedback, including Natalie Bazarova, danah boyd, Nicole Ellison, Keith Hampton, Kate Miltner, and Steve Schirra. Jeff Hall, Adrianne Kunkel, Kiley Larson, Andrew Ledbetter, Mei-Chen Lin, Michelle McCudden, Ryan Milner, Kate Miltner, and Yan Bing Zhang collaborated with me on some of my research discussed here. Kate Miltner, Natalie Pennington, Meryl Alper, Scott Campbell, Lynn Cherny, Alice Daer, Rebecca Hoffman, Holly Kruse, Adrianne Kunkel, Sonia Livingston, Alice Marwick, Joshua McVeigh-Schultz, and Jessica Vitak helped point me to additional readings. I also thank Kiley, Ryan, Kate, Steve, and Rebecca for editing and manuscript-preparation help. Markus Slivka has my eternal gratitude for letting me use him as an example and for his friendship. Many thanks to the cartoonists for such wonderful work and letting me use it, especially Joel Orff, Randall Munroe, and Rob Cottingham. This book owes much to the students who took my courses about personal relationships and new technology at the University of Kansas. There would be no second edition were it not for the people who have read and taught the first. This edition has been improved considerably by comments from and conversations with them in person, via email, on Skype, and on Twitter. It has also been deeply enriched by my colleagues and visitors at Microsoft Research. Finally, I wouldn't be who I am without my family, whose support sustains me in every medium. I thank them most of all.

1

New forms of personal connection

There have never been more ways to communicate with one another than there are right now. Once limited to face-to-face conversation, over the last several millennia we have steadily developed new technologies for interaction. The digital age is distinguished by rapid transformations in the kinds of technological mediation through which we encounter one another. Face-to-face conversation, landline telephone calls, and postal mail have been joined by email, mobile phone calls, text messaging, instant messaging, chat, web boards, social networks, photo sharing, video sharing, multiplayer gaming, and more. People have always responded to new media with confusion. In this time of rapid innovation and diffusion, it's natural to be concerned about their effects on our relationships.

When first faced with a new barrage of interpersonal communication media, people tend to react in one of two ways, both of which have long cultural histories. On the one hand, people express concern that our communication has become increasingly shallow. For many, the increased amount of mediated interaction seems to threaten the sanctity of our personal relationships. On the other, new media offer the promise of more opportunity for connection with more people, leading to stronger and more diverse relationships. Both perspectives reflect a sense that digital media are changing the nature of our social connections. Over time, as we get used to new communication media, people come to see them in more nuanced ways. Eventually they become so taken for granted they are all but invisible. These moments in which they are new and the norms for their use are in flux offer fresh opportunities to think about our technologies, our connections, and the relationships amongst them.

The purpose of this book is to provide a means of thinking critically about the roles of digital media and devices in personal relationships. Rather than providing exuberant accounts or cautionary tales, this book provides a theoretical and data-grounded primer on how to make sense of these important changes in relational life. I began paying attention to these issues in 1990, launched my first research project into interpersonal communication over the internet in 1991, and began teaching courses in communication and new technology in Communication departments in 1994. The material in this book draws on my research projects, observations, and the large and growing body of scholarship on how digital media affect our interpersonal lives, to offer frameworks for evaluating and understanding these changes.

New media, new boundaries

Digital media raise a variety of issues as we try to understand them, their place in our lives, and their consequences for our personhood and relationships with others. When they are new, technologies affect how we see the world, our communities, our relationships, and our selves. They lead to social and cultural reorganization and reflection. In her landmark study of nineteenth-century popular scientific magazines, Carolyn Marvin (1988) showed how a new technology such as electricity, the telegraph, or the telephone creates a point in history where the familiar becomes unfamiliar, and therefore open to change. This leads to anxiety. While people in ancient times fretted about writing and Victorians fretted about electricity, today we are in "a state of anxiety not only about the PC, but in relation to technology more generally" (Thomas, 2004: 219).

The fundamental purpose of communication technologies from their ancient inception has been to allow people to exchange messages without being physically co-present. Until the invention of the telegraph in the 1800s, this ability to transcend space brought with it inevitable time delays. Messages could take years to reach their audience. The telegraph changed that by allowing real-time communication across long distances for the first time. People may have reeled in the face of writing and publishing, but it was little compared to how we reeled and continued to reel in the face of this newfound power to collapse time and space. After millennia as creatures who engage in social interaction face-to-face, the ability to communicate across distance at very high speeds disrupts social understandings that are burned deep into our collective conscience. Digital media continue these disruptions and pose new ones. They raise important questions for scholars and lay people alike. How can we be present yet also absent? What is a self if it's not in a body? How can we have so much control yet lose so much freedom? What does personal communication mean when it's transmitted through a mass medium? What's a mass medium if it's used for personal communication? What do "private" and "public" mean anymore? What does it even mean to *be* real?

Kenneth Gergen (2002) describes us as struggling with the "challenge of absent presence," worrying that too often we inhabit a "floating world" in which we engage primarily with non-present partners despite the presence of flesh-and-blood people in our physical location. We may be physically present in one space, yet mentally and emotionally engaged elsewhere, a phenomenon on which Sherry Turkle dwells in her book *Alone Together* (2011). Consider, for instance, the dinner partner who is immersed in his mobile phone conversation. Since he is physically present, yet simultaneously absent, the very nature of self becomes problematic. Where is "he?" The borders between human and machine, the collapse of which was celebrated in Haraway's (1990) "Cyborg manifesto," and between self and body, are thrown into flux. In a time when some people feel that their "real self" is expressed best online (McKenna, Green, & Gleason, 2002), long-distance romances are built and maintained through electronic contact, and spaces for media are built right into the clothing we wear, how do we know where, exactly, true selves reside? Furthermore, what if the selves enacted through digital media don't line up with those we present face-to-face, or if they contradict one another? If someone is nurturing face-to-face, aggressive in one online forum, and needy in another online forum, which is real? Is there such a thing as a true self anymore? Was there ever?

The separation of presence from communication offers us more control over our social worlds yet subjects us to new forms of control, surveillance, and constraint. Naomi Baron (2008) argues that new media offer us "volume control" to regulate our social environment and manage our encounters. We can create new opportunities to converse. We can avoid interactions, talking into a mobile phone (or pretending to) to avoid a co-present acquaintance, or letting calls go to voice mail. We can manipulate our interactions, doing things like forwarding nasty emails or putting people on speakerphone. We can use nonverbally limited media such as text messages or emails to shelter us from anxiety-inducing encounters such as flirting or ending relationships. We can see where our contacts have checked in on Foursquare (now Swarm) or Facebook and choose to go elsewhere (Humphreys, 2011). But, just as we can use these media to manage others more strategically, others can also more easily manage us. Our autonomy is increasingly constrained by the expectation that we can be reached for communication anytime, anywhere, and we will owe an appropriate and timely response. We are trapped by the same state of "perpetual contact" (Katz & Aakhus, 2002) that empowers us. In light of revelations about government surveillance of mobile phone communication, web activities, and online games, it's evident that, even as we engage in increased control of our behaviors and relationships through digital media, the digital traces left by our activities are used for surveillance on a previously unimaginable scale.

One of the most exciting elements of new media is that they allow us to communicate personally within what used to be prohibitively large groups. This blurs the boundary between mass and interpersonal communication in ways that disrupt both. When people gather online to talk about a television show they are a mass communication audience, but the communication they have with one another is both interpersonal, directed to individuals within the group, and mass, available for anyone to read. If, as increasingly happens, the conversations and materials these fans produce for one another are incorporated into the television show, the boundaries between the production and reception of mass media are blurred as well.

Furthermore, what is personal may become mass, as when a young woman creates a videolog for her friends, which becomes widely viewed on YouTube. The ability for individuals to communicate and produce mediated content on a mass scale has led to opportunities for fame that were not available outside of the established culture industries before, but confusion about the availability and scale of messages has also led to unplanned broadcast of what was meant to be private, as when a politician inadvertently posts a sexually explicit selfie to his public Twitter feed rather than sending it through direct messaging.

This is just one way in which the boundaries between public and private are implicated in and changed by digital media. Internet users have been decried for revealing private information through online activities. Mobile phone users have been assailed for carrying on private conversations in public spaces (and shooting nasty looks at those who don't pretend not to notice). Puro (2002: 23) describes mobile phone users as "doubly privatizing" public space since they "sequester themselves non-verbally and then fill the air with private matters." Homes, especially in affluent societies, exhibit a "privatized media rich bedroom culture" (Livingstone, 2005) in which people use media to create privacy and solitude. All of this happens in a cultural moment when individualism is defined through consumerist prac-tices of purchasing mass-mediated and branded products (Gergen, 1991; Livingstone, 2005; Walker, 2008) and publicizing one's self through "self-branding" may be essential to career success (Marwick, 2013).

At the heart of this boundary flux is deep confusion about what is virtual – that which seems real but is ultimately a mere simulation – and what is real. Even people who hang out and build relation-ships online contrast it to what they do "IRL" (In Real Life), lending credence to the perception that the mediated is unreal. Digital media thus call into question the very authenticity of our identities, relation-ships, and practices (e.g. Sturken & Thomas, 2004). Some critics have noted that these disruptions are part and parcel of a movement from modern to postmodern times in which time and space are compressed, speed is accelerated, people are ever more mobile, com-munication is person-to-person rather than place-to-place, identities are multiple, and communication media are ubiquitous (e.g. Fornäs, Klein, Ladendorf, Sundén, & Sveningsson, 2002; Haythornthwaite & Wellman, 2002; Ling, 2004). Others have emphasized how, within these cultural changes, digital media are made mundane, boring, and routine as they are increasingly embedded in everyday lives and social norms coalesce around their use (e.g. Haythornthwaite & Wellman,

2002; Humphreys, 2005; Ling, 2004). The first perspective forms a necessary backdrop for contextualizing and making sense of the second, but the emphasis in this book is on the mundane and the everyday, on how people incorporate digital media into their routine practices of relating and with what consequences.

Plan of the book

In the remainder of this chapter I identify a set of key concepts that can be used to differentiate digital media, and which influence how people use them and with what effects. I then offer a very brief overview of the media discussed in this book and a discussion of who does and who doesn't make use of them. Chapter 2 is an orientation to the major perspectives used to understand the interrelationships between communication technology and society, and an exploration of the major themes in popular rhetorics about digital media and personal connection. Chapter 3 examines what happens to messages, both verbal and nonverbal, in mediated contexts. Chapter 4 addresses the group contexts in which online interaction often happens, including communities and social networks. The remaining two chapters explore dyadic relationships. Chapter 5 shows how people present themselves to others and first get to know each other online. Chapter 6 looks at how people use new media to build and maintain their relationships. Finally, the conclusion returns to the question of sorting myths from reality, arguing against the notion of a "cyberspace" that can be understood apart from the mundane realities of everyday life, and for the notion that online and offline flow together in the lifeworlds of contemporary relationships.

Seven key concepts

If we want to build a rich understanding of how media influence relationships, we need to stop talking about media in overly simplistic terms. We can't talk about consequences if we can't articulate capabilities. What is it about these media that changes interaction and, potentially, relationships? We need conceptual tools to differentiate media from one another and from face-to-face (or, as Fortunati, 2005, more aptly termed it, "body-to-body") communication. We also need concepts to help us recognize the diversity amongst what may seem to be just one technology. The mobile phone, for instance, is used for voice, texting, picture and video exchange, gaming, and, with the new dominance of smartphones, nearly endless other applications. The internet includes interaction platforms as diverse as YouTube, product reviews on shopping sites, email, and Instant Messaging (IM), which differ from one another in many ways. Seven concepts that can be used to productively compare different media to one another as well as to face-to-face communication are interactivity, temporal structure, social cues, storage, replicability, reach, and mobility.

The many modes of communication on the internet and mobile phone vary in the degrees and kinds of *interactivity* they offer. Consider, for instance, the difference between using your phone to select a new ringtone and using that phone to argue with a romantic partner, or using a website to buy new shoes rather than to discuss current events. Fornäs and his co-authors (2002: 23) distinguish several meanings of interactivity. Social interactivity, "the ability of a medium to enable social interaction between groups or individuals," is what we are most interested in here. Other kinds include technical interactivity, "a medium's capability of letting human users manipulate the machine via its interface," and textual interactivity, "the creative and interpretive interaction between users (readers, viewers, listeners) and texts." "Unlike television," writes Laura Gurak (2001: 44), "online communication technologies allow you to talk back. You can talk back to the big company or you can talk back to individual citizens." Indeed, these days customers often expect that, when they talk back, companies will respond swiftly. The social media marketing site Convince and Convert (2012) reports on a survey finding that everyone who contacts a brand, product, or company through social media expects a reply within a few days, and a third expect a response within half an hour. Rafaeli and Sudweeks (1997) posit that we should see interactivity as a continuum enacted by people using technology, rather than a technological condition. As we will see in chapters to come, the fact that the internet enables interactivity gives rise to new possibilities – for instance, we can meet new people and remain close to those who have moved away – as well as old concerns that people may be flirting with danger.

The *temporal structure* of a communication medium is also important. Synchronous communication, such as is found in face-to-face conversations, phone calls, and instant messages, occurs in real time. Asynchronous communication media, such as email and voice mail, have time delays between messages. In practice, the distinction cannot always be tied to specific media. Poor connections may lead to time delays in a seemingly synchronous online medium such as Instant Messaging. Text messaging via the telephone is often asynchronous, but needn't be. Twitter can function both ways. Ostensibly asynchronous email may be sent and received so rapidly that it functions as a synchronous mode of communication. Sites like Facebook may seem to be a single medium, but offer both asynchronous modes of interaction such as wall posts and messaging, and synchronous chat, and it is not unheard of for people to use comments on wall posts as a real-time chat medium.

The beauty of synchronous media is that they allow for the very rapid transmission of messages, even across distance. As we will see, synchronicity can enhance the sense of placelessness that digital media can encourage and make people feel more together when they are apart (Baron, 1998; Carnevale & Probst, 1997; McKenna & Bargh, 1998). Synchronicity can make messages feel more immediate and personal (O'Sullivan, Hunt, & Lippert, 2004) and encourage playfulness in interaction (Danet, 2001). The price of synchronicity, however, is that interactants must be able to align their schedules in order to be simultaneously engaged. Real-time media are also poorly suited to hosting interaction in large groups, as the rapid-fire succession of messages that comes from having many people involved is nearly impossible to sort through and comprehend, let alone answer. There is a reason that dinner parties are generally kept to a small collection of people, and guests at large functions are usually seated at tables that accommodate fewer than a dozen. Accordingly, most online chat rooms and other real-time forums have limits on how many can participate at one time.

With asynchronous media, the costs and benefits are reversed. Asynchronous communication allows very large groups to sustain interaction, as seen in the social network sites and online groups like fan forums, support groups, and hobbyist communities addressed in chapter 4. Asynchronicity also gives people time to manage their self-presentations more strategically. However, word may filter more slowly through such groups and amongst individuals. We can place fewer demands on others' time by leaving asynchronous messages for people to reply to when they like, but we may end up waiting longer than we'd hoped, or receive no reply at all. One of the biggest changes wrought by digital media is that even asynchronous communication can happen faster than before. Time lags are created by the time it takes a person to check for new messages and respond, not by the time messages spend in transit. In comparison to postal mail, the internet can shave weeks off interactions.

Most of the questions surrounding the personal connections people form and maintain through digital media derive from the sparse *social cues* that are available to provide further information regarding context, the meanings of messages, and the identities of the people interacting. As chapter 3 will address in more detail, rich media provide a full range of cues, while leaner media provide fewer. Body-to-body, people have a full range of communicative resources available to them. They share a physical context, which they can refer to nonverbally as well as verbally (for instance, by pointing to a chair). They are subject to the same environmental influences and distractions. They can see one another's body movements, including the facial expressions through which so much meaning is conveyed. They can use each other's eye gaze to gauge attention. They can see one another's appearance. They can also hear the sound of one another's voice. All of these cues – contextual, visual, and auditory – are important to interpreting messages and creating a social context within which messages are meaningful.

To varying degrees, digital media provide fewer social cues. In mobile and online interactions, we may have few if any cues to our partner's location. This is no doubt why so many mobile phone calls begin with the question "Where are you?" and also helps to explain some people's desire to share GPS positioning via mobile applications. The lack of shared physical context does not mean that interactants have no shared contexts. People communicating in personal relationships share relational contexts, knowledge, and some history. People in online groups often develop rich in-group social environments that those who've participated for any length of time will recognize.

Though, as we will address in more depth in chapter 6, much of our mediated interaction is with people we know face-to-face, some media convey very little information about the identities of those with whom we are communicating. In some circumstances, this renders people anonymous, leading to both opportunity and terror. In lean media, people have more ability to expand, manipulate, multiply, and distort the identities they present to others. The paucity of personal and social identity cues can also make people feel safer, and thus create an environment in which they are more honest. Chapter 5 examines these identity issues.

Media also differ in the extent to which their messages endure. *Storage*, the maintenance of messages on servers or harddrives over time, and, relatedly, *replicability*, the ability to make copies of messages, are highly consequential. Unless one makes an audio or video recording of telephone and face-to-face conversations (activities with laws governing acceptable practice), for the interactants they are gone as soon as they are said. Human memory for conversation is notoriously poor. To varying degrees, digital media may be stored on devices, websites, and company backups where they may be replicated, retrieved at later dates, and edited prior to sending (Carnevale & Probst, 1997; Cherny, 1999; Culnan & Markus, 1987; Walther, 1996). Synchronous forms like IM and Skype require logging programs that most users are not likely to have. Those that are asynchronous can be easily saved, replicated, and redistributed to others. They can also be archived for search. Government agencies, such as the United States' National Security Administration, may capture and save data and metadata from enormous amounts of internet and mobile phone traffic. Despite this, online messages may feel ephemeral, and, indeed, websites may be there one day and different or gone the next. The popular photosharing application Snapchat found its niche by emphasizing the ephemerality of its photos which, much like the mission instructions in *Mission Impossible*, self-destruct soon after viewing (although what actually happens is that the file extension changes and the photo remains cached).

Media also vary in the size of an audience they can attain or support, or *reach*. Gurak (2001: 30) describes reach as "the partner of speed," noting that "digitized discourse travels quickly, but it also travels widely . . . One single keystroke can send a message to thousands of people." Face-to-face communication is inherently limited to those who can fit in the same space. Even when amplified (a form of mediation in itself), physical space and human sensory constraints limit how many can see or hear a message as it's delivered. The telephone allows for group calls, but the upper limit on how many a group can admit or maintain is small. In contrast, many forms of digital communication can be seen by any internet user (as in the case of websites) or can be sent and, thanks to replicability, resent to enormous audiences. Messages can reach audiences both local and global. This is a powerful subversion of the elitism of mass media, within which a very small number of broadcasters could engage in one-to-many communication, usually within regional or geographic boundaries. The gatekeeping function of mass media is challenged as individuals use digital media to spread messages much farther and more widely than was ever historically possible (Gurak, 2001). Future chapters will address how enhanced reach allows people to form new communities of interest and new relationships.

Finally, media vary in their *mobility*, or extent to which they are portable – enabling people to send and receive messages regardless of location – or stationary – requiring that people be in specific locations in order to interact. The mobile phone represents the paradigm case of mobility, making person-to-person communication possible regardless of location. The trend toward mobile devices is further enhanced by the rise of tablets and "phablets" as well as the increasing preference for laptops over clunky personal computers tied to desks and landline phones. In addition to offering spatial mobility, some digital media allow us to move between times and interpersonal contexts (Ishii, 2006). Mobile media offer the promise that we need never be out of touch with our loved ones, no matter how long the traffic jam in which we find ourselves. When stuck with our families, we may import our friends through our mobile devices. As we'll see in chapter 6, mobile media give rise to microcoordination (Ling, 2004) in which people check in with one another to provide brief updates or quickly arrange meetings and errands. However, more than other personal media, mobile phones threaten autonomy, as we may become accountable to others at all times. Schegloff (2002), one of the first to study telephone-mediated interaction, suggests mobile media don't create perpetual contact so much as offer the perpetual possibility of making contact, a distinction some exploit by strategically limiting their availability (Licoppe & Heurtin, 2002).

These seven concepts help us begin to understand the similarities and differences between face-to-face communication and mediated interaction, as well as the variation amongst different kinds of digital interactions, even on the same web platform. Face-to-face communication, like all the forms of digital media we will be discussing, is interactive. People can respond to one another in message exchanges. Face-to-face communication is synchronous. It is also loaded with social cues that make one another's identities and many elements of social and physical context apparent (although, as we will return to in chapter 5, this does not guarantee honesty). Face-to-face conversations cannot be stored, nor can they be replicated. Even when recorded and, for example, broadcast, the recording loses many elements of the context that make face-to-face communication what it is. As discussed above, face-to-face communication has low reach, limiting how many can be involved and how far messages can spread. Face-to-face communication may be mobile, but only as long as the interactants are moving through space together. This combination of qualities grants face-to-face a sort of specialness. The full range of cues, the irreplicability, and the need to be there in shared place and time with the other all contribute to the sense that face-to-face communication is authentic, putting the "communion" in communication.

In contrast, some forms of mediated interaction are asynchronous, enabling more message planning and wider reach, but a potentially lower sense of connection. Media such as Skype or other video chat technologies offer many social cues – voice, facial expression, a window into the physical surroundings – but lack critical intimacy cues including touch and smell. Most digital media have fewer social cues than that, limiting interaction to sounds or even just words. By virtue of their conversion into electronic signals, all digital media can be stored, and often are even when individuals delete them (Facebook, for instance, saves drafts of messages that were never posted). Even when conversations and messages are not stored, however, they may leave traces such as records of which phone numbers called which other ones, which IP addresses visited which websites, or how many tweets a person has tweeted. Digital messages are easily replicated if they are asynchronous, but less so if they are synchronous. The reach of digital media can vary tremendously depending on the medium. A phone call generally remains a one-to-one encounter, as does much instant messaging and chat, but social network sites, emails, mailing lists, discussion groups, and websites are among the digital modes that can have extraordinary reach. Digital media are becoming increasingly mobile as the internet and mobile phone converge into single devices, meaning that these technologies make communication possible in places where it wasn't before, but also that they can intrude into face-to-face conversations where they never could before. As a result, people can have very different experiences with different media, yet none may seem to offer the potential for intimacy and connection that being face-to-face does. These distinctions and convergences all bring with them important potential social shifts, which the remainder of this book will address.

Digital media

Just as it's important to clarify core concepts that may shape mediated social interaction, it's helpful to walk through the media in question. It's also important to recognize that the media we use today have historical precedents whose traces may have been as disruptive in their own time and traces linger today. Tom Standage's 2013 book *Writing on the Wall: Social Media – The First 2,000 Years* offers a lively walk through such precedents, including literal writing on walls in ancient Rome, as does William Powers's (2010) *Hamlet's Blackberry*. Asa Briggs and Peter Burke's (2009) *A Social History of the Media* demonstrates the precedents of earlier technologies, and also the continuities between old and new media. Such books reveal that many of the phenomena and concerns associated with new media began long before electricity, let alone digital media – a topic the next chapter will address.

I assume readers are familiar with the mobile phone, so I focus below on a brief historical overview of the internet. I emphasize the extent to which the interpersonal appeal of digital media shaped their development. Unlike the mobile phone, the internet was not built as a personal communication medium, let alone a way for fans to connect around their objects of pleasure, for people to find potential romantic partners, for employers to find or investigate potential hires, or any such social processes. It was developed to safeguard military knowledge. When the first internet connection was made in 1969 through what was then called ARPANET, funded by the US Department of Defense, no one envisioned that an interpersonal communication medium had been launched. However, what became the internet was not the only networked computing system being built at that time. Hobbyists built dial-in bulletin board systems for interactive file exchange, interaction, and games. Universities developed computer networks such as PLATO. Indeed, as a child in Urbana, Illinois, home of the University of Illinois where PLATO was developed, in the mid 1970s I used to stay after school to read jokes, play games, and chat with anonymous PLATO users in other locations (little did my classmates and I realize how ahead of our time we were!). In those same early years, bulletin board systems users dialed into servers in people's homes to chat. As Kevin Driscoll has written (2014), the received history of the internet as having begun with ARPANET, covered in detail in Janet Abbate's (1999) history, is one of several origin stories that could be told about "the internet." It is beyond the scope of this book to cover either the technological or social development of the internet. First, though, a disclaimer: trying to list specific types of digital media is frustrating at best. Between this writing and your reading there will be new developments, and things popular as I write will drop from vogue. Let this be a reminder to us of the importance of remaining focused on specific capabilities and consequences rather than the media themselves.

The textual internet

For its first quarter-century, the internet was text-only. With its limited social cues, it seemed a poor match for personal interaction. Yet it took mere months for its developers (who were also its primary users) to realize the medium's utility for personal communication. Within three years of the first login, email was in use, and within four years, three-quarters of online traffic was email (Anderson, 2005). By 2000, the ability to use email was a significant reason that people first got online and one of the main reasons that those already online stayed online (Kraut, Mukhopadhyay, Szczypula, Kiesler, & Scherlis, 2000).

Synchronous person-to-person and small-group communication also developed early in the internet's history. "Talk" was an early synchronous internet communication genre. When using Talk, a horizontal line divided the top and lower halves of the screen, each half showing messages from one interactant. It was as minimalist and purely textual as a communication medium could be. Talk remained in regular usage into the early 1990s. When I began using the internet in 1990, I used it almost daily to tell my then-boyfriend that dinner was ready – I couldn't call since his phone line was tied up with his modem's internet connection. Talk provided a convenient work-around. Talk was followed by Internet Relay Chat (IRC) and, later, chat rooms that allowed distributed groups to converse in real-time. Instant Messaging, developed in the 1990s, can be seen as an advanced version of Talk. A person-to-person medium, IM was distinctive in its use of a buddy list and provision of continual information about who on that list was online and available for contact.

Not long after email, mailing lists were developed, in which a single email could be sent to a large group of subscribers, all of whom would receive it and (usually) be able to respond. Although the technological specifications of email and mailing lists are the same, there are some important differences. Specifically, on mailing lists, senders may very well not know most (or any) of the recipients. Mailing lists are often large. For instance, the Association of Internet Researchers' mailing list, AIR-L, has approximately 5,000 subscribers in many nations. In contrast, others are small private lists of family and friends. A colleague of mine, faced with a family member's cancer, created a mailing list of family members so that they could all share news with a single message. Private mailing lists may also be made up of school friends who have graduated or other such small groups of people seeking to stay in touch as a group.

In the early 1980s, another means of asynchronous group

discussion with wide reach developed. Usenet newsgroups are asynchronous topic-based discussion forums distributed across multiple servers. Although these groups have become magnets for spam, they continue to house discussion. Originally, one read newsgroups through newsreaders built into Unix operating systems. This later developed into stand-alone newsreaders. Now most people access Usenet through the web, most notably through Google groups, where they may well not recognize them as Usenet newsgroups. These provided an early model for the topical web boards and social media groups so common now. They were also my own entrée into online group communication and the subject of my earliest work on online communication.

On some early sites, developers and participants used words and code to create a rich geographical context for synchronous interactions, and a highly developed range of characters. In the late 1970s, Richard Bartle and Roy Trubshaw developed MUD1, an interactive online role-playing game. Around the same time, Alan Klietz independently developed Sceptre of Goth, a MUD game (Bartle, 2004). Readers who play World of Warcraft or related massively multiplayer online role-playing games will recognize MUDs as their precedent. MUD stands for either Multi-User Domain or the less antiseptic Multi-User Dungeon, which better captures the phenomenon's origin in the role-playing game Dungeons and Dragons. Many MUDs offered predetermined categories by which to define one's character. People might choose their sex (often from a list with more than two choices) and race. Depending on the MUD, people might choose to be elves, fairies, cats, dragons, trolls, vampires, and other fantasy creatures.

Lambda MOO (Multi-User Domain Object-Oriented, a distinction that is of minimal importance here) and other MUDs, MOOs, MUCKs, MUSHes, and other oddly acronymed parallel sites followed, many of which were simply creative environments in which fictional rooms and landscapes served as spaces for social interaction, not games. Though MUDs and MOOs have always been obscure uses of the internet (unlike the later graphical games they inspired), they were the object of an inordinate amount of early research about the internet.

The World Wide Web

A major transformation in digital communication occurred in the 1990s when a group of physicists led by Sir Tim Berners-Lee at the Swiss physics laboratory CERN developed the World Wide Web. This heralded a shift from communication that was purely text-based to multimedia communication, and gave rise to more new forms of mediated interaction than I can cover here. These include web boards, blogs, wikis, social network sites, video and photosharing sites, and graphically intensive virtual worlds.

In the 1990s, web boards took up where the promise of Usenet left off, facilitating asynchronous topic-based group interaction amongst people who did not need prior connections. Blogs, authored by either single people or collectives, are websites in which recent updates appear above previous updates, creating a reverse chronology of messages. Their content may be personal, political, or anything else, and their audiences may be anything from zero to millions. By convention and design, blogs almost always include a list of hyperlinks to other blogs (a "blog roll"), which serves to create connections and drive traffic amongst blogs. Groups of bloggers may read one another and comment on each other's blogs, creating communities of like-minded individuals and semi-organized grassroots social movements.

Also during this time, websites such as Active Worlds began to develop graphically rich environments. These have exploded in the early 2000s, in the form of massively multiplayer online role-playing games (MMORPGs – an acronym usually pronounced "more pigs"), such as World of Warcraft, League of Legends, and non-game spaces such as Second Life.

The 2000s brought what has been called "Web 2.0," the hallmark of which is often taken to be user-generated content. But, having been through the paragraphs just above, one must wonder what content on the textual internet and much of Web 1.0 was not generated by users. Wikis, the most famous of which is Wikipedia, are among the stars of this generation of digital media. Wikis are collective encyclopedia-authoring sites in which people can collaborate to produce informative entries. Though this may sound sterile, behind the editing of entries are rich social worlds of interconnected users with shared histories, conventions, and practices. Social network sites (SNSs) such as Facebook or Sina Weibo, in which individuals have profiles to which they can upload many diverse media (photos, videos, music, links, and more) and connect their profiles with others through "friending," have been wildly successful and are near-ubiquitous, especially amongst young people, in some countries. boyd and Ellison (2007) locate the origins of SNSs in the advent of SixDegrees.com in 1997, followed by AsianAvenue, BlackPlanet, and MiGente, then LiveJournal and Cyworld (1999) and LunarStorm (2000). MySpace began in 2003, and Facebook in 2005. The professional SNS, Linked In, began in 2003. Video and photosharing sites such as Instagram (owned by Facebook), YouTube (owned by Google), and Flickr (owned by Yahoo!) may be considered a subset of SNS. Other popular, more specialized platforms that could be considered SNSs include Tumblr and Spotify. In these sites, people can create personal accounts, upload their own materials, and share them with others publicly or only amongst approved recipients. Social network sites are unique in combining multiple modes of communication and, hence, in the breadth of and control over social cues they may provide. As more people have acquired mobile phones with data plans, locative media such as Swarm, which allow people to "check in" from their locations, have become more common.

The move from the early internet to the Web and mobile phone can be seen in part as the rise of "platforms" and, more recently, apps. Tarleton Gillespie (2010: 348) argues that platforms have inherent politics, shaped by the incentives of their creators as they position themselves relative to users, clients, advertisers, and policy makers. These platforms have become "the primary keepers of the cultural discussion as it moves across the internet." José van Dijck (2013), in her critical history of social media *The Culture of Connectivity*, shows how the human desire for *connection* that drove the growth of the internet has been parlayed into *connectivity* – the making and storing of connections between individuals and sites (think of how Facebook Like buttons appear on so many sites other than Facebook). While early internet media such as Usenet or mailing lists were public-sector-financed and focused on connecting users for the users' own benefit, the culture of connectivity is driven by commercial platforms primarily interested in commodifying personal connections in order to derive profits for owners and venture capitalists, generally through advertising. Furthermore, rather than simply displaying the content that has appeared since you last visited, most contemporary platforms use proprietary algorithms in order to determine which content is made visible to which users at which times.

As this brief review suggests, even as we are concerned with their overall impact, we must avoid the temptation to look at new media only as a whole. Each of these media, as well as the mobile phone, offers unique affordances, or packages of potentials and constraints (Gibson, 1977; Norman, 1988), for communication. Even as we think in terms of which qualities any given medium offers, we must also understand that we live in a "polymedia" environment where media can be embedded in one another and all media form contexts for the others (Madianou & Miller, 2012a, 2012b). In this media ecosystem, a person's choice to convey a message through one medium rather than another becomes part of its relational meaning (Gershon, 2010; Madianou & Miller, 2012a, 2012b). To understand how we use media, and with what consequences, we need to consider them both separately and holistically. We also need to understand how people used and made sense of earlier forms of digital media if we are going to make claims about what is and isn't new. It is for that reason that you will find so many studies of modes of online communication that are no longer as popular in the pages that follow.

Who uses new digital media?

The story of online media history is also a story of changing users, and we need to keep questions of whom we are talking about in mind as we think about how new media and social life intertwine. In its early years, the only people using the internet were the ones developing it, almost all of whom were located in the United States and the UK (Abbate, 1999). By the 1980s, scientists at universities had begun to use it, and, by the end of that decade, college students were using it too. But the internet of the 1980s was funded almost entirely by the National Science Foundation (NSF), an agency of the United States government. Commercial activity was prohibited, and almost all users gained access through a university affiliation, or a government lab or agency. Computer networks connecting people with home computers, such as CompuServe, Prodigy, and America Online, began in the 1980s, as did many private bulletin board systems that had major impacts on the sociality of the later internet (Driscoll, 2014). These provided home hobbyists with a means to get online, but they were not integrated with each other or with the internet.

Throughout the 1980s and the early 1990s, access to the internet gradually spread to other countries. It was not until the mid 1990s that the diffusion of the internet into everyday life for many Americans and people in some other parts of the world (most notably the UK and northern Europe) began in earnest. The years 1994 and 1995 were huge for the internet. The NSF pulled out of its funding, making commercial activity feasible, and the World Wide Web moved from concept to realization. Internet Service Providers such as America Online began to connect to the internet, and Americans began to come online in droves, leading to all kinds of culture clashes between those who had been online for years and this new class of users. By the end of the decade, most Americans were online.

Globally, the story is different, however, as it remains within some segments of the American population. Online media are far from universal, either across or within populations. Many books and articles have been written addressing the issues of the "digital divide" (e.g. Norris, 2001; Warschauer, 2004). As a whole, digital divide research has little to say about interpersonal connection, the topic of this book. Its focus is usually on issues such as political participation, career advancement, and the use of financial and health information (e.g. Hargittai & Hinnant, 2008). This research indicates that those most able to use new media improve their lives in ways that those who do not use them do not, increasing social and economic disparity. Everything this book will discuss needs to be understood as happening in a context which only some sectors of the global population can access or engage.

The digital divide is often framed as a simple division between those who have access to the internet and those who do not. Even within countries, there are clear trends in which populations use the internet and which don't. Within the United States, survey research by the Pew Internet & American Life Project (*Who's Online*, 2014) has consistently found demographic differences in which Americans use the internet. In their May, 2013, random phone survey of American adults, Whites were 10 percent more likely to use it than Hispanics. Among young people (18–29 years old), 98 percent used the internet, while only 56 percent of those over 65 did. Income also correlated strongly with internet use. Only 76 percent of people in households earning less than $30,000/year reported using the internet, while 96 percent of those earning $75,000 or more did. Education was also an influence, as those who had not graduated from high school reported 59 percent usage compared to the 96 percent of those who had graduated from college. Location also matters. People living in urban and suburban communities were both 16 percent more likely to use the internet than people living in rural areas. Finally, people with disabilities are significantly less likely to use the internet. Pew data (Fox & Boyles, 2012) show that only 54 percent of Americans who identified as having a disability that inhibits daily functioning (approximately 27 percent of Americans) used the internet in mid 2012.

Globally, the disparities are even more striking. The website Internet World Stats (Miniwatts Marketing Group, 2013), which tracks this, estimates that 76.8 percent of North Americans use the internet, 67.6 percent of those in Oceania/Australia do, 63.2 percent of Europeans, 42.9 percent in Latin American / Caribbean countries, 40.2 percent of Middle Easterners, 27.5 percent of Asians, and only 15.6 percent of Africans. On average, just over a third of the world's population use the internet. Within these parts of the world, the factors that affect Americans (education, age, etc.) affect further which members of the population are among the internet users.

In many regions where internet use is lower than in North America, mobile phone use is far more pervasive. The United Nations' International Telecommunications Union (2013) estimated that, while 41.3 percent of the world's households have internet access and 38.8 percent of individuals use the internet, 96.2 percent used mobile phones. The report also draws attention to the fact that not all internet access is the same – only 9.8 percent of the global population have access to broadband services through a fixed internet connection, and only 29.5 percent have it through mobile connections. In developed countries, 74.8 percent of the population have mobile broadband and 27.2 percent have fixed, but in developing countries, those numbers are only 19.8 percent and 6.1 percent respectively, demonstrating that although mobile broadband subscription increased considerably in developing countries, it is still beyond the financial reach of those with low incomes. The Pew Internet and American Life Project (Horrigan & Rainie, 2002) found that broadband access is important in shaping whether a person merely reads the internet or contributes content to it.

A 2001 UN Human Development Report is no doubt outdated in its precise numbers, but their analysis of global trends is still apt (UN, 2001). Much of the global population is illiterate. Worldwide, most internet users remain male and college-educated, and earn higher-than-average incomes. Women are in the minority of users in both developed and developing countries. The 2013 ITU report finds that, while it is lessening, gender disparity remains an issue. Men are more likely than women to use the internet, by an 11 percent margin globally (2 percent in developed nations, 16 percent in developing nations).

In the time between this book's first edition and this one, many of these disparities have begun to shrink. However, as the point about broadband suggests, access does not tell the whole story. Even if one sometimes uses a medium, other factors affect how much one is likely to gain from its use. Jung, Qiu, and Kim (2001) developed the Internet Connectedness Index to assess the varying degrees of connectivity that "internet use" may actually entail. Among the variables they identified as important were whether or not one owned a home computer, for how long one had owned one, from how many places a person could access the internet, how much time people spend online, and how many things a person can do online.

Eszter Hargittai's work has pointed to the importance of skill. She (2002) describes a "second level digital divide" that speaks to the differences in skill levels (e.g. understanding internet terminology, searching for and evaluating information) that internet users may have. Hargittai and Hinnant (2008) surveyed a random sample of US young adults. They found that women, people who had not graduated from college, and those who did not use the internet at home reported lower skill levels and were less likely to visit sites with the potential to improve one's life, such as those offering news, or government, health, financial, and product information sites. Helsper and Eynon (2013) identified overlapping sets of technical, social, creative, and critical skills that can affect digital inclusion, and found that different kinds of social exclusion (education, gender, age, etc.) are related to different types of skills, helping to explain the cycle between social and digital exclusion.

In sum, we are still standing on shifting ground in our efforts to make sense of the capabilities of digital media and their social consequences. New media are constantly developing, new populations are taking up these tools, and new uses are emerging. Who is excluded from or enabled by digitally mediated interaction is neither random nor inconsequential. The same tools may take on very different meanings for different populations in different contexts or different times. It is too soon to tell what the final consequences will be, but it seems unlikely that they will ever be universal or stable. Nonetheless, we do know a great deal from nearly forty years of research. In the rest of this book we'll work with what data we have to fill in what we know now. I hope that astute readers will read between the lines to consider also how much more we have to learn.

2

Making new media make sense

When faced with a new communication medium, the immediate challenge for scholars, users, and non-users is to make sense of it. What is it good for? What are its risks? What benefits might it bring? I once asked students to brainstorm what hopes and fears the internet raised for them. Among other things, they hoped the internet might facilitate new connections, cross-cultural interaction, more social support, and tighter family ties, but they feared losing face-to-face interaction as well as the rise of false relationships, deception, stalking, and new levels of vulnerability to strangers. To understand new media and their potential consequences, we need to consider both the technological features of a medium and the personal, cultural, and historical presumptions and values those features evoke.

In chapter 1, I raised the notion that new media cause cultural anxieties, and articulated several technological concepts that help us to think about how new media may differ from earlier forms of communication as well as from one another. Most anxieties around both digital media and their historical precursors stem from the fact that these media are interactive. Especially in combination with sparse social cues, interactivity raises issues about the authenticity and well-being of people, interactions, and relationships that use new media. Other anxieties arise out of the temporal structure of digital media, which seem to push us toward continuous interaction. The internet's ability to store and replicate information without regard to its content leads to fears about what that content might include and how this power might be abused in harmful ways. The mobility of some new media means that we can now have conversations when we are in public that would have once been held in our homes and that we can be with others wherever we are, feeding into a related set of concerns about privacy and companionship.

In addition to technological qualities, social forces also shape the anxieties we have and the questions we pose about new communication technologies. This chapter explores the messages that circulate around new media in order to show how social forces influence technological interpretation and use. New media appear in the stories we tell each other about what happened during our day and in the domestic squabbles over whose turn it is to use the computer. They are represented in mass media, where technologies play starring and peripheral roles in news stories, magazine articles, films, and television shows. Popular films such as *You've Got Mail* or *The Net*, both released shortly after the internet became popular in the USA, provide modern-day fairy tales that serve as cultural referents for understanding online romance or identity theft. The film and subsequent television show *Catfish* has become a touchstone that frames concerns about online deception. In *Her*, a man falls in love with his device's artificial intelligence, symbolizing concerns that machines could be more attractive than humans. The messages in popular media, examples of which we'll see below, show the social elements we bring to understanding new communication technologies and help to shape how people understand and design new technology.

Through communication, people assign symbolic meanings to technologies. The messages we communicate about technology are *reflective*, revealing as much about the communicators as they do about the technology (Sturken & Thomas, 2004). When we communicate about digital media, we are communicating about ourselves, as individuals, groups, and societies. As we represent these unfamiliar interpersonal tools through our words, conversations, stories, metaphors, images, and so on, we collectively negotiate what interpersonal relationships are and what we want them to be. When we talk about technology, we are sharing "the visions, both optimistic and anxious, through which modern societies cohere" (2004: 1). In addition to telling us about a medium, communication about technology is also one of the best places to see "the desires and concerns of a given social context and the preoccupations of particular moments in history" (2004: 1).

Communication about technology is also productive, generating new meanings for technologies, new uses of technologies, and even new technologies (Sturken & Thomas, 2004). As early as the sixteenth century, there was an urban legend about "sympathetic needles" that allowed people to communicate instantaneously across distance, a legend that helped to inspire the telegraph (Standage, 1998). William Gibson's 1984 science fiction novel *Neuromancer* gave us the term "cyberspace," and both his writings and those of Neal Stephenson, especially the novel *Snow Crash* (1992), provided models of virtual worlds such as Second Life that were developed in their aftermath. Hannu Rahaniemi's novel *The Quantum Thief* (2010) serves us a future in which people wear "entanglement rings," share a collective "exomemory," and can protect their privacy by activating "guvelot" which makes them appear blurry to observers and the exomemory. When the book's hero receives a message from his girlfriend through his ring, he muses: "sending brain-to-brain messages directly through a quantum teleportation channel seems like a dirty, invasive way to communicate" (2010: 38). This sounds fantastical until one realizes that prototypes of technologies that allow people to control computers through thoughts already exist, developers are hard at work on rings that display messages, and Facebook and Google already function as proto-exomemory.

When people explain the consequences of a new medium in terms of technological or social forces, or some combination of these, they rely on theoretical assumptions about causality. This chapter is organized around the major theoretical frameworks for understanding the causal flow between technology and society. There is a strong tendency, especially when technologies are new, to view them as causal agents, entering societies as active forces of change that humans have little power to resist. This perspective is known as *technological determinism*. When media are new, most popular messages about them are deterministic. A second perspective, the *social construction of technology*, argues that people are the primary sources of change in both technology and society. The *social shaping* perspective sees technology and society as continually influencing one another. Ultimately, over time, people stop questioning individual technologies. Through a process of *domestication*, they become taken-for-granted parts of everyday life, no longer seen as agents of change. In the remainder of this chapter, we'll look at each of these four perspectives, drawing on rhetorics of technologies old and new to illustrate how they work.

Technological determinism

Machines change us

In a widely read essay in the *Atlantic* (2008), Nick Carr posited that Google is "making us stupid." Before discussing other people's stories and neuroscience, he described his own dumbing down:

> Over the past few years I've had an uncomfortable sense that someone, or something, has been tinkering with my brain, remapping the neural circuitry, reprogramming the memory. My mind isn't going – so far as I can tell – but it's changing. I'm not thinking the way I used to think. I can feel it most strongly when I'm reading. Immersing myself in a book or a lengthy article used to be easy. My mind would get caught up in the narrative or the turns of the argument, and I'd spend hours strolling through long stretches of prose. That's rarely the case anymore. Now my concentration often starts to drift after two or three pages. I get fidgety, lose the thread, begin looking for something else to do.

As Carr tells it, "someone, or something," changed him. He was the passive recipient transformed by an outside force. As he himself articulates, Carr's essay is in keeping with a long-standing tradition of technological determinism in which the technology is conceptualized as an external agent that acts upon and changes society.

A year after Carr worried that Google was sapping our intelligence, widespread news coverage of a forthcoming academic lecture compared Facebook's ability to "enhance intelligence" with Twitter's power to "diminish it." The UK paper the *Telegraph* (Cockroft, 2009) described University of Stirling memory expert Tracy Alloway's take on how asynchronous and synchronous interaction online differentially affect the brain:

> Sudoku also stretched the working memory, as did keeping up with friends on Facebook, she said. But the "instant" nature of texting, Twitter and YouTube was not healthy for working memory. "On Twitter you receive an endless stream of information, but it's also very succinct," said Dr Alloway. "You don't

have to process that information. Your attention span is being reduced and you're not engaging your brain and improving nerve connections."

Problematic as they may be, concerns like this should not be dismissed. However, they should be understood in the theoretical and historical context of the reception of new technologies. Popular visions of new technology have tended toward technological determinism as far back as Ancient Greece. In *Phaedrus*, Socrates (Plato, *c.*370 BCE) decried the invention of the alphabet and writing as a threat to the oral tradition of Greek society (Ong, 1982). Anticipating what his nation's newspapers would write more than 2,000 years later (Koutsogiannis & Mitsikopoulou, 2003, to whom we will return in the next chapter), Socrates, paraphrasing an Egyptian God, warned the inventors of the alphabet:

> this discovery of yours will create forgetfulness in the learners' souls, because they will not use their memories; they will trust to the external written characters and not remember of themselves. The specific which you have discovered is an aid not to memory, but to reminiscence, and you give your disciples not truth, but only the semblance of truth; they will be hearers of many things and will have learned nothing; they will appear to be omniscient and will generally know nothing; they will be tiresome company, having the show of wisdom without the reality. (Plato, 2008 [360 BCE]: 69)

The language and forms of evidence may have changed, but the concern that communication technologies make us dumber is as old as writing. There is, as Lynn Spigel (2004: 140) put it, a "compulsion to repeat the same ideas, even as the society itself has noticeably changed." Reading books such as Marvin's *When Old Technologies Were New* (1988), *The Victorian Internet* (Standage, 1998), or Fischer's *America Calling* (1992) about the telephone's early days, the parallels between today's discourse, especially about the internet, and earlier rhetorics of technology are striking.

There are several variants of technological determinism. One, often linked to thinkers such as Canadian media theorist Marshall McLuhan, who coined the phrase "the medium is the message," is that technologies have characteristics that are transferred to those who use them. Claude Fischer calls this an "impact-imprint" perspective in which technologies change history by transferring "their essential qualities" to their users, imprinting themselves on users' individual and collective psyches (1992: 10). Fischer uses the example of Meyrowitz's influential book *No Sense of Place* (1985), which argued that, because physical and social spaces are separated through electronic media, people who use them lose their own sense of place. Arguments that the rapid-fire editing of current television film creates short attention spans, or that playing violent video games leads to violent behavior, represent other takes on this perspective. Seen this way, "a technology enters a society from outside and 'impacts' social life" (Fischer, 1992: 12).

Such direct effects of technology may be strongest when a technology is new because people do not yet understand it. Rather than "using" it, people may be "used by it" (Fischer, 1992: 12). Direct effects are also tied to thinking of technologies in a simplistic way: the more you use them, the more they use you, and the more you are influenced by them. For instance, many studies of internet use, some of which will be addressed in chapters 4 and 6, measure time spent online, divide people into heavy and light users, or users vs. non-users, and then correlate that measure with outcome variables such as loneliness or time spent with family. What a person was doing online is not addressed, collapsing such diverse activities as keeping in touch with one's mother, banking, researching political information, and looking at pornography into a single causal agent: The Internet.

In a milder form of technological determinism, media choice, technological features are seen as having direct consequences, but people are seen as making strategic, and usually rational, choices about which media they use for differing purposes. According to this perspective, "individuals will effectively employ media whose inherent characteristics are congruent with task demands" (Fulk, Steinfeld, Schmitz, & Power, 1987: 531). A later variant of this perspective, niche theory, developed by John Dimmick (2003), argues that different media allow for different exchanges of resources. For instance, instant messaging "appears to be for contacts with friends late at night while at home," while the landline phone is "for contacts made while at work" (Dimmick, Feaster, & Ramirez, 2011: 1278).

From a media choice perspective, change happens at an individual rather than societal level. By extension, this means that people are

THE ART OF LETTER-WRITING IS FAST DYING OUT. WHEN A LETTER COST NINE PENCE, IT SEEMED BUT FAIR TO TRY TO MAKE IT WORTH NINE PENCE ... NOW, HOWEVER, WE THINK WE ARE TOO BUSY FOR SUCH OLD-FASHIONED CORRESPONDENCE. WE FIRE OFF A MULTITUDE OF RAPID AND SHORT NOTES, INSTEAD OF SITTING DOWN TO HAVE A GOOD TALK OVER A REAL SHEET OF PAPER.

THE SUNDAY MAGAZINE

1871

IT IS, UNFORTUNATELY, ONE OF THE CHIEF CHARACTERISTICS OF MODERN BUSINESS TO BE ALWAYS IN A HURRY. IN OLDEN TIMES IT WAS DIFFERENT.

THE MEDICAL RECORD

1884

WITH THE ADVENT OF CHEAP NEWSPAPERS AND SUPERIOR MEANS OF LOCOMOTION ... THE DREAMY QUIET OLD DAYS ARE OVER ... FOR MEN NOW LIVE THINK AND WORK AT EXPRESS SPEED. THEY HAVE THEIR MERCURY OR POST LAID ON THEIR BREAKFAST TABLE IN THE EARLY MORNING, AND IF THEY ARE TOO HURRIED TO SNATCH FROM IT THE NEWS DURING THAT MEAL, THEY CARRY IT OFF, TO BE SULKILY READ AS THEY TRAVEL ... LEAVING THEM NO TIME TO TALK WITH THE FRIEND WHO MAY SHARE THE COMPARTMENT WITH THEM ... THE HURRY AND BUSTLE OF MODERN LIFE ... LACKS THE QUIET AND REPOSE OF THE PERIOD WHEN OUR FOREFATHERS, THE DAY'S WORK DONE, TOOK THEIR EASE ...

WILLIAM SMITH, MORLEY, ANCIENT AND MODERN

1886

CONVERSATION IS SAID TO BE A LOST ART ... GOOD TALK PRESUPPOSES LEISURE, BOTH FOR PREPARATION AND ENJOYMENT. THE AGE OF LEISURE IS DEAD, AND THE ART OF CONVERSATION IS DYING.

FRANK LESLIE'S POPULAR MONTHLY, VOLUME 29

1890

INTELLECTUAL LAZINESS AND THE HURRY OF THE AGE HAVE PRODUCED A CRAVING FOR LITERARY NIPS. THE TORPID BRAIN ... HAS GROWN TOO WEAK FOR SUSTAINED THOUGHT.

THERE NEVER WAS AN AGE IN WHICH SO MANY PEOPLE WERE ABLE TO WRITE BADLY.

ISRAEL ZANGWILL, THE BACHELORS' CLUB

1891

THE ART OF PURE LINE ENGRAVING IS DYING OUT. WE LIVE AT TOO FAST A RATE TO ALLOW FOR THE PREPARATION OF SUCH PLATES AS OUR FATHERS APPRECIATED. IF A PICTURE CATCHES THE PUBLIC FANCY, THE PUBLIC MUST HAVE AN ETCHED OR A PHOTOGRAVURED COPY OF IT WITHIN A MONTH OR TWO OF ITS APPEARANCE, THE DAYS WHEN ENGRAVERS WERE WONT TO SPEND TWO OR THREE YEARS OVER A SINGLE PLATE ARE FOR EVER GONE.

JOURNAL OF THE INSTITUTE OF JAMAICA, VOLUME I

1892

SO MUCH IS EXHIBITED TO THE EYE THAT NOTHING IS LEFT TO THE IMAGINATION. IT SOMETIMES SEEMS ALMOST POSSIBLE THAT THE MODERN WORLD MIGHT BE CHOKED BY ITS OWN RICHES, AND HUMAN FACULTY DWINDLE AWAY AMID THE MILLION INVENTIONS THAT HAVE BEEN INTRODUCED TO RENDER ITS EXERCISE UNNECESSARY.

THE ARTICLES IN THE QUARTERLIES EXTEND TO THIRTY OR MORE PAGES, BUT THIRTY PAGES IS NOW TOO MUCH. SO WE WITNESS A FURTHER CONDENSING PROCESS AND, WE HAVE. THE FORTNIGHTLY AND THE CONTEMPORARY WHICH REDUCE. THIRTY PAGES TO FIFTEEN PAGES SO THAT YOU MAY READ A LARGER NUMBER OF ARTICLES IN A SHORTER TIME AND IN A SHORTER FORM AS IF THIS LAST CONDENSING PROCESS WERE NOT ENOUGH THE CONDENSED ARTICLES OF THESE PERIODICALS ARE FURTHER CONDENSED BY THE DAILY PAPERS, WHICH WILL GIVE YOU A SUMMARY OF THE SUMMARY OF ALL THAT HAS BEEN WRITTEN ABOUT EVERYTHING.

THOSE WHO ARE DIPPING INTO SO MANY SUBJECTS AND GATHERING INFORMATION IN A SUMMARY AND SUPERFICIAL FORM LOSE THE HABIT OF SETTLING DOWN TO GREAT WORKS.

EPHEMERAL LITERATURE IS DRIVING OUT THE GREAT CLASSICS OF THE PRESENT AND THE PAST ... HURRIED READING CAN NEVER BE GOOD READING.

G. J. GOSCHEN, FIRST ANNUAL ADDRESS TO THE STUDENTS, TOYNBEE HALL, LONDON

1894

THE EXISTENCE OF MENTAL AND NERVOUS DEGENERATION AMONG A GROWING CLASS OF PEOPLE, ESPECIALLY IN LARGE CITIES, IS AN OBVIOUS PHENOMENON ... THE MANIA FOR STIMULANTS ... DISEASES OF THE MIND ARE ALMOST AS NUMEROUS AS THE DISEASES OF THE BODY ... THIS INTELLECTUAL CONDITION IS CHARACTERIZED BY A BRAIN INCAPABLE OF NORMAL WORKING ... IN A LARGE MEASURE DUE TO THE HURRY AND EXCITEMENT OF MODERN LIFE, WITH ITS FACILITIES FOR RAPID LOCOMOTION AND ALMOST INSTANTANEOUS COMMUNICATION BETWEEN REMOTE POINTS OF THE GLOBE ...

THE CHURCHMAN, VOLUME 71

1895

IF WE TEACH THE CHILDREN HOW TO PLAY AND ENCOURAGE THEM IN THEIR SPORTS ... INSTEAD OF SHUTTING THEM IN BADLY VENTILATED SCHOOLROOMS, THE NEXT GENERATION WILL BE MORE JOYOUS AND WILL BE HEALTHIER THAN THE PRESENT ONE.

PUBLIC OPINION: A COMPREHENSIVE SUMMARY OF THE PRESS THROUGHOUT THE WORLD, VOLUME 18

1895

THE CAUSE OF THE ... INCREASE IN NERVOUS DISEASE IS INCREASED DEMAND MADE BY THE CONDITIONS OF MODERN LIFE UPON THE BRAIN EVERYTHING IS DONE IN A HURRY. WE TALK ACROSS A CONTINENT, TELEGRAPH ACROSS AN OCEAN, TAKE A TRIP TO CHICAGO FOR AN HOURS TALK ... WE TAKE EVEN OUR PLEASURES SADLY AND MAKE A TASK OF OUR PLAY ... WHAT WONDER IF THE PRESSURE IS ALMOST MORE THAN OUR NERVES CAN BEAR.

G. SHRADY (FROM P. C. KNAPP) "ARE NERVOUS DISEASES INCREASING?" MEDICAL RECORD

1896

Cartoon 2.1 *"The pace of modern life,"* xkcd

THE MANAGERS OF SENSATIONAL NEWSPAPERS ... DO NOT TRY TO EDUCATE THEIR READERS AND MAKE THEM BETTER, BUT TEND TO CREATE PERVERTED TASTES AND DEVELOP VICIOUS TENDENCIES. THE OWNERS OF THESE PAPERS SEEM TO HAVE BUT ONE PURPOSE, AND THAT IS TO INCREASE THEIR CIRCULATION.

MEDICAL BRIEF, VOLUME 26

1898

TO TAKE SUFFICIENT TIME FOR OUR MEALS SEEMS FREQUENTLY IMPOSSIBLE, ON ACCOUNT OF THE DEMANDS ON OUR TIME MADE BY OUR BUSINESS ... WE ACT ON THE APPARENT BELIEF THAT ALL OF OUR BUSINESS IS SO PRESSING THAT WE MUST JUMP ON THE QUICKEST CAR HOME, EAT OUR DINNER IN THE MOST HURRIED WAY, MAKE THE CLOSEST CONNECTION FOR A CAR RETURNING ...

LOUIS JOHN RETTGER,
STUDIES IN ADVANCED PHYSIOLOGY

1898

IN THESE DAYS OF INCREASING RAPID ARTIFICIAL LOCOMOTION, MAY I BE PERMITTED TO SAY A WORD IN FAVOUR OF A VERY WORTHY AND VALUABLE OLD FRIEND OF MINE, MR. LONG WALK?

I AM AFRAID THAT THIS GOOD GENTLEMAN IS IN DANGER OF GETTING NEGLECTED, IF NOT FORGOTTEN. WE LIVE IN DAYS OF WATER TRIPS AND LAND TRIPS, EXCURSIONS BY SEA, ROAD AND RAIL- BICYCLES AND TRICYCLES, TRAM CARS AND MOTOR CARS ... BUT IN MY HUMBLE OPINION, GOOD HONEST WALKING EXERCISE FOR HEALTH BEATS ALL OTHER KINDS OF LOCOMOTION INTO A COCKED HAT.

J. THATCHER, 'A PLEA FOR A LONG WALK',
THE PUBLISHERS' CIRCULAR

1902

THE ART OF CONVERSATION IS ALMOST A LOST ONE. PEOPLE TALK AS THEY RIDE BICYCLES-AT A RUSH-WITHOUT PAUSING TO CONSIDER THEIR SURROUNDINGS ... WHAT HAS BEEN GENERALLY UNDERSTOOD AS CULTURED SOCIETY IS RAPIDLY DETERIORATING INTO BASENESS AND VOLUNTARY IGNORANCE. THE PROFESSION OF LETTERS IS SO LITTLE UNDERSTOOD, AND SO FAR FROM BEING SERIOUSLY APPRECIATED, THAT ... NEWSPAPERS ARE FULL, NOT OF THOUGHTFUL HONESTLY EXPRESSED PUBLIC OPINION ON THE AFFAIRS OF THE NATION, BUT OF VAPID PERSONALITIES INTERESTING TO NONE SAVE GOSSIPS AND BUSY BODIES.

MARIE CORELLI,
FREE OPINIONS FREELY EXPRESSED

1905

THERE IS A GREAT TENDENCY AMONG THE CHILDREN OF TODAY TO REBEL AGAINST RESTRAINT, NOT ONLY THAT PLACED UPON THEM BY THE WILL OF THE PARENT, BUT AGAINST ANY RESTRAINT OR LIMITATION OF WHAT THEY CONSIDER THEIR RIGHTS ... THIS FACT HAS FILLED WELL MINDED PEOPLE WITH GREAT APPREHENSIONS FOR THE FUTURE.

REV. HENRY HUSSMANN,
THE AUTHORITY OF PARENTS

1906

THERE IS A GREAT TENDENCY AMONG THE CHILDREN OF TODAY TO REBEL AGAINST RESTRAINT, NOT ONLY THAT PLACED UPON THEM BY THE WILL OF THE PARENT, BUT AGAINST ANY RESTRAINT OR LIMITATION OF WHAT THEY CONSIDER THEIR RIGHTS ... THIS FACT HAS FILLED WELL MINDED PEOPLE WITH GREAT APPREHENSIONS FOR THE FUTURE.

REV. HENRY HUSSMANN,
THE AUTHORITY OF PARENTS

1906

OUR MODERN FAMILY GATHERING, SILENT AROUND THE FIRE, EACH INDIVIDUAL WITH HIS HEAD BURIED IN HIS FAVOURITE MAGAZINE, IS THE SOMEWHAT NATURAL OUTCOME OF THE BANISHMENT OF COLLOQUY FROM THE SCHOOL ...

THE JOURNAL OF EDUCATION, VOLUME 29

1907

PLAYS IN THEATRES AT THE PRESENT TIME PRESENT SPECTACLES AND DEAL OPENLY WITH SITUATIONS WHICH NO PERSON WOULD HAVE DARED TO MENTION IN GENERAL SOCIETY FORTY YEARS AGO ... THE CURRENT REPRESENTATIONS OF NUDE MEN AND WOMEN IN THE DAILY JOURNALS AND THE ILLUSTRATED MAGAZINES WOULD HAVE EXCLUDED SUCH PERIODICALS FROM ALL RESPECTABLE FAMILIES TWO DECADES AGO ... THOSE WHO HAVE BEEN DIVORCED ... FORTY AND FIFTY YEARS AGO LOST AT ONCE AND IRREVOCABLY THEIR STANDING IN SOCIETY, WHILE TO-DAY THEY CONTINUE IN ALL THEIR SOCIAL RELATIONSHIPS, HARDLY CHANGED ...

EDITORIAL, THE UNITED PRESBYTERIAN

1908

WE WRITE MILLIONS MORE LETTERS THAN DID OUR GRANDFATHERS, BUT THE INCREASE IN VOLUME HAS BROUGHT WITH IT AN AUTOMATIC ARTIFICIAL MACHINE-LIKE RING ... AN EXAMINATION OF A FILE OF OLD LETTERS REVEALS NOT ONLY A REMARKABLE GRASP OF DETAILS, BUT A FITNESS AND COURTLINESS TOO OFTEN TOTALLY LACKING IN THE MECHANICAL CURT CUT AND DRIED LETTERS OF TO-DAY.

FORREST CRISSEY, HANDBOOK OF
MODERN BUSINESS CORRESPONDENCE

1908

A HUNDRED YEARS AGO IT TOOK SO LONG AND COST SO MUCH TO SEND A LETTER THAT IT SEEMED WORTH WHILE TO PUT SOME TIME AND THOUGHT INTO WRITING IT. NOW THE QUICKNESS AND THE CHEAPNESS OF THE POST SEEM TO JUSTIFY THE FEELING THAT A BRIEF LETTER TO-DAY MAY BE FOLLOWED BY ANOTHER NEXT WEEK-A 'LINE' NOW BY ANOTHER TO-MORROW.

HERBERT HOLMES BOYNTON, PRINCIPLES OF COMPOSITION

1915

able to avoid technological influence by avoiding the technology. According to Lynne Markus (1994), however, the key issue is not which features have which effects. Instead, "it is the degree to which the outcomes, whether positive or negative, are the inevitable results of technological characteristics, or whether they might be subject to other influences" (1994: 122). Markus argues that technological determinism is ultimately an optimistic theory. If negative outcomes can be traced to technological causes, then they can be eliminated with better technology. It is also, however, a disempowering perspective that positions people as powerless to stop these changes unless they invent new, better, or different technologies or eschew technology altogether.

As the similarities amongst Socrates', Carr's, and Alloway's articulation of new media's effect on wisdom suggest, deterministic rhetorics tend to be formulaic and hyperbolic (Turkle, 2004). Predictable negative stories are met with predictable positive alternatives in a familiar contradictory binary. In the 1920s, for instance, people anticipated that radio would "provide culture and education to the masses, eliminate politicians' ability to incite passions in a mob, bring people closer to government proceedings, and produce a national culture that would transcend regional and local jealousies" (Douglas, 2004 [1999]: 20). Now, Douglas continues, "we've been witness to all sorts of overheated and contradictory predictions about the Internet: it will re-create political and cultural communities in cyberspace; it will bring pornographers, stalkers, and credit-card scammers into our homes, corrupting our kids and ransacking our privacy." The cartoonist Randall Munroe demonstrated this beautifully in his cartoon "The Pace of Modern Life" (cartoon 2.1).

The historian David Nye (1997) has carried out extensive research on how nineteenth-century Americans responded to new technologies of the time. As he summarized in a later article (2004), Americans could have used many narratives to make sense of new technology, but in practice usually used six, three *utopian*, envisioning a world improved by technology, and three *dystopian*, visions of a world made worse. In the utopian stories, technologies are seen as natural societal developments, as improvements to daily life, or as forces that will transform reality for the better. Dystopian reactions emphasize fears of losing control, becoming dependent, and being unable to stop change. In the three dystopian rhetorics Nye identifies, technology may be seen as a way for elites to control the masses, as agents of doom, or as malevolent tricksters that promise positive change but in the end only make our lives more difficult. "The long history of popular culture's alternately fearful and euphoric representations of electronic communication," wrote Boddy (2004: 4), "suggests the continuing historical relevance of such ephemeral fantasies of pleasure and terror." Even in his dystopian article, Carr (2008) offered utopian visions, arguing that "the new technology did often have the effects [Socrates] feared," yet also that Socrates "couldn't foresee the many ways that writing and reading would serve to spread information, spur fresh ideas, and expand human knowledge (if not wisdom)."

Recurrent themes in the reception of new technology

We are surrounded by messages that treat media qualities as a cause of social consequences. In this section, I identify common recurring themes regarding new media and social life that appear in popular media. In addition to previous theorists and cultural historians of technology, I make use of Janna Quitney Anderson's (2005) compilation of predictions and descriptions of the internet from newspapers, magazines, and other American sources from the early 1990s. I also use cartoons from the *New Yorker* – an influential and long-lived magazine that has been questioning our relationship to technology through humor since its inception in the 1920s – and letters from the two most popular American advice columns, "Ann Landers" and "Dear Abby." The *New Yorker* reached a sector of the American population – urban, educated, and affluent – most likely to be early adapters of the internet and earlier new technologies. "Ann Landers" and "Dear Abby" together reached as many as 110 million readers daily and, especially in the mid 1990s, could well have been the only mass messages about the role of the internet in intimate relationships that many people encountered. Though these sources might seem trivial, silly, or even gossipy, they should not be underestimated in their capacity to reflect pervasive cultural attitudes. Writers and editors design mass-mediated messages in order to resonate with their audience's concerns. Their livelihood depends upon it. Though other kinds of messages, including scholarly reports such as those we'll turn to in the remaining chapters, may be better sources of accurate information about new media effects, mass-mediated messages are considerably more likely to influence how people think about new technology and, as we'll return to below, how they subsequently behave. The themes I'll consider in this section include issues of the authenticity of mediated communication and relationships, the quality of mediated interactions, the formation of new relationships, the effects of anonymity (honesty, deception, liberation, and the potential erasure of status), and the effects on existing close relationships (will they become closer, be replaced with mediated relationships, be forgone altogether?). I postpone my discussion of the themes about children, specifically their status as potential victims and as dangerously empowered, until the section on social construction that follows.

Socrates' idea that writing provides "not truth, but only the semblance of truth" remains very much with us. At the core of most, if not all, of the rhetorics about mediated forms of personal connection is a persistent sense that mediated interaction and the relationships sustained through it are not *real*. Many "fear that actual human connection has been irretrievably lost," although others hope "that communication technologies can promote human connectivity" (Sturken & Thomas, 2004: 3). In the telephone's early years, some worried it could sustain "only a semblance of 'real' relations" (Fischer, 1992: 224). The common use of the term "virtual" to describe online relationships and groups, and of the acronym "IRL" (in real life) to describe offline connections, are evidence of this deep-seated presumption.

People often question the *quality of mediated interactions*, believing technological mediation takes away the social cues that provide rich meaning (a topic explored in depth in the next chapter). Walter Benjamin (2009 [1935]) famously argued that the "aura" of tangible art provides much of its value, a value lessened in the age of mechanical reproduction. Replicating this concern, internet critic Stoll (1995, cited in Anderson, 2005: 65) wrote that, in comparison to letters, electronic interaction was cold: "The paper doesn't age, the signatures don't fade. Perhaps a future generation will save their romances on floppy disks [but] give me a shoebox of old letters."

Electronic messages are frequently portrayed as vacuous. A 2009 study by market research firm Pear Analytics, for instance, created a category called "pointless babble" into which they placed 40 percent of Twitter messages, echoing oft-heard complaints that mobile phones lead to empty conversation, sustained for the sake of interacting even when we have nothing to say ("Twitter tweets are 40% 'babble,'" 2009). The idea that new media cause pointless babble could also be seen in a 1927 *New Yorker* cartoon in which a luxuriantly robed, very made-up, clearly affluent, woman reclining on a couch said: "Hold the line a minute, dear ... I'm trying to think what I have on my mind" (cartoon 2.2).

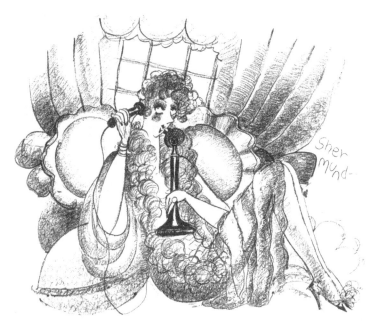

Cartoon 2.2 "Hold the line a minute dear . . . I'm trying to think what I have on my mind."

One of the hopes surrounding the internet is that it can *broaden our pool of potential relational partners* and lead to new relationships (a topic we will return to in chapter 5). For instance, this testimonial from "A Netizen in Chicago" appeared in "Ann Landers" in 1996:

> I met my girlfriend on the Net. She is Canadian. I live in Illinois. We have gotten together, face to face, only once, but over the last few months, we have gotten to know each other well. We have fallen in love. We have four meetings planned and call each other twice a week. We e-mail every night.
>
> I also have made many friends on the Net. Most of us will never meet, but we offer our support when one of us is feeling blue and our accolades when things are going great.
>
> On our news group alone, many friendships have developed. There have been four marriages so far, and several relationships are now in progress that will probably end up in marriage. None of us is hooked on the Net, but we do check frequently to see how our on-line pals are doing.

At the same time, many question whether relationships formed this way can ever be as real as those formed face-to-face. Cartoon 2.3, from 2006, plays off the befuddled faces of older parents against the smiling faces of a young – mediated – couple, showing both the

SIPRESS

Cartoon 2.3 "We met online."

utopian hope for new relational opportunities and the wary uncertainty that surrounds them.

One reason for uncertainty in mediated environments is that, with fewer visual and auditory social cues, people are not sure whether or not they can *trust* other people to be who they claim to be. This is the central problem of anonymity. Perhaps the best encapsulation of the binary between hope and dread that the anonymity of the internet provides is Peter Steiner's famous 1993 *New Yorker* cartoon of two dogs, one seated on a chair at the computer, the other sitting on the floor watching (cartoon 2.4). The computing dog explained to the other, "On the Internet, nobody knows you're a dog," a caption which, writes Anderson (2005: 228), "will live forever as an online-culture touchstone." This cartoon has been reproduced in numerous scholarly

Cartoon 2.4 "On the Internet, nobody knows you're a dog."

articles and books, has its own Wikipedia page, and has become one of the most popular *New Yorker* cartoons ever, as indicated by its high rank on requested reprint and presentation rights. A Google search for its caption in 2009 turned up more than 250,000 hits, and by 2013 it turned up nearly 53 million. Its transnational appeal can be seen in its appearance on the cover of an Estonian book about the internet (Institut Za Etnologiju I Folkloristiku, 2004).

Although Steiner has said he didn't know what the cartoon was about when he drew it, *New Yorker* cartoon editor Robert Mankoff said it "perfectly predicted both the Internet's promise and its problems" (2004: 618). Whether this cartoon represents a dream or a nightmare depends on whether one is the dog or the fool unknowingly talking to the dog.

Of course, no one really expects house pets to go online and pretend to be people, but they often expect that sparse social cues will cause people to lie about themselves. As one man explained in a 1994 letter to "Ann Landers":

> Every woman on a computer line describes herself as Cindy Crawford, and every guy is Tom Cruise. Women lie about their marital status, weight, age and occupation. And get this, Ann, some women are actually guys.

Authentic self-representation is not always a simple question of true and false, as we will address in chapter 5. With its potential to liberate people from the constraints of their social context, people may also be seen as becoming *more honest* in mediated encounters. This advice column letter-writer admitted to Abby that she had presented a deceptive identity online, yet claimed the emotions and relationships predicated upon it were real:

> I am deeply in love with a man who is handsome, smart and loving. We are engaged and happy together. The problem? We met on the Internet. Abby, he thinks I am 26, but I'm not. Everything I've said to him has been a lie. I am really 12.

On a societal level, anonymity opens the possibility of *liberation* from the divisions that come about from seeing one another's race, age, gender, disabilities, and so on. Standage (1998) tells of an interracial relationship formed via telegraph without either party's knowledge of

Cartoon 2.5 "How the hell does Facebook know I'm a dog?"

the other's racial identity. Early rhetoric about the internet often speculated that the reduction of social cues would lead to people valuing
one another's contributions for their intrinsic worth rather than the
speaker's status. The internet would lead to the world Martin Luther
King Jr. dreamed of, in which people would be judged by the content
of their character rather than the color of their skin. A now-legendary
telecommunication company advertisement that ran during the 1997
Superbowl described it like this: "There is no race, there are no
genders, there is no age, there are no infirmities, there are only
minds. Utopia? No, the Internet." Sites like Facebook and (for a time)
Google+ have insisted that all accounts belong to individuals who use
real names and have encouraged everyone to enter many identifying
pieces of information that tie them to particular verifiable places and
times. This stance is both mocked and critiqued in Rob Cottingham's
2010 twist on Steiner's dog cartoon (cartoon 2.5).

On the other hand, many people, especially in the middle and
upper classes, view social divisions as useful and necessary means
of protecting themselves and their families from unwanted outside
influences and dangers (Marvin, 1988; Spigel, 1992). For them, the

specter of technological *erasure of social status information* is frightening. Communication technologies have long been represented as a source of stress for families, making it too easy for people to engage in "irregular courtship" with people outside the community (Marvin, 1988: 73). The telephone was feared for its potential to enable the "wrong kinds" of sociability across age, class, and racial lines (Fischer, 1992: 225). When the telephone was new, articles criticized ordinary people who called New York City's mayor regularly, simply because they now could. Those placing the calls might have understood this as a utopian outcome of the technology – allowing them greater access to those of significantly higher status and greater ability to participate in governance – but, for the mayor and other members of the elite, it demonstrated an intrusive threat. Furthermore, even when people themselves do not enter the sanctuary of the privileged, their communication artifacts might. The phonograph and radio were often viewed as corrupting because they raised the specter of interracial interaction (and sex!) by bringing ragtime and jazz music written and performed by black artists into affluent white homes (Douglas, 2004 [1999]).

Building new online relationships has been both touted and decried as a way for a person to "assemble his or her own electronic neighborhood" (Dertouzos, 1991, in Anderson, 2005: 49). Though some, such as Dertouzos, see this as a perk, others worry that, rather than lessening differences in social class, social divides will be reproduced or increased by technology. "The superhighway may connect us more to other people of similar interests and beliefs," worried Brown in the *Seattle Post-Intelligencer* (1995, cited in Anderson, 2005: 64), "But we'll have less communication with those who are different. Socially we may find ourselves returning to a form of tribalism, as we separate ourselves along group lines – racial, ethnic, ideological – choosing access to only the information that speaks to our identities and beliefs." Eli Pariser's (2011) book *The Filter Bubble* makes a similar argument, raising concerns that algorithms shape what people see, based on assumptions about what will interest them.

Technologically deterministic rhetorics also frame new communication media as improving and damaging the close personal relationships people sustain face-to-face. The telephone was seen as a means to bring people closer together, build communities, and decrease loneliness (de Sola Pool, 1977; Fischer, 1992). Electricity was going to decrease the divorce rate since it would make domestic chores easier to do and lessen the conflict they created (Marvin, 1988). The automobile spawned dreams of family togetherness (Fischer, 1992), as seen in the recurrent motif of the car-based family vacation. Early ads for the radio and phonograph often showed happy families where clean children looked approvingly at their parents as they gathered around the technology in their living rooms. As Spigel (1992: 3) shows in her analysis of popular communication during television's early years, the television "was depicted as a panacea for the broken homes and hearts of wartime life . . . shown to restore faith in family togetherness . . . however . . . equally dystopian discourses warned of television's devastating effects on family relationships and the efficient functioning household."

In the context of contemporary digital media, the hope remains that new communication technologies will *bring families and loved ones together*. Today, we hear of people staying in touch with their children through Skype, or using mobile "family plans" to keep the family in continuous contact. A 1995 article in *Wired* predicted that the family would rise to the top of a new communication hierarchy: "Every family will have its own mailing list carrying contributions from its members. . . . I sense that the rules will be something like this: friends over strangers; family over friends; and within those categories, the geographically or chronologically close over the distant" (Hapgood, 1995, cited in Anderson, 2005: 64).

The dystopian alternative is usually articulated as a fear that new media will take people away from their intimate relationships, as they *substitute* mediated relationships or even media use itself for face-to-face engagement. Fischer (1992) described early twentieth-century concerns that the telephone would replace visiting. The fear of substituting mediated for meaningful relationships also occurred around television. A 1962 *New Yorker* cartoon, for instance, showed a husband and wife seated at the dinner table, his face buried in a newspaper (cartoon 2.6). The wife watched a television depicting a couple sharing a romantic dinner. The image on the screen simulated intimacy while media old (newspaper) and new (television) kept the spouses from connecting with each other. A popular photo passed

Cartoon 2.6

around social networks in 2013 specifically drew this same connection, depicting an historic black-and-white image of a train full of men, backs to the camera, all reading newspapers. The tagline? "All this technology making us anti-social."

A common motif in stories of digital media damaging relationships is the "cyberaffair." One of the most recurrent metaphors advice columns used to describe the internet during its early American diffusion was "homewrecker." Published letters and replies repeatedly described men and women who, upon getting access to the internet, found a new love (or pornography), and ruined their marriage. A 1995 letter to "Ann Landers" begged Ann to warn readers about "an insidious monster about to pounce on the American people. It will destroy more marriages and lives than anything the world has ever known. It's called the Internet." Ann Landers cast the phenomenon as rampant, writing in 1998, "My mail tells me that the Internet may become the principal home-wrecker of the next century."

In addition to ruining close relationships, the internet and other new media are frequently depicted as causing *social isolation*. In the *Wall Street Journal*, Hays speculated that "Connecting with one and all in the electronic ether could leave people more disconnected than ever before, as the necessity of face-to-face contact diminishes. If a troubled or shy office worker easily finds solace and approval on the networks, will she be less inclined to seek out friends on the job?" (1993, cited in Anderson, 2005: 96). Writers to "Ann Landers" and "Dear Abby" in the late 1990s frequently described internet users as "junkies" who get "addicted" to the internet, destroying their close relationships. One wrote:

> My husband of 22 years has become a recluse. He refuses social invitations, has quit attending our children's activities and lies to me about the amount of time he spends surfing the 'Net. Like an alcoholic, he apologizes and promises to do better, but once the computer clicks on, he sits there, transfixed, until the wee hours of the morning. (1998)

"People are not going to want to leave their homes when they can have more fun in cyberspace," warned futurist Faith Popcorn in the London *Independent* (Anderson, 2005: 67–8). In *US News & World Report*, Neal Postman offered a futuristic scenario that summarized the dystopian fears concisely:

> Public life will have disappeared because we did not see, in time to reverse the process, that our dazzling technologies were privatizing almost all social activities. . . . We replaced meeting friends with the video telephone and electronic mail . . . We became afraid of real people and eventually forgot how to behave in public places, which had become occupied almost entirely by criminals. The rest of us had no need to be with each other. (1993, cited in Anderson, 2005: 96)

To summarize, technologically determinist rhetorics of digital media, like those of previous communication technologies, often focus on the authenticity of identity and the well-being of "real" relationships. Utopian rhetorics emphasize the happy prospect that technology will liberate true selves from the constraints of geography and the shackles of marginalized social identities and empower them to enrich their offline relationships and engage in new ones online. These visions are pitted against tangled dystopian scenarios of deception, tribalism, and the erasure of social class distinctions. These perpetuate fears that communication technologies will take us farther apart from one another, leading us to cocoon in highly selective groups of like others, embracing machines instead of people. These rhetorics are predictable, and tell us as much – if not more – about society than they tell us about technologies. They point to our deep need to trust, connect with, and protect one another and ourselves, and the perpetual struggles these needs engender. Once again, xkcd cartoonist Munroe summarizes the issues concisely (cartoon 2.7).

Social construction of technology

People have the power

In the examples I have just discussed, and the historical trends they represent, technology is positioned as causing us and our social lives to change. Determinism views technology as arising independent of social contexts and then affecting them. Other perspectives share concern about the same issues, but do not grant technology as much causal agency. The Social Construction of Technology (SCOT) perspective focuses on how technologies arise from social processes. SCOT proponents view technologically deterministic perspectives as "inadequate as explanations and dangerously misleading [because] human beings, not machines, are the agents of change, as men and women introduce new systems of machines that alter their life world" (Nye, 1997: 180). One focus of social constructivism is how social forces influence the invention of new technologies (e.g. Bijker, Hughes, & Pinch, 1987; Bijker & Law, 1992). From a SCOT perspective, inventors are embedded in social contexts that make it feasible to use a garage to create a personal computer or a bicycle repair shop to invent an airplane. The choices that designers and developers make as they develop technology are seen as dependent on their social contexts which are, in turn, shaped in part by communication. In the contemporary context, one might look at the female avatars available in online games, characters that are almost uniformly shaped like pornographic fantasy figures, and posit that this is related to their having been designed by people – primarily male – who are embedded in a

THE
SIMPLE ANSWERS
TO THE QUESTIONS THAT GET ASKED ABOUT EVERY NEW TECHNOLOGY:

WILL [____] MAKE US ALL GENIUSES?	**NO**
WILL [____] MAKE US ALL MORONS?	**NO**
WILL [____] DESTROY WHOLE INDUSTRIES?	**YES**
WILL [____] MAKE US MORE EMPATHETIC?	**NO**
WILL [____] MAKE US LESS CARING?	**NO**
WILL TEENS USE [____] FOR SEX?	**YES**
WERE THEY GOING TO HAVE SEX ANYWAY?	**YES**
WILL [____] DESTROY MUSIC?	**NO**
WILL [____] DESTROY ART?	**NO**
BUT CAN'T WE GO BACK TO A TIME WHEN—	**NO**
WILL [____] BRING ABOUT WORLD PEACE?	**NO**
WILL [____] CAUSE WIDESPREAD ALIENATION BY CREATING A WORLD OF EMPTY EXPERIENCES?	**WE WERE ALREADY ALIENATED**

Cartoon 2.7 "Simple answers," xkcd

patriarchal culture that views women as sex objects and thinks of their primary audience as men and boys.

Furthermore, SCOT theorists see technological development as influenced by many factors beyond the inventors. Investors – both private and governmental – have priorities that shape which technologies are deemed worthy of pursuit and given the resources to enable their success. Competitors drive development in different directions, as seen, for instance, in Microsoft turning from a DOS interface to Windows in emulation of Apple's graphic operating system, or Facebook's efforts to capitalize on the success of Twitter with revisions of its own site. Government agencies may shape technological development with their dispersion of grant monies, policies that prescribe what machines and sites can and cannot do, and actions that influence companies (as when some companies began using secure connections by default to lessen the likelihood of NSA eavesdropping on their customers). Furthermore, users shape development, especially, as Fischer (1992) notes, when they are organized. These differing sources of influence do not always agree. Indeed, they are often in conflict with one another, and the shape of any given technology is often a matter of compromise.

SCOT proponents also focus on what happens during technological adoption, arguing that a wide range of social, economic, governmental, and cultural factors influence how people take up and use media. In his study of the adoption of the telephone, Fischer (1992: 269) argued for a "user perspective." "Users," he wrote, "try to put a new technology to their own ends, which can lead to paradoxical outcomes not easily deducible from the straightforward logic of the technology." Lister, Dovey, Giddings, Grant, and Kelly (2003: 81) draw on media theorist Raymond Williams to argue that "whatever the original intention to develop a technology might be, subsequently other social groups, with different interests or needs, adapt, modify or subvert the uses to which any particular technology is put." Communication about technology, as seen in the messages discussed above, is one important force in these processes. The telegraph, radio, refrigerator, and internet are all technologies whose unexpected uses became their most common (Nye, 2004). The internet, conceived as a military back-up system, exemplifies technology re-envisioned and transformed by its users.

Though it's important to understand the power users have, it's easy to grant too much influence to individuals, when, as Fischer (1992) notes, there are other social structures at play, including access, availability, price, and marketing. Texting is an interesting example of this. It used to be that when I mentioned using mobile phones to send text messages, most of my college students – almost all of whom had mobile phones in their pockets – stared blankly. They'd never heard of such a thing, despite the fact that this had become a major use of mobile phones in other countries in Asia and Europe years earlier. Regulatory and pricing decisions in the United States had hindered its diffusion (Ling, 2012). Around 2005, pricing plans on US cell phone contracts changed to make texting inexpensive. Then my students all used this feature of the phone. They no longer stared blankly. Indeed, some of them were too busy texting under their desks to register what I was saying.

The social influence model proposed by Janet Fulk (1993) draws attention to the influence of peers on individuals' perceptions and subsequent uses of media. In her work on adoption of new media (specifically email) in an organizational context, she found that the perspectives of peers, especially "attractive" peers – those who are friends as well as good colleagues – were strong influences on individuals' attitudes toward email. In a study of attitudes toward mobile phones in the midwestern United States, Campbell and Russo (2003) also showed that attitudes toward behaviors, such as whether or not you should turn off your mobile in a restaurant, were shaped by the attitudes of peers. As people discuss new media, and as those media are represented in other media such as television, print, and film, devices themselves come to carry social meaning (so that some phones look cool, and others look dorky). Media are also discursively associated with genders, so that computers are often cast as male, and telephones as female (Rakow, 1992; Hijazi-Omari & Ribak, 2008), and the disembodied voices of Siri and Cortana are female.

Moral panic

As we saw in our discussion of technological determinism, new media often stir up fears of moral decline. These fears, which take form in dystopian rhetorics, can lead to important policy decisions at personal, household, governmental, and design levels. In other words, the communication about the technologies becomes more important than the technologies in shaping the uses and effects of new media. Such rhetorics often focus on the well-being of children, and especially on the well-being of teenage girls. Concerns about protecting children seem to arise almost instantaneously in the wake of any new communication medium. Children are often seen as innocents who can be corrupted, damaged, and permanently transformed by technology in ways that adults such as parents, teachers, and political leaders are powerless to prevent (Facer, 2012; Marvin, 2004; Sturken & Thomas, 2004). "The relationship of children and media culture, and the larger social context in which this relationship is forged," wrote Marvin (2004: 283), "is constantly debated and rehashed in the popular press and in public discourse." In the United States, the automobile led to fears that teenagers would isolate themselves from their families (Fischer, 1992). Among the media that have been charged with causing children to mature too soon and/or become juvenile delinquents are books, movies, comic books, and television (Fang, 2008). In American history, dime novels, so popular in the mid 1800s, spawned concern about the intellectual development of their readers, potential increases in anti-social behavior, and criminality, but also fostered hopes that the new medium could be used for enlightenment (Fang, 2008).

These days, children are seen as likely to be exposed to (or, worse yet, exploited for) pornography and sexual encounters and to encounter pervasive cyberbullying. The most prominent examples of this in the discourse around the internet concern sexual predation. To hear much of the public representation of the internet is to imagine a world in which sexual crimes are reaching new heights as unwitting innocents are drawn into deceptive relationships that end in molestation, abduction, and even death. Adult men do sometimes use the internet to lure girls into inappropriate relationships. This is surely awful, but it is very unusual. When adult men and under-aged girls do meet through the internet for sexual encounters, it is usually consensual (inasmuch as an under-aged person is capable of consent) and honest, if morally dubious (Cassell & Cramer, 2007; Wolak & Finkelhor, 2013). Cassell and Cramer's close analysis of US federal crime-report data regarding crimes against children shows that crimes against people 12–17 years old fell between 46 percent and 69 percent after 1993–5, despite the fact that millions of young people integrated the internet into their lives in that time frame. Sexual predation between strangers remains extremely infrequent relative to sexual predation within existing relationships, and assaults between those who met online are but a tiny proportion of stranger crimes (Internet Safety Technical Task Force, 2008).

However, the perception that this is a serious risk to most young people who use the internet is a classic case of a "moral panic" in which anxieties over uncontrollable social forces become the focus of efforts to understand a new cultural trend (Cohen, 1972). Panics displace our anxieties over something more important onto the technology, perhaps because they are too difficult or threatening to face directly (Thomas, 2004). One could just as easily argue that the internet has protected teens by keeping them home. Sexual predation is terrible, but if your goal is to reduce sexual crimes against children or women, the internet is the wrong place to focus. It is, however, a much easier target than our own marriages, homes, neighborhoods, places of worship, and schools, where most crimes against children and women occur (Internet Safety Technical Task Force, 2008).

Similarly, media reports of cyberbullying (often ending in a teenage suicide) are not entirely inaccurate, but are deceptive. Online bullying is almost always rooted in offline bullying (Livingstone & Smith, 2014). A 2013 overview of youth internet safety surveys conducted between 2000 and 2010 (Jones, Mitchell, & Finkelhor, 2013) attributed what seems to be an increase in online harassment to more female friends interacting more often through the internet, with the consequence that more offline aggression bleeds into online environments.

In a review of all the peer-reviewed empirical research they could find on child risk and harm online, Livingstone and Smith (2013) concluded that approximately 20 percent of adolescents are affected by online aggression, strangers seeking contact, sexting, or pornography. Despite increases in young people's access to online experiences in recent years, exposure to risk and actual harm have not become more frequent (Livingstone & Smith, 2014). Parents, however, tend to overestimate how often their children encounter distressing material online (Sorbring & Lundin, 2012). This is not to argue that children do not experience harm online. For the small percentage of young people who both encounter sexual materials or predators online and find those experiences distressing, the harm can be very real (Livingstone & Smith, 2014). Yet it is important to recognize that, on average, the harms children experience through digital media are in line with, or less than, those they experience without new media.

The flip side to children's abilities to do new things outside parental supervision through technology is that children are often seen not just as endangered, but as dangerous. Advertisements for early computers, targeted at parents in hopes they would buy them for their children, presented young people as natural users, even if parents were constructed as naïve, setting the stage for the perception that parents are clueless, and children naturals (Facer, 2012). Although children neither have nor think they have all the digital skills that are attributed to them (Livingstone, 2008), some children do develop skills and use technologies in ways that limit how much parents and others can control them (Banet-Weiser, 2004; Marvin, 2004). In one of my son's middle schools, for instance, students thwarted the district's efforts to keep them off social media on school machines by creating a system of hidden folders that gave them access to sites they continued to use.

The phenomenon of teen sexting, sharing naked selfies with each other via their mobile phones, combines the fear of children's sexuality and its potential negative consequences with the fear of children's empowerment. A comprehensive review of sexting research, media coverage, and educational resources in Australia, combined with focus group research, found that teens viewed "sexting" as an adult term that did not reflect their practices and experiences (Albury, Crawford, Byron, & Mathews, 2013). Given the regularity with which prominent adults are publicly humiliated for committing behaviors such as sending photographs of their genitalia through Twitter, one has to wonder how much adults' fear of children's behavior reflects fear of their own activities.

Fears about children can also be understood as arising from adults' fear of losing control over them, a problem inherent in child rearing, regardless of whatever technologies may or may not be present. Since fear is often displaced onto seemingly more manageable technology, parents, child welfare bodies, clinicians, teachers, and governments often try to protect children by implementing surveillance systems, legislating policy limitations on children's access to technology, and creating new technologies to limit children's interaction with technology (Marvin, 2004: 281). Displacing our anxieties about children's safety onto the internet and mobile phones makes our fear more manageable, but does little to protect children, and may keep them from realizing the benefits new technologies can offer them (Cassell & Cramer, 2007; Ito et al., 2010; Livingstone, Haddon, & Görzig, 2012; Livingstone & Helsper, 2013).

In sum, social constructivism provides a polar alternative to technological determinism. Rather than viewing social change as a consequence of new media, it views new technologies and their uses as consequences of social factors. From this perspective, the utopian and dystopian rhetorics I discussed above tell us little about the technology, but do provide insight into how technologies come to be and how they come to be understood and used. The example of moral panics shows how deterministic rhetorics can give rise to understandings of technology and to policy decisions which in turn shape the uses and consequences of those media, though not always as intended.

Social shaping of technology

If technological determinism locates cause with the technology, and social constructivism locates cause with people, a third perspective, sometimes called social shaping (MacKenzie & Wajcman, 1985/1999), emphasizes a middle ground. From this perspective, the consequences of technologies arise from a mix of "affordances" (Gibson, 1977; Norman, 1988) – the capabilities configurations of technological qualities enable – and the unexpected and emergent ways that people make use of those affordances. Expectations of how technologies will be used are built into their design (Gershon, 2010; Nardi, 2010), yet those influences do not necessarily dominate experience. Katz and Aakhus (2002) speak of technologies having "logics" or "apparatgeists" that influence but do not determine use. "Machines," wrote Douglas (2004 [1999]: 21), "do not make history by themselves. But some kinds of machines help make different kinds of histories and different kinds of people than others." Machines "can and do accelerate certain trends, magnify cultural weaknesses, and fortify certain social structures while eroding others" (Douglas, 2004 [1999]: 20). Social media platforms engineer particular kinds of sociality even as their users develop norms around their use (van Dijck, 2013).

People, technologies, and institutions all have power to influence the development and subsequent use of technology. They are "interrelated nodes in constantly changing sociotechnical networks, which constitute the forms and uses of technology differently in different times and places for different groups" (Lievrouw, 2006: 250). Historical analyses demonstrate that social shaping is "a process in which there is no single dominant shaping force" (MacKenzie & Wajcman, 1985/1999: 29). For instance, with Jean Burgess (Burgess & Baym, 2014), I studied the development of the @-reply, hashtag, and retweet conventions on Twitter. Each of these features was developed and used by lead users before Twitter incorporated them in its design. From the social shaping perspective, we need to consider how societal circumstances give rise to technologies, what specific possibilities and constraints technologies offer, and actual practices of use as those possibilities and constraints are taken up, rejected, and reworked in everyday life.

Domestication of technology

The fact that we no longer engage in either utopian or dystopian discourses about the landline telephone or, for that matter, the alphabet is evidence of how successfully earlier technologies have been domesticated. What once seemed marvelous and strange, capable of creating greatness and horror, is now so ordinary as to be invisible. Life without them can become unimaginable (my son once asked how we used the internet before computers were invented). When others don't use them – as when someone refuses to have a mobile phone, text, or use Facebook – it can become a problem not just for them, but for us (Ling, 2012).

British and Norwegian media and technology studies in the 1990s developed the "domestication" approach to technology in order to continue where the social shaping of technology leaves off (Haddon, 2006). This approach concurs with social shaping in seeing both technology and society as influences in the consequences of new media, but it is particularly concerned with the processes at play as new technologies move from being fringe (wild) objects to everyday (tame) objects embedded deeply in the practices of daily life. Early domestication work showed that, by the time most users encounter technologies, they are already laden with the social meanings given them by advertisement, design, and the kinds of rhetorics we have been discussing. Nonetheless, "both households and individuals then invest them with their own personal meanings and significance" (Haddon, 2006: 196). This is particularly true early on, in the "mastery" stage of domestication, when how we use and display our technologies and the ways we rework them to fit our needs can have most influence on their subsequent development (Ling, 2012). The process of domestication plays out at societal levels, but also in daily interactions as people figure out where to place devices, and, more importantly, who gets to use them for what and who doesn't (Silverstone, Hirsch, & Morley, 1992).

As technologies are integrated into everyday life, they come to be seen as offering a nuanced mix of both positive and negative implications. In the case of the mobile phone, despite near-ubiquitous adoption, there are still competing narratives between phones as ostentatious, expensive, stressful, and prone to creating bad manners and phones as assuring safety, autonomy, access to others, and control over the flow of daily life (Ling, 2012). Syntopian perspectives (Katz & Rice, 2002) view new technologies as simultaneously enabling and disabling. The extremes may persist, but in between we use communication to negotiate a vast realm of detail, contradiction, and complexity. In closing this chapter, I want to consider how we move from a period where new technologies are threatening or exciting to one in which they are ordinary and barely worthy of remark. The advice columns I drew on above serve as a remarkable microcosm through which to see domestication of the internet in action.

In early letters, particularly those prior to 2000, there was a very clear norm that the internet was dangerous. Internet users were often described as junkies, addicts, recluses, or, at best or on average, "fairly decent people" (as Ann Landers wrote in 1994). Both columns had readers who were having different experiences, however, and the columns provided a venue in which those having good experiences were able to resist the negative image of the technology being constructed in others' letters and in Ann's and Abby's responses. A Netizen in Chicago's 1996 letter (seen above) explaining all the positive relationships he had built online is one example. Similar letters from many others singing the praises of the internet poured in. The mail, wrote Landers in 1996, was "staggering, and most of the readers agree."

Letter writers defended the internet against dystopian visions in many ways. One was through the use of metaphor, comparing the internet to fire, parks, knives, and, in one letter (which I swear I did not write), the telephone, as seen in these 1996 examples:

> Saying the Net is destructive because it can be used incorrectly is like saying humankind would be better off without fire because it can be dangerous.

> Get a clue, Ann. Condemning the Internet because some people meet scoundrels on-line is like condemning parks because some pedophile exposed himself to children in a park.

> The problem with people and the Internet is not the Internet but what people do with it. The same is true of a knife. I was under the knife having lifesaving surgery the same day someone across town was murdered by one.

> Wary of the Internet, Ann? I'll bet if you had been around in the 1880s, you'd have been suspicious of the telephone because it could be used for "nefarious purposes." Anything new needs time to be accepted.

As seen in this comparison between the telephone and the internet, letter writers who defended the internet often took a social constructivist perspective on the relationship between technology and society. Some explicitly challenged Ann's, Abby's, and other letter writers' construction of the technology's status as cause rather than symptom:

> You have said that the Internet has disrupted relationships between couples and destroyed marriages. That is not the fault of the Internet. Those relationships were already in trouble. (1996)

> People who stay up all night on their computers don't have an Internet problem. They have an addiction problem. (1997)

Others took a social shaping stance in which the internet was positioned as a contributing factor when combined with other problems:

> Our 19-year marriage had been rather rocky, what with career problems, financial woes, children and other pressures. Then, my husband, "Ron," discovered the chat lines. (1996)

Mark my words, Ann, mid-life and the Internet are an explosive combination that spells double trouble. (1996)

By the end of the 1990s, both columnists took a social shaping perspective on the relationship between the internet and social problems. The technology was seen as enabling some new possibilities for trouble, but the troubles belonged firmly to the people perpetrating the behaviors. Ann Landers eventually wrote that the internet posed a threat to "sterile" marriages (1996), but was not "a 'killer of marriages' any more than TV was when it first entered our living rooms" (1998). "Get out the wet noodle," Landers wrote in her inimitable style, "My readers have convinced me that the Internet, when used properly, has a lot more to offer than I thought" (1999).

Once this more nuanced understanding had been reached, the internet continued to appear as a character in letters to advice columns, but the tone changed considerably. For instance, the writer of a 2004 letter about a fiancé who had placed a personal ad on an online dating site was told that her fiancé "does not understand the responsibilities and obligations of marriage" and that "he might run off with the neighbor's wife." In contrast to earlier replies in which Ann and Abby bemoaned an "epidemic" of home-wrecking due to the internet, the internet was not even mentioned in this response. By 2004, it had become almost invisible.

That the internet and mobile phone have been largely domesticated does not mean that all anxieties surrounding them have been resolved. Digital media still appear in advice columns, in *New Yorker* cartoons, in all other popular media, and in everyday conversations. Just as one form of mediated communication becomes domesticated, another arises with some new twist to confuse us. The social concerns that we voice when we discuss technology are concerns we would have even if there were no technology around. They are questions of what it means to be truly yourself, to have meaningful relationships with others, and to be situated in a world of others who are very different from the people with whom we were raised.

Social shaping and domestication differ in where they put the emphasis on the social processes involved in making sense of the technology–society relationship, but agree that the direction of influence is, at the very least, two-way. Rather than being deterministic, they see the consequences of technology for social life as *emergent*. Even if we knew all the factors that influence us at the start (an impossible feat), we would not be able to precisely predict the social interactions, formations, and changes that result from their ongoing interplay as people use technologies in specific situations.

This book adheres to social shaping and domestication perspectives, arguing that, to connect digital media to social consequences, we need to understand both features of technology and the practices that influence and emerge around technology, including the role of technological rhetorics in those practices. If you turn the page expecting to find simple answers to the question of what computers and mobile phones do to our personal connections, you will be disappointed. They do many things, and which ones they do to which people depends on many forces, only some of which are predictable. As the chapters that follow will show, sometimes these media are used in ways that are predictable given media affordances (people call to say they are running late more because they have mobile phones on hand through which to do it), surprising (the American social network site Orkut came quickly to be dominated by Brazilians and later Indians, Friendster became the dominant social network site in Southeast Asia), disruptive (people form close relationships before meeting in person), and affirming (people use the mobile phone to increase family cohesion). The complexity of the social shaping and domestication perspectives does not mean we should throw up our hands and despair of gaining any insight. We should, however, always be wary of simple explanations.

3

Communication in digital spaces

If asked to share general thoughts about communicating face-to-face, on the telephone, and on the internet, many people are likely to say something like this:

> Face-to-face is much more personal; phone is personal as well, but not as intimate as face-to-face. The internet is the least personal but it's always available.

> Face-to-face: I enjoy the best. I like to see facial reactions, etc. Phone: nice to hear their voice, but wish I could see their reactions. Internet: like it, but can't get a true sense of the person.

> I am more apt to be more affectionate and personable face-to-face. Over the phone, I can try to convey them, but they don't work as well. The internet is much too impersonal to communicate feelings.

> Internet would definitely be the least personal, followed by the phone (which at least has the vocal satisfaction) and the most personal would be face-to-face.

These responses to a survey I conducted in 2002 framed the comparison in terms of the extent to which nonverbal social cues ("hear their voice," "see their reactions," "vocal satisfaction") affected the perceived intimacy of each medium.

In the first chapter, we saw that a medium's ability to convey social cues about interactants and context is an essential component of its communicative possibilities and constraints. In chapter 2, we saw historical and contemporary visions, both hopeful and fearful, of how limited social cues may affect people, relationships, and social hierarchies. Media with fewer social cues often trigger hopes that people will become more equal and more valued for their minds than their social identities, but also raise fears that interactions, identities, and relationships will become increasingly shallow, untrustworthy, and inadequate.

This chapter asks what happens to communication itself – the messages people exchange – when it's digitally mediated. We begin by examining the perspective seen in the quotes at the start of this chapter, that mediation is impoverishment. We'll look closely at the practice of "flaming," or extremely argumentative communication, as a test case for considering the extent to which a lack of cues can be considered a cause of how people behave. Having established that there's more going on than can be explained by a mere shortage of nonverbal cues, we'll see how people inject sociability into mediated communication, showing emotion, expressing closeness and availability, having fun, and building new social structures. I'll argue that mediated interaction should be seen as a new and eclectic mixed modality that combines elements of face-to-face communication with elements of writing, and that increasingly uses images, rather than as a diminished form of embodied interaction. In the closing section of the chapter, we'll consider how messages online are influenced by and potentially reshape social identities that transcend media, including gender and culture.

Mediation as impoverishment

Reduced social cues

The quotes that opened this chapter demonstrate a formulaic tendency to think about media in ranked order and to position the one that seems to offer the widest range of verbal and nonverbal social cues on top and the one seeming to offer the least on the bottom. As we saw in chapter 2, this is in keeping with popular discourses throughout history and may well resonate with your own intuitions. It is also in keeping with early research approaches that conceptualized face-to-face conversations as the norm against which other kinds of communication could be compared. From this point of view, mediated communication is seen as a diminished form of face-to-face conversation. Taking embodied co-present communication as the norm, early research often saw the telephone and internet as lesser versions of the real thing, inherently less intimate, and, therefore, less suited to personal connections.

The first research comparing mediated interaction to face-to-face communication began in the 1970s. At this time, audioconferencing, videoconferencing, and networked computer systems were being installed in large organizational contexts. Research was driven by managerial concerns about when to choose each medium. Put simply, both managers and scholars wanted to know when they could hold a teleconference and when they would need to get employees together face-to-face. The first two theories of media choice, Social Presence Theory (Short, Williams, & Christie, 1976) and Media Richness Theory (Daft & Lengel, 1984), both tried to match media capabilities, defined as their ability to transmit social cues, with task demands.

Short and his collaborators (1976) were interested in how different degrees of social cues invoked differing senses of communication with an authentic person during synchronous interaction. They defined social presence as "the degree of salience of the other person in the interaction and the consequent salience (and perceived intimacy and immediacy) of the interpersonal relationships" (1976: 65). Thurlow, Lengel, and Tomic (2004: 48) describe social presence as the "level of interpersonal contact and feelings of intimacy experienced in communication."

Social presence is a psychological phenomenon regarding how interactants perceive one another, not a feature of a medium. However, the perception of social presence was attributed to the nonverbal cues enabled or disabled by mediation. Important nonverbal cues include facial expression, direction of gaze, posture, dress, physical appearance, proximity, and bodily orientation. In body-to-body communication, these nonverbal cues serve important functions (e.g. Wiemann & Knapp, 1975). For example, looking at someone, turning your torso toward them, nodding your head, and using fillers such as "uh huh" are all ways in which we demonstrate attentiveness (e.g. Goodwin, 1981). We rely on gestures to keep our audience tuned in and to illustrate our words. Nonverbal "emblems" such as the American thumbs-up gesture have direct verbal translations (in this case, "yes," "good job," or "can I have a ride?" although the same gesture might directly translate into something far more provocative elsewhere). Facial expressions including smiles, furrowed brows, and clenched teeth convey interpersonal attitudes of liking and aversion, as well as cognitive states such as confusion and understanding (e.g. Andersen & Guerrero, 1998). Given the importance of these nonverbal cues in coordinating interaction and conveying meaning, especially emotional meaning, it makes sense that people question how well mediated communication can successfully serve social functions.

Social Presence theorists argued that if you knew which social cues served which functions in conversation, and you knew which media transmitted which cues, you would be able to predict how much social presence people using a medium would experience. In particular, they expected that groups completing tasks that involved maintaining personal relationships would require media that conveyed more social cues than groups performing tasks in which people were primarily acting out social roles. In experiments, they found that people experienced more sense of social contact in face-to-face encounters than in videoconferences (Short et al., 1976). As Fulk and Collins-Jarvis (2001: 629) summarize, in several related studies people were found to perceive the least social presence of all in audio meetings "which are seen as less personal, less effective for getting to know someone, and communicate less affective content than face to face."

Social Presence Theory focuses on the perception of others as real and present. Media Richness Theory, developed by Daft and Lengel (1984), is closely related, but focuses directly on the medium. Daft and Lengel (1984) defined a medium's richness as its information-carrying capacity, which they based on four criteria: the speed of feedback, the ability to communicate multiple cues, its use of natural language rather than numbers, and its ability to readily convey feelings and emotions (a factor I find conceptually difficult to tease apart from the conveyance of multiple cues). Media Richness scholars compared rich and lean media for their suitability for solving tasks differing in equivocality and uncertainty. In contrast to Social Presence researchers, most Media Richness research focused on asynchronous communication (Fulk & Collins-Jarvis, 2001). The expectation was that tasks high in uncertainty with many possible answers, such as resolving personnel issues, would work better in rich media, while unequivocal tasks like telling someone you're running late would be best served by lean media (Daft & Lengel, 1984).

These two theories – developed in a time when all online interaction was text-only – and related work from around that time can be considered "cues filtered out" approaches (Walther, Anderson, & Park, 1994). In their simplest forms, cues filtered out approaches assume that, to varying degrees, mediated communication is lean and therefore impedes people's ability to handle interpersonal dimensions of interaction. Because computer-mediated interactants are unable to see, hear, and feel one another, they can't use the usual cues conveyed by appearance, nonverbal signals, and features of the physical context. Mediated communication may be better than face-to-face interaction for some tasks, but for those involving personal identities and feelings, mediation was depicted as inherently inferior (Fulk & Collins-Jarvis, 2001).

Cues filtered out studies examining how reduced cues affected social qualities of communication (e.g. Baron, 1984; Kiesler, Siegel, & McGuire, 1984) had several expectations, which resonate with much of the public discourse we saw in the previous chapter. First, mediation would make it more difficult to maintain conversational alignment and mutual understanding. Messages would be harder to coordinate. This would mean that communicators would have to work harder to achieve their desired impact and be understood.

Second, because social identity cues would not be apparent, interactants would gain greater anonymity. Their gender, race, rank, physical appearance, and other features of public identity are not immediately evident. As a result, people would be "depersonalized," losing their sense of self and other. This impersonal environment would make these media inherently less sociable and inappropriate for affective bonds. On the other hand, anonymity was also expected to result in a redistribution of social power, echoing the visions of blurred social status seen in chapter 2. With the cues to hierarchy (e.g. age, attire, seating arrangement) missing, participation would become more evenly distributed across group members. This egalitarian balance would make it difficult for people to dominate and impose their views on others (Baron, 1984; Walther, 1992). For those seeking speedy task resolution, the plurality of voices could mean tasks would take longer to accomplish. When everyone voices opinions, it often takes longer to reach a decision, complete a task, or achieve consensus (Sproull & Kiesler, 1991).

Cues filtered out researchers also expected that the lack of social cues would result in contexts without social norms to guide behavior (Kiesler et al., 1984; Rice, 1984, 1989; Sproull & Kiesler, 1991). Where face-to-face communication is regulated by implicit norms made apparent in the social context (for example, that this is a formal situation and it would not be appropriate to stand up enraged and start swearing), computer-mediated discourse was seen as a social vacuum in which anything went. Among other predictions, this was expected to lead to less social and emotional (socioemotional) communication and, somewhat paradoxically, more negatively loaded emotional communication. Instead of following the social norms mandating politeness and civility, rendered anonymous by the absence of social cues we would be meaner to one another than we would ever be in person.

These theories made enduring contributions to our understandings of communication media. The concepts of social presence and media richness continue to influence the ways scholars think about the consequences of mediation for interaction, and have become important pieces of later analytic frameworks. Social Presence continues to be an important thread in internet research (e.g. Cortese and Seo, 2012). Furthermore, cues filtered out predictions about task accomplishment have held up well in research and in practice. However, their expectations about social interaction turned out to be problematic at best and sometimes downright wrong. Certainly, some people do become aggressive sometimes under some circumstances, a phenomenon to which we'll return below, but people also build warm loving relationships and provide one another with all kinds of social support, phenomena for which these approaches failed to account. Despite their contributions, they fall short as ways to describe and explain mediated communication's social consequences.

One reason for this is that scholars tended to use experimental research strategies that were unrealistic, usually involving small groups in short-term one-shot interactions in which they were supposed to accomplish an assigned task (Rafaeli & Sudweeks, 1997;

Walther et al., 1994). Furthermore, their research findings, and findings from other lines of research, provide grounds for empirical criticisms. Lab studies did find statistically significant differences between face-to-face and computer-mediated communication, but the differences were very small (Walther et al., 1994).

More importantly, the few field studies in which researchers spent time in naturally occurring contexts in which computer systems were already being used demonstrated that socioemotional communication not only existed, but was more likely to be prosocial than antisocial (Hiltz & Turoff, 1978). The social cues reported in early field studies included typographical art, salutations, the degree of formality of language, paralanguage, communication styles, and message headers (Hiltz & Turoff, 1978; Lea, O'Shea, Fung, & Spears, 1992). In a content analysis of transcripts from a professionally oriented CompuServe forum, Rice and Love (1987) found that socioemotional content (defined as showing solidarity, tension relief, agreement, antagonism, tension, and disagreement) constituted around 30 percent of messages, and was mostly positive.

Cues filtered out approaches can also be criticized for how they conceptualize the forces at play. The very definition of media richness distinguishes the conveyance of emotion from the ability to convey social cues, though they are profoundly interrelated. Many studies counted all emotional expression as evidence of disinhibition (Lea et al., 1992), with the result that friendly asides were seen as evidence of a norm-free medium. In fact, as we'll discuss in the next chapter, over time, mediated groups develop strong communicative norms that guide behavior. Furthermore, positive consequences of disinhibition, such as increased honesty and self-disclosure, of the sort we will see in chapter 5, were also overlooked or assumed to be negative.

The perspective that mediated communication is a diminished form of face-to-face communication ignores many other factors that affect mediated communication, such as people's familiarity with the technology, whether they know one another already and what sort of relationship they have, whether they anticipate meeting or seeing one another again, their expectations and motivations for interacting, and the social contexts in which interactions are embedded. But, more significantly, it sells people short, failing to recognize the extent to which we are driven to maximize our communication satisfaction and interaction. This "communication imperative" (Walther, 1994) pushes us to use new media for interpersonal purposes and to come up with creative ways to work around barriers, rather than submitting ourselves to a context- and emotion-free communication experience.

The example of antagonism

Despite its problems, as the comments with which I opened this chapter and some of the technological rhetorics seen in chapter 2 demonstrate, the cues filtered out approach still rings true for many. I would be the first to insist that nothing can replace a warm hug. But even if we accept that face-to-face communication provides a kind of social connection that simply cannot be attained with mediation, it does not follow that mediated communication, even in lean media, is emotionally or socially impoverished, or that social context cannot be achieved.

In chapter 2, I argued that our best shot at understanding the social consequences of mediated communication is a social shaping stance that recognizes both technological and social influences on behaviors. Research on flaming helps to illustrate how both qualities of the medium and emergent group norms influence online group behavior. Walther et al. (1994) defined flaming as messages that include swearing, insults, name calling, negative affect, and typographic energy. Flaming is exactly the kind of behavior that cues filtered out approaches predict and it is widely perceived as both common and unpleasant online. If cues filtered out theory were going to be able to fully explain one thing about social interaction, this should be it.

This flame from the Usenet newsgroup rec.arts.startrek.current from 1993 remains one of my favorites for its ability to illustrate how virulent, petty, mean, and yet entertaining flames can be:

>>Just fine by me. Personally I'd like to involve Lursa and her sister (the
>> Klingons) too. Now THAT would be a fun date.
>>
>> ·Jim Hyde

> Will you stupid jerks get a real life. Everyone with half a brain or more
> know that a human and a Kligon can not mate. The Klingon mating
> procedure would kill any human (except one with a brain like you).
> Stay of the net stoopid!

Oh really. Hmmmm. And I suppose Alexander and his mom are just
clones or something? If you recall, she is half human, and Alexander is 1/4.
Romulans don't seem any more sturdy than humans, and we saw hybrids
there as well.

Looks like I'm not the one with half a brain. Check your facts before you
become the net.nazi next time pal. This isn't just a forum for us to all bow
down and worship your opinion you know. You might also do well for yourself
to learn how to spell, stooopid.

-Jim Hyde

These messages occur predictably in online group interactions
and often lead to "flame wars" in which flames are met with hostile
retorts. The hostilities escalate, drawing in more participants. Other
participants chime in urging the original participants to move the discussion off-list or ignore the hostilities. Eventually people lose interest
and the discussion dies out. Many sources on the internet can be
found describing this pattern and offering "netiquette" tips to prevent
flame wars (e.g. Shea, n.d.).

But flaming is not always as laughable as this example, especially
when it merges with trolling (Hardaker, 2010). Hate speech against
both individuals and ethnic groups is common online and raises
significant policy issues around regulation (Citron & Norton, 2011).
YouTube comments are famous for their aggression – as a musician
I interviewed told me, "I think there's something about YouTube.
The people that comment on there, I think, if you put them together
and gave them weapons and put them in uniform, they could take
over the world, 'cause they are the nastiest people I've ever come
across." Twitter has come under fire for the virulently misogynistic
attacks on women that take place there, such as the case of Caroline
Criado-Perez whose (successful) campaign to get a woman who was
not royalty (the author Jane Austen) on the British £10 bank note
unleashed a torrent of rape and murder threats, ultimately leading to

at least one arrest and a campaign urging Twitter to be more active in reining in abusive tweets. When the female Asian-American chancellor of the University of Illinois at Urbana-Champaign did not cancel classes on a particularly cold day in 2014, she was attacked by both men and women on Twitter in the crudest of sexist and racist terms. Many news sites have begun requiring commenters to log in through platforms with an expectation of real names such as Facebook and Google+ in hopes that people posting under real names will behave better. (As a glance at many Facebook groups will show, there is little evidence that they do).

There's no question that flaming and abusive online behavior are real. To some extent, this is surely facilitated by what cues filtered out scholars describe. The lack of social presence and accountability in a reduced-cues medium is seen by some as a platform for launching attacks. However, if flaming were caused by reduced social cues, it ought to be very common online. Yet it is perceived as more common than it actually is. In Rice and Love's (1987) study, only 0.2 percent of the messages were antagonistic. We may overestimate the amount of flaming because single messages may be seen by so many people and because hostile messages are so memorable (Lea et al., 1992). The fact is that most people in online groups are far more likely to be nice than to flame (e.g. Preece & Ghozati, 1998; Rice & Love, 1987). Even those who have been the targets of abuse such as Criado-Perez report experiencing more supportive messages than abusive once their abuse became known.

If reduced cues cause flaming, we should also see equal amounts of flaming in all interactions in a medium. But the amount and tolerance of hostility varies tremendously across online groups. Martin Lea and his collaborators (1992) argued that, contrary to the cues filtered out explanation that flaming occurs because of a lack of norms, flaming occurs *because* of norms. Groups with argumentative communication styles encourage people to conform to the group's style, while those with more civil styles invoke more courteous behavior. The predominantly female soap opera discussion group I studied had almost no flaming; what little there was came from outsiders (Baym, 1996, 2000).

Furthermore, rather than occurring in the absence of social norms, people often flame in ways that demonstrate their awareness that they are violating norms (Lea et al., 1992). They may substitute punctuation marks for letters in swear words or use the html inspired "<flame on>" and "</flame off>" designations to bracket the abrasive message. Flames are also used to discipline people for behaving inappropriately, thus maintaining group norms. Norms are also negotiated through flaming, as participants in discussion forums work out what kinds of activities they are taking part in. For example, people in a cancer support group flamed as a means of determining whether or not venting was appropriate (Aakhus & Rumsey, 2010). In some groups, flaming is a form of playful sport. Although women flame too (Savicki, Lingenfelter, & Kelley, 1996), flaming has been linked to masculinity, or "the chest-thumping display of online egos" (Myers, 1987a: 241). The misogynistic trolls of Twitter come there from communities on sites like Reddit that support and foster their abusive behavior.

Putting social cues into digital communication

Instead of asking what mediation *does to* communication, we can also ask what people *do with* mediated communication. People appropriate media characteristics as resources to pursue social and relational goals (O'Sullivan, 2000). People show feeling and immediacy, have fun, and build and reinforce social structures even in the leanest of text-only media. As a consequence of people's enthusiasm for digital social interaction, developers have created ever-richer means for us to communicate. Facebook is the world's largest photo repository, Tumblr is overwhelmingly image-based, Instagram (owned by Facebook) is entirely image-based, and image-based memes have become pervasive throughout online communication. "Selfie" was the *Oxford English Dictionary*'s 2013 Word of the Year. YouTube has enabled people to communicate via video, and Skype has become a common means of communication for people in long-distance relationships, including romantic partners but also immigrants, around the world (e.g. Lingel, 2013; Madianou & Miller, 2012a, 2012b). However, even text-only interaction, on which we'll focus here given how much more research is about text-based communication, can be used to accomplish relational and social connection, leaving no question that we can do it with additional cues such as video, images, and voice.

In 1972, just three years into ARPANET's existence, Carnegie Mellon University professor Scott E. Fahlman proposed that punctuation marks could be combined like this :-) to mark jokes (Anderson, 2005). Fahlman's innovation responded to the now-familiar problem that emotional information can be difficult to convey without facial expression and vocal intonation. Sarcasm can be particularly tricky. Conflict often results. The smiley face, used by many and reviled by some, has spread into elaborate lexicons of *emoticons*, most of which show feelings, but some of which are simply playful. Emoticons have now been built into new media to the extent that when I first typed that punctuation combination, my word processor automatically translated it into this graphical representation: ☺. Emojis (a Japanese term combining "picture" and "letter") now extend far beyond facial expressions and are standardized in smartphone keyboards. Most emoticons and emojis originated in novel uses of punctuation to illustrate feeling or to convey how the words were meant to be interpreted (Dresner & Herring, 2010). Emoticons and emojis have not entirely solved the confusion about what words mean and the emotions behind them, but they have helped.

There are other ways in which people convey nonverbal social cues when limited to textual communication. We use asterisks as brackets, upper-case lettering, and letter and punctuation repetition to indicate emphasis, as in "I am *so* busy" (my word processor automatically transforms the asterisked word into boldface), "I am SO busy," "I am sooooooo busy," or "I am so busy!!!!!!" (e.g. Darics, 2010; Herring, 2001). People also simply use words or abbreviated phrases to describe their nonverbal reactions in textual media. The people discussing soap operas I studied frequently used phrases like "I laughed so hard everyone knew I wasn't working" or the more oblique "does anyone know how to clean coffee off a keyboard?" to describe nonverbal reactions to others' humorous messages. Someone in a music fan group I followed described herself dancing on her couch while listening to the song under discussion. The acronyms LOL (for either "lots of laughs" or "laughing out loud") is even more ubiquitous than its oft-used forerunners ROTFL or the now more common ROFL ("rolling on the floor laughing"). We also display immediacy online, engaging in behaviors that reduce psychological distance and increase affiliation (Mehrabian, 1971).

We show others that we are approachable, and that we are interested in them, through immediacy cues (O'Sullivan et al., 2004). The language of immediacy is informal, filled with non-standard spellings, deletions, casual and slang vocabulary, greetings, and sign offs (Baron, 2008; O'Sullivan et al., 2004), and other linguistic markers. In my Twitter feed as I write, for instance, highly educated friends have written "yer" (your) and "tho," "Hahaha," "LOL," and "sammich" (sandwich). "Tho" shows how we delete letters. We may also leave out subject pronouns ("gotta go now"), vowels, punctuation, and, in text messages, spaces, adjectives, and adverbs (Hård af Segerstad, 2005; Ling, 2005). Deletions may be partially driven by the formal limitations of message space and time constraints (especially in synchronous media) and the physical discomforts of too much typing, but they can also create immediacy. Together, these many linguistic variations serve as ample resources for building friendly conversationality.

People also appropriate qualities of digital media as resources for play. In her book *Cyberpl@y*, Brenda Danet (2001) traced the playful quality of much online interaction, especially when synchronous, to several influences, including interactivity and synchronicity, anonymity, the lack of clear authorities and formal governing structure, and the legacy of hacker culture with its love of wordplay, puns, irony, flippancy, and irregular uses of typography and spelling. On Twitter, people play with fonts.

Many people have noted how common humor is in mediated communication contexts, whether it's the use of mobile phones to share dirty jokes amongst teenagers (Oksman & Turtiainen, 2004), the forwarding of humorous emails and links, displays of creativity in online groups (e.g. Baym, 1995; Myers, 1987a), or signifyin' amongst Black users of Twitter (e.g. Brock, 2012; Florini, 2013 – I return to this below). Rafaeli and Sudweeks (1997) found that more than 20 percent of the thousands of messages they coded from international discussion forums contained humor. In my soap group study, I found that, even in the discussion of a dark storyline the fans disliked and found disturbing, 27 percent of the messages were humorous. Group members indicated in my surveys and in their responses to one another that humor was one of their main criteria for assessing the quality of messages and one another.

There are many other kinds of creative play in textual media. In ASCII art, the symbols available on a keyboard are used to draw images. A particularly clever account, @Glitchr, exploits glitches in the code to create tweets with letters and symbols that extend outside of the box meant to constrain the content of the tweet, disrupting the appearance of Twitter itself. An IRC group Danet (2001) studied used the keyboard in combination with colored fonts to create illustrations with many qualities found in traditional folk designs, such as those in rugs and other textiles. People invent new words and even dialects in textual interaction. The widespread LOLcat phenomenon, in which short grammatically incorrect phrases rife with misspellings (e.g. "I can haz cheezburger?" or "Literecy cat is amaized at ur perfick grahmar") are juxtaposed with pictures of cats (among other things), has given rise to a new grammatical dialect which can, in fact, be done incorrectly. "You me give cheezburger?" is bad grammar, but it is not LOLspeak (Lefler, 2011). More recently, a similar dialect, "doge," emerged, based on imagined canine speech. We also see playful humor in the creation and spread of "memes" such as Socially Awkward Penguin, Success Kid, and the others catalogued at knowyourmeme.com (Milner, 2012; Shifman, 2013). These kinds of humor require particular kinds of literacies in "vernacular creativity" (Burgess, 2006; Milner, 2012; Miltner, 2014), otherwise they will not be funny or accepted by the communities in which they circulate.

As people appropriate the possibilities of textual media to convey social cues, create immediacy, entertain, and show off for one another, they build identities for themselves, build interpersonal relationships, and create social contexts, topics to which we will return in coming chapters. Performing well can bring a person recognition, or at least lead to a sense that there is a real person behind otherwise anonymous text. Our expressions of emotions and immediacy show others that we are real, available, and that we like them, as does our willingness to entertain them. Our playful conventions and in-jokes may create insider symbols that help groups to cohere. These phenomena are only enhanced by the additional cues found in shared video, photography, sound, and other multimedia means of online interaction that have developed over time.

Digital language as a mixed modality

If comparing mediated text to face-to-face communication doesn't work adequately, it might be more fruitful to think of digital communication as a mixed modality that combines elements of communication practices in embodied conversation and in writing. Instead of approaching mediated interaction as face-to-face communication and finding it wanting, we draw from our existing repertoire of communication skills in other modes to make a medium do what we want it to do as best we can.

Online language has been called an "interactive written register" (Ferrara, Brunner, & Whittemore, 1991), a hybrid (Danet, 1997), a creole (Baron, 1998), and an "uncooked linguistic stew" (Baron & Ling, 2003) that blends elements of written and oral language with features that are distinctive to this medium, or at least more common online than in any other language medium. Mediated interaction in several languages (including English, French, Swedish, and Norwegian) resembles both written language and oral conversation (Baron, 2000; Baron & Ling, 2003; Baym, 1996; Danet, 1997; Ferrara et al., 1991; Hård af Segerstad, 2005; Herring, 2001; Ling, 2005).

Online interaction is like writing in many ways. In detailed analyses of naturally occurring messages, Baron (2008) argues that, on balance, emails, instant messages, and text messages look more like writing than speech, but fall on a spectrum in between. Like writing, textual interaction online often bears an address. Messages can be edited prior to transmission. The author and reader are physically (and often temporally) separated. Messages can be read by anonymous readers who may not respond and it is not possible for interlocutors to overlap one another or to interrupt. Context must be created through the prose so that messages are often explicit and complete. There is rarely an assumption of shared physical context. Messages are replicable and can be stored.

On the other hand, there are many ways in which online language resembles speech. As we saw in the discussion of immediacy above, misspellings and deletions often foreground phonetic qualities of language. Despite the challenges to conversational coordination (Herring, 2001), messages are generally related to prior ones, often through turn-taking. The audience is usually able to respond and often does so quickly, resulting in reformulations of original messages. Topics change rapidly. The discourse often feels ephemeral, and often is not stored by recipients despite the capacity for storage.

The specter of a new language form, neither spoken nor written yet both, raises dual fears about the degeneration of spoken conversation and written language. Newspaper articles have worried, for instance, that the brief exchanges of Instant Messaging (IM) will lead to an inability to conduct face-to-face conversations, or that non-standard spelling and punctuation will decimate grammar as we know it. Teachers in Finland, where text messages are full of non-standard Finnish, worry about negative consequences for student writing (Kasesniemi & Rautiainen, 2002), echoing concerns heard in seemingly every nation that uses these media.

The scant evidence so far does not offer strong reasons for concern. There are far fewer such deviations from standard language forms than people think (Baron & Ling, 2003). Baron (2008) found few abbreviations, acronyms, contractions, misspellings, emoticons, or missing punctuation in American college students' Instant Messages. Furthermore, like flaming, few of the non-standard features of language are due to inattention or lack of awareness of standards (Herring, 2001). Most are deliberate adaptations of the technical and social contexts of interactions for social purposes. The language of mediated interaction is "at most a very minor dialectal variation" (Baron, 2008: 163).

The discourse of fear and language decay surrounding these media (reflected in the rhetorics of new media discussed in chapter 2) can be understood as part of a cultural reaction to the growing informality of public life. Baron (2008) argues that, culturally, formality has increasingly been replaced by casualness, something that extends to writing across media. Writing standards, she argues, are declining as we rarely linger over the written word. Social attitudes to proofreading and perfect writing have changed so that writing is done more quickly. In a survey, 68 percent of US Advanced Placement and National

Writing Project teachers expressed concern that digital tools make students more likely to take shortcuts and put less effort into their writing (Purcell, Buchanan, & Friedrich, 2013). "Computers are not the cause of contemporary language attitudes and practices," Baron writes (2008: 171), but, "like signal boosters, they magnify ongoing trends."

People also usually understand that not all textual digital media, or circumstances in which they are used, are alike, and adapt accordingly. Messages in IM, chat, and SMS are considerably shorter than those in most other forms of online interaction, for instance, due to the temporal and software structures of those modalities. Any instance of digital language use depends on the technology, the purpose of the interaction, the norms of the group, the communication style of the speakers' social groups offline, and the idiosyncrasies of individuals. There is no standardized "digital language."

However, even if there is little reason for concern about wholesale devolutions of language in other contexts, there is still disagreement about which elements of digital style are appropriate to use when. These are value questions we are still resolving. In one particularly prominent example, Jerry Yang, then CEO of Yahoo!, wrote an entirely lower-case email to all employees to announce the layoff of thousands of workers. Yang's letter spread widely across the internet where the lack of capitalization generated controversy. While some saw it as a means of creating immediacy, thus showing compassion for the workers, and others saw it as a goofy personality quirk, some found all-lower-case entirely inappropriate in these professional and difficult circumstances. Most teachers can tell tales of students who use immediacy cues in email that seem inappropriate for that relationship. For instance, I often received emails from students asking favors of me that opened with "Hey Nancy," even when we had not met. Some professors have taken to writing guides for appropriate email and including them with their syllabi (general rule: whenever you are communicating with someone more powerful, err on the side of too formal and too polite).

What was once a complex hybrid between writing and speech has become even more complicated now that we blend and incorporate styles from conversations and writing with stylistic and formal elements of film, television, music videos, and photography, and other genres and practices. In an analysis of "Instafame" – the amassing of large numbers of followers through the Instagram platform without being famous outside of that site – Alice Marwick (in press) shows that many of the Instafamous post selfies that appropriate the poses and props seen in celebrity culture. As Alper (2013) puts it, they use a particular "visual lexicon," which in this case draws on clothing, poses, and settings familiar from shoots of famous people. In contrast to words alone, pictures – especially selfies – can feel "more 'real' than text" (Van House, 2011: 131).

Contextual influences on online communication

Thus far we've focused on technological and social drivers of online communication. Communication is also shaped by larger social forces we carry with us into our mediated interactions. A quick look at how gender and culture play out online speaks to how social contexts shape and are shaped by mediated communication.

Gender

All cultures have different customs, rules, and expectations for behavior from men and women. Early discourses of the internet suggested that gender might become irrelevant or reinvented online. Some online contexts do take gender as a subject for linguistic play. One much-studied Multi-User Domain, Lambda MOO, offered participants multiple gender options for their identity, each with its own set of pronouns (Danet, 1998). In addition to male, female, and neuter, people can choose to identify as: either Spivak, splat, plural, egotistical, royal, or 2nd person. Third-person descriptions of each of these options would be he, she, it, s/he, E, e*, they, I, we, and you.

Several language-oriented researchers have compared men's and women's mediated messages and concluded that gender influences mediated interaction just as it influences unmediated communication. Rather than being liberated from gender, people perform gender through the ways they communicate (e.g. Herring, 1996). Most studies of gendered communication find men and women are far more similar in their communication than different, but women are socialized to attend more to relational dimensions of conversation while men are reared to specialize in the informative dimensions (Burleson & Kunkel, 2006; Kunkel & Burleson, 1999).

Not surprisingly, gender differences appear in mediated interaction. Statistical analysis of large samples of communication from Usenet groups found that the influence of gender on language style was present, but modest (Savicki et al., 1996). Kasesniemi and Rautiainen (2002: 185) described Finnish girls' text messages as "full of social softening, extra words and emotional sharing of experiences. Boys tend to write only about what has happened, and where and how . . . girls contemplate the reasons." Women are more likely to use a supportive/attenuated style oriented toward affiliation. Messages written by women are more likely to include qualifications, justifications, apologies, and expressions of support (Herring, 1996). In blogs written by young Iranians, Bordbar (2010) found that women were more likely to use cooperative and accommodating language than men, who were more likely to use aggressive and motion-oriented language. Women's IM closings take twice as many turns and are nearly three times as long as male closings. Women are also nearly three times more likely to begin SMS interactions with openings (Baron, 2008; Baron & Ling, 2003). Kapedzic and Herring (2011) found that teens' word choice in synchronous chat was determined primarily by topic, but that all other speech acts, tone, and the appearance in profile images were shaped by gender identity and conformed to gender stereotypes. In her work comparing discussion groups oriented toward male and female topics, Larson (2003) found that women used a wider range of nonverbal cues online than men. Groups with more men use more factually oriented language and calls for action, less self-disclosure, and fewer attempts at tension prevention and reduction (Savicki et al., 1996). Men may be more likely to use an adversarial style in their messages (Herring, 2001), though the data on flaming is mixed (Savicki et al., 1996). One MUD developed a term for the behavior of its male members: "MAS" for "Male Answer Syndrome" (Kendall, 2002). Gender can also influence how messages are perceived: men may be more likely to see aggressive messages as evidence of freedom of speech, candor, and healthy debate, while women are more likely to see them as hostile and unconstructive (Herring, 1996).

As we have seen with the Twitter attacks mentioned earlier, like gender, sexism persists and is amplified online. Women with unpopular positions are routinely attacked for being women while men with unpopular ideas are attacked for their ideas (Gurak, 1997). Women are depicted as sexual objects. When someone mentions seeing a woman in one MUD, for instance, a typical response is "did you spike 'er?" (Kendall, 2002: 85). When people sell their characters in role-playing games, female avatars go for 10 percent less than their male counterparts, even when they have comparable skill levels (Castronova, 2004). Kishona Gray (2012) studied Black women's experience in Xbox Live gaming environments where people can hear one another speak in addition to seeing what they write and how they play. She found these women received sexist comments complicated by racist ones. The result is different experiences of gender for women of color than for white women.

Culture

Gender has received a good deal of attention from scholars interested in new technology. The topic of cultural identity, including nationality, language, and race and ethnicity, has received less. Miller and Slater's (2000) ethnographic analysis is an exception, showing how Trinidadian identity permeated online interaction. "Trinis" living both at home and abroad communicated in a style that displayed "being Trini and representing Trinidad" for one another and for outsiders. This ranged from engaging in "limin'," an often risqué form of playful banter, to including links to Trinidadian national sites on their personal webpages. Ananda Mitra's (1997) analysis of the soc.culture. indian Usenet group showed how diasporic Indians used communication that both maintained their Indian identity and recreated India's internal ethnic divides. Paula Uimonen (2013) analyzed profile photos of Tanzanian college students, showing how they moved between representing themselves as globe-trotting cosmopolitans and as distinctly Tanzanian. One young woman, for instance, used a photo of herself lying in a pile of autumn leaves, marking her as being out of Tanzania, but later changed it to a picture of the Tanzanian flag.

Lisa Nakamura (2002) and David Silver (2000) have drawn attention to how race is represented or erased through the interfaces of online spaces. Race is often "routed around" online, rather than brought to the front (Silver, 2000). For example, many online sites that make users select gender and even species do not make them select race. This may be celebrated as an erasure of an unnecessary social division, but it can also be read as an assumption that most users are White. Listings of discussion groups on Yahoo! Groups were typical in that they designated many racial and ethnic groups, constructing for their users a range of social identities with which they may or may not identify. "White" did not appear in Yahoo!'s list of racial and ethnic categories. Discussion groups that do label themselves "White" are often supremacist. Like sexism, racism thrives online, and groups that do self-identify as "White" are often replete with horrifying demonstrations of racial animosity toward others. Even when one can select a non-White race, online spaces often offer highly stereotypical portrayals (Nakamura, 2002). Asian men, for instance, are frequently sword-wielding or nerdy. Asian women, so often the subjects of online pornography, often appear as passive sex toys.

In contrast, many African-Americans on Twitter have drawn on the site's use of hashtags to make themselves visible and connect with each other, resulting in a phenomenon dubiously labeled "Black Twitter" (Brock, 2012; Florini, 2013). As mentioned above, Black Twitter draws on traditions of African-American communication that favor verbal dexterity and performance, often, though not always, using Black Vernacular English or indicating "an intended oral delivery" (Florini, 2013: 11). This may be done through phonetic spellings such as "wit" in place of "with," or "tryna" in place of "trying to," and has led to standardization of Black Vernacular English on Twitter with words like "talmbout" for "talking about" becoming widely used and expected (Florini, 2013). What is important about Black Twitter is that it uses language styles associated with a marginalized and oppressed cultural group in order to claim an online space. That this has met with hostility from non-Black users (Brock, 2012) is disappointing, though sadly not surprising.

Cultural identity also manifests through the language we use. As discussed in chapter 1, the internet was created in the English-speaking world, and the influence and spread of English online remains disproportionate to its speakers. It's only in the last few years that English has come to represent less than half of the internet's language, but it is still (for now) the most common language used online. Until recently, online writing was restricted to the ASCII character set, which is designed exclusively for the Latin alphabet. With the advent of Unicode, people can now write with other alphabets and emojis; however, this technology is neither available to nor used by all. The result has sometimes been considered a form of "typographical imperialism" (Herring & Danet, 2003) with potential social, political, economic, and linguistic consequences. For instance, I've mentioned the outcry about the devolution of language in Greece and its echoes of Socrates' warnings about the alphabet. This centers on "Greeklish," the online version of written Greek using the Latin alphabet, which has been decried in Greek papers for destroying the language (Koutsogiannis & Mitsikopoulou, 2003).

The business Translate to Success (2009) compiled data from a variety of surveys of internet users to estimate that, in 2004, 38.3 percent of internet users spoke English. Chinese, Japanese, and Korean are also popular, constituting 11.2 percent, 10 percent, and 4.1 percent respectively. Only 1 percent of the world's internet users speak Arabic. Fewer than 0.1 percent speak any African language. A now-defunct effort to conduct a language census of blogs (www.hirank.com/semantic-indexing-project/census/lang.html; *Languages*, n.d.) indexed over 2 million blogs. More than half of these were in English, followed in dramatically smaller numbers by those in Catalan, French, Spanish, and Portuguese. German, Italian, Chinese, Farsi, Japanese, and Dutch were the only other languages found in more than 10,000 blogs each. Herring, Paolillo, Ramos-Vielba, et al. (2007) studied blogs on the site LiveJournal, where two-thirds of users report being outside the USA and pages can be set to appear in 32 different languages. They found that the blogs were 84 percent English, 11 percent Russian, 0.4 percent Portuguese, 0.3 percent Finnish, Spanish, Dutch, and Japanese, and 2.3 percent mixed language. All other languages combined only made up 0.8 percent of the site's user-generated content. According to WordPress.com (2014), a blogging platform with more than 69 million users worldwide, more than half of its blogs are in English, followed in dramatically smaller numbers by those in Spanish, Portuguese, and Indonesian. Italian, German, French, Russian, Vietnamese, and Swedish, though also in the top-ten most-used languages, each accounted for only 1–2 percent of all blogs.

These statistics are obviously profoundly skewed in comparison to the distribution of speakers in the global population, and reflect economic and social conditions in these parts of the world. The over-representation of languages used in wealthy countries, especially English, has often given rise to a sentiment that the internet represents a further colonization of poor nations by those with greater wealth, particularly the United States. Many of the world's voices and communicative styles are simply absent from online communication.

Summary

Mediated online messages are shaped by both technological and social qualities, both of which affect the consequences they may have. From a deterministic perspective, the two primary forces that influence online language use are the paucity of social cues, or media leanness, and the potential asynchronicity of a medium. Together, these are taken to have a host of effects, foremost among them decreasing the intimacy or personal quality of interactions (and subsequently relationships) and increasing the hostility of mediated interactions. There is a grain of truth in those claims, but they are inadequate to explain what people do with language online. Rather than giving up and accepting limited cues as a directive to live without emotion and caring in their mediated interactions, a communication imperative inspires people to appropriate the cues that are on offer in creative ways so they can show feeling, play, perform, and create identities, relationships, and group contexts.

Social forces, both online and off, shape communication online and in mobile texting, their signal boosted by mediation. People's familiarity with the medium is an influence, as are their motivations for participating. Relational and group contexts, which may themselves be shaped through online discourse, matter. Most online communication happens against a backdrop of a shared history, whether that involves two individuals or a group that has had time to develop norms to guide appropriate behavior. People draw on long-standing practices in other media like writing, oral conversation, film and photography to guide their verbal and nonverbal activity in new media. Social identities including (but by no means limited to) gender and culture affect how people act and how their messages are perceived. The ways people communicate in these media have reshaped the media themselves, as developers respond to user creativity by automating emoticons, adding new ways to represent social cues (e.g. color, images, sound), and making it possible to use diverse alphabets through the technologies. In sum, mediated communication demonstrates many new qualities, but continues to display and reinforce the broader cultural forces that influence messages in all contexts.

4

Communities and networks

After inventing one-to-one communication systems, it took the developers of what became the internet almost no time to develop platforms for group communication. Among the first such groups was SF-Lovers, a mailing list for science fiction fans. Accompanied by influential bulletin board systems such as the Bay Area counterculture hangout, The Well (Rheingold, 1993), and early multiplayer games, these group communication platforms were followed by thousands, then millions, of topically organized mailing lists, Usenet newsgroups, and websites. The advent of social network sites (SNSs) in the late 1990s provided another platform for groups and simultaneously posed challenges for them by foregrounding more loosely bound networks of individuals. Yet communities continue, even if it means creating Twitter hashtags.

Many online groups develop a strong sense of group membership. They serve as bases for the creation of new relationships as people from multiple locations gather synchronously or asynchronously to discuss topics of shared interest, role play, or just hang out. Participants have extolled the benefits of being able to form new connections with others regardless of location and to easily find others with common interests, the round-the-clock availability of these groups, and the support they provide. Members of these groups often describe them as "communities." Internet proponents such as Howard Rheingold (1993) touted a new age of "virtual community" in which webs of personal connection transcended time and distance to create meaningful new social formations. My own research on the newsgroup rec.arts.tv.soaps (r.a.t.s.) conceptualized the group as a community.

Given its emotional force, it's not surprising that this use of "community" generated strong counter-reactions from those such as Lockard (1997: 225) who warned that "to accept only communication in place of a community's manifold functions is to sell our common faith in community vastly short." Early critics such as Stoll (1995) raised fears of a "silicon snake oil" that replaced genuine and deep connections with shallow and inadequate substitutes. The specter of people isolated indoors substituting Gergen's "floating world" of connection for meaningful contact with their neighbors sends a shudder through those concerned that, as Robert Putnam (1995, 2000) famously put it, we are already doing far too much "bowling alone."

If you hear echoes of the hopes and concerns about mediated interaction that have reverberated through the history of communication technologies, you should. As we've seen in previous chapters, people tend to doubt the authenticity of social connections sustained through new media and question their impact on interpersonal, civic, and political engagement. Historical changes occurring in conjunction with and facilitated by communication technologies have led many to worry that people are losing connections to their local communities, with towns, cities, and nations suffering the consequences. Digital technologies have potential to engage us more closely in communal connections but, if they take us away from embodied local interactions, they could threaten the real thing.

In this chapter we'll look at how people organize into groups and networks online. First, we'll ask what is meant when people label an online group "community." We turn then to social networks, exploring how these more recent platforms have afforded more personalized and diffuse yet centralized connections. In closing the chapter we'll look at how digital media connect with participation in geographically grounded communities.

Online community

What did it mean when YouTube, with its millions of users, prominently featured the term "community" on its navigation bar, as though its millions of users were united into a common group through mere use of the site? What kind of "community" was being invoked when the digital services company Sparta Networks (n.d.) boasted on their website that they built a client "a highly scalable, function rich, flexible online community . . . in less than a third of the time it would have taken them to build the community internally?" These technological definitions of "community" appeal to developers and also to marketers (Preece & Maloney-Krichmar, 2003) who can create a site, call it a "community," and hope to reap the benefits of the term's warm connotations without having to deal with questions of what actually happens on-site. Different technological platforms do lend themselves to different sorts of group formations, and differences in digital affordances lead to differences in group behavior. Yet one need only peek below the surface of any one online platform to see that technologically based definitions of "community" fall apart in the face of variety. YouTube, as Burgess and Green (2009) show, is far from a single collective. Instead it is comprised of many subgroups, each with its own practices and purposes, which are sometimes at odds with the other groups. Thus, when Oprah decided to join YouTube, many of the amateur media producers resented her and her fans' presence, just as the female vloggers resented the sexist commenting practices of male subgroups with which they had to contend. The mere existence of an interactive online forum is not community, and one platform can host many different groups.

Whether you are willing to consider any digitally based group a "community" depends first and foremost on which of many definitions of "community" you choose. No one has ever been able to agree what exactly "community" means. "Ever since sociological theorist Ferdinand Tönnies declared community to be an essential condition for the development of close, primary social bonds," wrote Mary Chayko (2008: 6), "sociologists have not been able to agree on how, or whether, definitions of community should be updated." Despite (or perhaps because of) the term's openness to a variety of interpretations, it remains useful. Chayko conducted electronic interviews with 87 people who self-identified as active users of group communication online, in order to explore their perspectives of mediated social dynamics. Although she did not use the word "community" in her interview questions (2008: 212–13), her interviewees repeatedly invoked it to describe their online experiences, saying things like "I feel I am part of a tight-knit community" and "You can definitely feel the community on the board" (2008: 7). Like Chayko, I am reluctant to drop the term altogether. "Community" has provided a resonant handle for members, developers, analysts, marketers, and even critics as they've tried to understand online groups. Rather than debate which definition is correct, and hence whether or not online communities are "real," I will identify five qualities found in both online groups and many definitions of community that make the term resonate for online contexts. These are the sense of space, shared practice, shared resources and support, shared identities, and interpersonal relationships.

Space

Those who argue online groups cannot be communities often consider common geography a necessary condition of "community." From early on, geographical communities such as Berkeley and Santa Monica, California, turned to the internet as a means of building local community, creating community networks to foster civic engagement and provide access for those without internet connections. Schuler (1996) runs through several examples of efforts to create online networks to support local communities. One of the earliest, Santa Monica's PEN system, had five objectives, including providing city residents with: easy electronic access to public information; an alternative means of communication, delivery, and creating awareness of public services; and the opportunity to learn about computer technology. The PEN system also sought "to provide an electronic forum for participation in discussions of issues and concerns of residents in order to promote an enhanced sense of community" (quoted in Schuler, 1996: 120).

Most online groups are not so tied to geographical space, yet people who are involved in online groups often think of them as shared places. The feeling that online groups meeting on software and hardware platforms constitute "spaces" is integral to the language often used to describe the internet. Consider the term "cyberspace," coined by science fiction author William Gibson, or the western United States metaphor in the subtitle of Rheingold's now classic

1993 book *The Virtual Community: Homesteading on the Electronic Frontier.*

The metaphor of space is particularly applicable in visual online environments such as massively multiplayer online role-playing games (MMORPGs) where fictional worlds built through code are experienced as semi-physical realities. Second Life, in which users create buildings, parks, and other emulations of physical spaces, also lends itself to spatial understandings of "community." The immersive graphics of World of Warcraft, combined with participants' organiza-tion into guilds, shapes the sense of community – or communities – in that environment (Nardi, 2010). Schuler (1996) organizes the second chapter of his book around Ray Oldenburg's concept of a "third place." Similarly, in their analysis of two MMORPGs, Steinkuehler and Williams (2006) use Oldenburg's ideas to argue that these envi-ronments function similarly to the "cafes, coffee shops, community centers, beauty parlors, general stores, bars and hangouts that get you through the day" in well-functioning cities and towns (Oldenburg, 1989: front cover). Third places, neither work nor home, are vital sites of informal social life, critical to social cohesion. Steinkuehler and Williams's analysis of MMORPGs as third places shows how they provide sites of neutral ground, equal status, sociable conversation, easy access, known regulars, playful interaction, (sometimes) homely aesthetics, and a homelike atmosphere.

Textual groups can also be metaphorically based on space, as was the case in the official board for fans of television show *Buffy the Vampire Slayer* documented by Stephanie Tuszynski (2007) in her ethnographic film *IRL: In Real Life.* This board was called "The Bronze" after a hangout in the television show. Members Tuszynski interviewed frequently referred to the board as a place, one even laugh-ing at herself for saying goodbye to her partner before walking down the hall to go to The Bronze, as though she were leaving the apartment to go elsewhere. Furthermore, online groups can be organized with reference to geographical location. People form groups to discuss national and regional issues or to share the things that make their locations special to them (e.g. the Facebook group called "MAN !!!! LOOK AT THIS THING I SAW IN A LAWRENCE, KANSAS ALLEY !!!"). People also form groups to discuss cultural materials tied to particular regions, as I've described in the context of Swedish independent music's international fans (Baym, 2007). With the rising use of social media in social protests (to which I will return below), many ad hoc groups emerge throughout Twitter, Facebook, and elsewhere, enabling rapid organization but also governmental surveillance.

Shared practice

A metaphorical sense of shared space is thus one criterion that people use when they label digitally mediated groups "communities." Community can also be found in the habitual and usually unconscious practices – routinized behaviors – that group members share. Communities of practice include occupational, educational, and recreational groups as well as regional ones (e.g. Dundes, 1977; Lave & Wenger, 1991). Because language is the primary tool through which digitally mediated groups cohere, the concept of "speech community," which foregrounds shared communication practices, has been particularly useful for many of us studying online groups. Speech communities have distinctive patterns of language use which enact and recreate a cultural ideology that underpins them (Philipsen, 1992).

Online speech communities share ways of speaking that capture the meanings that are important to them and the logics that underlie their common sensibilities. Groups share insider lingo and literacies including acronyms, vocabulary words, genres, styles, and forms of play. In my book *Tune In, Log On* (Baym, 2000), I wrote about a soap opera fan group (r.a.t.s.) on Usenet. I spent years reading the group and conducted close analysis of the ways in which language created a social context akin to community. Members of r.a.t.s. used many terms comprehensible to insiders, including the acronym "IOAS" for "It's Only A Soap" and numerous nicknames for characters.

Though I would not consider Twitter a single community, any more than YouTube, its users do share some practices, shaped both by technological affordances (the 140-character limit) and by other internet trends such as LOLspeak (see chapter 3). The power of being able to speak like a Twitter insider was evident when the four founders of Swedish file-sharing site The Pirate Bay went on trial in

2009. One defendant tweeted from the courtroom. With posts such as "EPIC WINNING LOL" he quickly won the hearts of his followers (if not the court), who saw one of their own in his use of language. They did not win the trial, but the Swedish election of a member of the Pirate Party to the European Parliament in the wake of their conviction was evidence of the popular support they had gained. The discussion of Black Twitter (Brock, 2012; Florini, 2013) in the previous chapter provides one example of playful language use that serves to build a distinctive community. Image memes, which often emerge on the site 4Chan and then move to Reddit and Imgur, and are old news by the time they appear on Facebook, are another example of shared practice that requires a sense of group identity (Milner, 2012; Miltner, 2014; Shifman, 2012).

These terms and genres are markers of insider status and hence help to forge group identity (see further discussion of this below). They also indicate groups' core values. IOAS did not just mean "it's only a soap opera," it also meant that the group valued soap operas and understood that one could be involved enough to find them frustrating yet not be the lifeless idiots represented by the soap viewer stereotype. The phrase simultaneously validated group members' shared love of the genre, self-representation as intelligent, and their shared frustrations. Tweeters' use of "epic" demonstrates the shared values of humor and irreverence. Rage Comics' frequent representations of socially awkward young white men, like the Socially Awkward Penguin meme, speak to the shared masculine geek culture of sites like 4Chan and Reddit (Milner, 2012). Summer postings of "hot dog legs" on Instagram demonstrate the values of leisure, luxury, and the body amongst young female Instagrammers.

Shared practices entail *norms* for the appropriate use of communication. In a piece on norms and their violations on Facebook, McLaughlin and Vitak (2011: 300) define norms as "a framework through which people determine what behaviors are acceptable and unacceptable." Norms can be explicitly stated, but they are often implicit, negotiated without discussion. Ongoing groups develop standards that guide members' behavior. The "NSFW" (Not Safe For Work) Tumblr community Katrin Tiidenberg studied (e.g. 2014) had distinct norms about sexiness, emphasizing that every woman's body can be appealing, and training one another in the aesthetics of what constitutes a sexy image. Violations of these norms are often met with critical response from other users. In an early study, McLaughlin, Osborne, and Smith (1995) collected messages from Usenet in which participants had been castigated for misbehavior. Analyzing those instances, they identified several issues that spanned Usenet groups, including incorrect use of technology, bandwidth waste, network-wide conventions, newsgroup-specific conventions, ethical violations, inappropriate language, and factual errors. Online groups that discuss television shows and movies often have a norm that the word "spoilers" should be included in the subject lines of posts which give away the story ahead of time. This enables those who don't want the show spoiled by this advance information to avoid such posts. Other groups are devoted entirely to sharing spoilers.

In the last chapter, we saw groups differ in their attitude toward flaming (Lea et al., 1992); the soap opera group I studied would have none of it, while other groups tolerate and even encourage it. The discussion board for my favorite band tolerated a great deal of rudeness, particularly when people violated norms, but attended carefully to an implicit norm that people must be thanked when they share materials with the group. Users of r.a.t.s. shared a commitment to friendliness, which could be seen in the details of how they disagreed with one another. Their disagreements were packed with qualification ("I might be wrong but I thought that . . ."), partial agreement ("I agree that . . ., but I still thought that . . ."), and other linguistic strategies designed to minimize offense and maximize affiliation (Baym, 1996). Group members do not have to think about these norms as they formulate their messages. Instead, becoming a group insider involves a process of being socialized to these norms and values so that they guide one's communication without having to be considered. On Wikipedia, adherence to norms is critical to remaining an editor or rising through the editorial ranks. In his analysis of the use of the word "community" by Wikipedians, Pentzold (2011) describes Wikipedia as an "ethos-action community" committed to ideals of openness, fairness, objectivity, consensus, and following the guidelines. No one enters the community with trust, but new editors are able to earn it by acting in accordance with that ethos.

Social norms also emerge in social network sites (SNSs). Fono and Raynes-Goldie (2006) interviewed users of LiveJournal about their reasons for friending people on that site and the issues that arise around friending. boyd (2006) interviewed users of MySpace and Friendster. Both studies found friending norms, although they were not uniform and, as we will return to in chapter 6, caused confusion and interpersonal conflict. Donath (2007) argues that SNSs develop norms for what constitutes truth in terms of "the mores of our community." Humphreys (2007) observed the short-lived location-sensitive SNS Dodgeball for one year and performed in-depth interviews with users in seven American cities. She found that there were norms regulating things such as how often one should post one's location to the network. Just as the norms around friending are uncertain, "normative Dodgeball use is not only emerging but contested"; subgroups "may have different tolerance levels, expectations, and definitions of acceptable or 'correct' Dodgeball use" (Humphreys, 2007). On Facebook, the undergraduates interviewed by McLaughlin and Vitak (2012) voiced norms regarding whether to accept or deny friend requests (accepting was generally preferred), not posting too many status updates, not writing overly emotional updates, fighting, or tagging pictures of other people that reflect negatively on them. How people responded to violations of those Facebook norms depended on both the nature of the violation and the relationship.

Community norms of practice are displayed, reinforced, negotiated, and taught through members' shared behaviors. They are also enshrined through FAQs (Frequently Asked Questions files). Early on, these appeared as regularly occurring posts in message boards. Web boards often include them as a link. Hansen and his collaborators studied a question-and-answer mailing list for web developers that also maintained a wiki repository that worked as a FAQ and as an alternative space that allowed members to keep the list discussion on-topic (Hansen, Ackerman, Resnick, & Munson, 2007). They performed both qualitative thematic analysis and quantitative content analysis of all the wiki pages as well as samples from several thousand of the group's 90,000 emails, and conducted semi-structured interviews. They found that the wikis served several normative functions in the group. When people broached irresolvable disputes over topics such as font size, they could be gently referred to the wiki. This allowed the list to avoid irresolvable "holy wars," maintain the "friendly and professional tone," and socialize new members without losing old members who had been through those questions many times before.

Online groups also share norms for what constitutes skilled communicative practice. The Pirate Bay founder who knew to use the phrase "epic winning" and the acronym "LOL" demonstrated not just his insider status, but also his Twitter skill. Participants in r.a.t.s. valued humor and insight in their posts, and, in surveys I conducted, particularly funny posters were those most frequently mentioned as "good" contributors. In fan communities, those who write particularly good fan fiction might be celebrated, while those who give especially helpful advice might be considered the best contributors to support communities. Friends who post status updates at the right frequency with the right mix of humor, self-deprecation, and thoughtfulness might be most appreciated on Facebook. Good-looking people whose selfies best capture the aesthetic of celebrity photographs may achieve fame on Instagram (Marwick, in press).

Normative standards always implicate power structures. Hierarchies form online, giving some people more say than others in creating and regulating behavioral standards within group contexts. Stivale, for example, examined the variants of what counts as spam in LambdaMOO and argued that "the ambiguity of what is appropriate or not suggests once again the ongoing struggle between centripetal and centrifugal forces, i.e. forces that seek some unified central 'command' versus those seeking to contest such unification from the margins" (Stivale, 1997: 139). Many groups are moderated, meaning that power structures are both explicit and built into the group's very structure. Some of the norm-maintaining jobs that moderators do include keeping the group on-topic, deleting posts that they deem inappropriate or distracting, and fixing problematic formatting. In unmoderated groups, power structures may be implicit and emergent (Preece & Maloney-Krichmar, 2003). The contrast between this and optimistic predictions that the absence of social cues in online interaction would eliminate hierarchy and render all participants equal should be obvious.

Social norms are also rooted within the behavioral contexts in which users live, as we saw in the last chapter. On social network sites, where people may be "aware that their friends and colleagues are looking," they are likely to feel pressured to conform to those groups' norms (Donath, 2007). Walther, Van der Heide, Kim, and Westerman (2008) conducted an experiment in which they first had focus groups describe what constituted good and bad peer behaviors. They then manipulated Facebook profiles to demonstrate those behaviors and assessed perceptions of those profiles. They found that college student participants did rely on societal and peer group standards when forming impressions online. Wall posts describing excessive and questionable behavior result in more negative perceptions, although this was only true for women's profiles. In an analysis of the metadata from 362 million fully anonymized private messages and "pokes" exchanged by 4.2 million North American Facebook users through that site, Golder, Wilkinson, and Huberman (2007) found that messaging was guided by strong temporal rhythms that were often grounded in local norms. For instance, messaging took place at night and peaked Tuesdays and Wednesdays and was at its lowest during the "college student weekend" beginning mid-afternoon Friday and lasting through mid-afternoon Sunday. Studies of millions of images posted to Instagram from different cities likewise demonstrate temporal and color patterns, displaying distinctive "visual rhythms" in each city (Hochman & Manovich, 2013; Hochman & Schwartz, 2012).

Shared resources and support

Communities are often defined as "composed of broadly based relationships in which each community member felt securely able to obtain a wide variety of help" (Wellman, 1988: 97). The supportive exchange of resources is often implied when people use the term "community" in digital contexts. Closely related to social support is "social capital" (Coleman, 1988). Social capital, as Ellison, Steinfeld, and Lampe (2007) explain, is "an elastic term with a variety of definitions." In essence, it refers to the resources people attain because of their network of relationships. When people provide and receive social support in online groups, they are contributing to one another's accumulated social capital. Social capital may be either "bonding" or "bridging" (Putnam, 1995, 2000). Bridging capital is exchanged between people who differ from one another and do not share strong relationships. The internet and social network sites lend themselves to and expand the potential for this kind of capital (Hampton, Lee, & Her, 2011). In contrast, bonding capital is usually exchanged between people in close relationships. While the former is a "sociological lubricant," the latter is "a kind of social superglue" (Steinkuehler & Williams, 2006). Many online groups provide bridging capital, exchanged in relationships that are highly specialized, yet it is also common to find members of online communities and social networks providing one another with the sort of emotional support often found in close relationships. Indeed, supportive exchanges between weak ties may be more stress-reducing than those between strong ties (Wright, Rains, & Banas, 2010).

Social support offers many benefits to its recipients. Documented positive effects include better psychological adjustment, higher perceptions of self-efficacy, better coping, improved task performance, better disease resistance and recovery, and lowered risk of mortality (Burleson & MacGeorge, 2002). Some online communities are explicitly support groups. Forums abound for people with medical conditions, addiction, traumas, and other debilitating or stigmatizing life circumstances. Though one might be inclined to think of support as inherently good, there are cases that push or cross that boundary – what Haas, Irr, Jennings, and Wagner (2011) call "online negative enabling support groups." The "pro-ana" sites they studied provide support to those who view anorexia as a life-style choice rather than a disease. Extreme body modification communities support those interested in changing their bodies in ways practitioners embrace as self-expression, but which many consider mutilation and which may be illegal (Lingel & boyd, 2013).

Walther and Boyd (2002) conducted an email survey of a sampling of people who had posted to Usenet support groups. Their research identifies four motivations for people to seek this kind of support online, including the security provided by anonymity, the ease of access to these groups, the ability to manage one's interaction within them, and the social distance from others. Online support can allow people access to bonding and bridging resources without the entanglements and threats of close relationships. These groups are also important for those without local support groups.

The provision of social support is common even in groups that are not explicitly designated as supportive (Wellman & Gulia, 1999). There are several, often overlapping, kinds of social support (Cutrona & Russell, 1990). *Social integration* or *network* support:

> enables people to feel part of a group whose members have common interests and concerns. Such relationships reflect more casual friendships, which enable a person to engage in various forms of social and recreational activities. (Cutrona & Russell, 1990: 322)

Online fans and hobbyist groups exemplify this, as their very existence is predicated on a desire to organize around common interests for social and recreational purposes. Consider the *Survivor* spoiler fan "knowledge community" described by Jenkins (2006). Members of this group collaborated to figure out the identities of all the contestants and even the winner of the sixth season's contest before the entrants had been officially announced or the first show had aired. In the short term, this group was "just having fun on a Friday night participating in an elaborate scavenger hunt involving thousands of participants." In the long term, Jenkins posits that they were coming to understand "how they may deploy the new kinds of power that are emerging from participation within knowledge communities" (2006: 29). The recreational information exchanged amongst fans online becomes a form of subcultural capital that can bolster individuals' status within and outside of the fan group (Kibby, 2010).

Emotional support represents "the ability to turn to others for comfort and security during times of stress, leading the person to feel that he or she is cared for by others" (Cutrona & Russell, 1990: 322). In one striking example, Heather Spohr, a prominent "mommy blogger," had been writing about her daughter since her premature birth at 29 weeks. She and her readers built strong connections. When Spohr's daughter passed away unexpectedly at 17 months, the *Los Angeles Times* (Bermudez, 2009) described an outpouring of support that crashed the servers and generated more than $20,000 in donations to the March of Dimes, a nonprofit organization working to help prevent birth defects. While emotional support may be more common in explicit support groups, a content analysis of diverse online groups found that most demonstrate empathic communication and provide emotional support (Preece & Ghozati, 1998).

Esteem support bolsters "a person's sense of competence or self-esteem" through the provision of "individual positive feedback on his or her skills and abilities or expressing a belief that the person is capable" (Cutrona & Russell, 1990: 322). McKenna and Bargh (1998) surveyed people who posted to Usenet groups for homosexuals. They found that newsgroups contributed to "identity demarginalization." As people participated within the newsgroups and received positive feedback for their gay identities, their self-acceptance increased and sense of estrangement dropped. As a direct result, they were more likely to come out to their loved ones. McKenna and Bargh concluded that the anonymity of online groups allows people to engage in riskier self-disclosure and, when that is affirmed, such groups can create positive changes in people's self-concepts. In contrast, the pro-ana groups studied by Haas et al. (2011) supported one another in their negative self-appraisals, affirming one another by accepting without contradiction their expressions of self-loathing and worthlessness. The men Elija Cassidy (2013) studied in Brisbane, Australia, used Grindr and Facebook to connect with other gay young men, but in so doing often came to abhor images of gay masculinity and to feel marginalized and unattractive within that community.

Informational support offers "advice or guidance concerning possible solutions to a problem" (Cutrona & Russell, 1990: 322). Advice may be about topics as diverse as writing CSS or managing one's love life. Much of the communication on Oprah's web board exemplified informational (and emotional) support, as seen in this exchange when Brokenhearted girl wrote about her ex-boyfriend's on-again off-again affections for her. Phyllis g advised:

> Listen to what all frosting1112 had to say to you today . . . she is wise and what she said is right-on!! I, too, think your ex-boyfriend is trying to keep you hanging on!! Guys do this all the time. They will break your heart . . . knowing that you love them. and then feel some sort of . . . male "thing" when you cry about them.. It makes me sick!! Girl.. Maybe it's time you just start setting some of those boundaries for yourself!! Your pain is very genuine to me. I know and

can feel threw the computer and threw your words that you need help . . . but . . . if you keep focusing on him and never really try working this out for yourself. You are going to continue to stay sick!! And, you are sick . . . he is like a drug for you. YOU got to make a step . . . toward recovery!! He is an addiction!! (Phyllis g)

Frosting 1112 later returned to the thread, offering emotional support:

Hi again. Hope things are getting better for you girl.. You still sound a little confused and upset to me.. I hope and shall keep you in my prayers. And know God will bring you peace if you let him!! (Frosting 1112)

In response, Brokenhearted girl provided the others in the thread with esteem support:

I wanted to thank you all for you beautiful reply. I could only hope to be as beautiful as the sweet spirit that I know from all of you!!

This exchange demonstrates the cyclical and self-reinforcing nature of much supportive behavior in online communities, a point I'll return to in discussing people's motivations for providing strangers and casual acquaintances with resources. In groups supporting marginalized identities – including extreme body modification and anorexia – informational support becomes fraught, as people simultaneously seek information and seek to hide that information-seeking from others in their lives (Haas et al., 2011; Lingel & boyd, 2013). Information within such groups may be managed in ways designed to keep outsiders out, or, as one of the body modifiers interviewed by Lingel & boyd put it, "keep it secret, keep it safe."

When people support one another with money, by doing things for them, and by providing them lodging and other services, Cutrona and Russell call this *tangible aid*. When one of the regular writers at Daily Kos, a left-leaning political blogging site, suffered extreme damage to his home, members of the site sent him money to help him to recover. People often provide traveling members of online groups places to stay, or at least meals, when they visit their towns. In recent years, increasing numbers of artists and entrepreneurs have turned to their online communities and networks to crowdfund their projects through sites like Kickstarter and Indie Go-Go. The musician Amanda Palmer, for instance, was able to raise US$1.2 million for an album from her fans, though she initially requested $100,000. On a more modest yet still impressive scale, Jill Sobule was able to motivate her online community to donate $74,000 for her album *California Years*. (In the realm of absurdity, Zach Danger Brown of Columbus, Ohio raised more than $60,000 on Kickstarter to make a potato salad for which he had initially sought $10.)

As they share resources in public group contexts, people participating in online groups collaboratively build a replenishing repository of public goods that can be used by unknown recipients one might never encounter again and whom one can't expect to reciprocate immediately (Kollock, 1999). One might ask why people do this. It makes obvious sense to take the time and financial and emotional risks to support those you already know and love, but why provide this kind of support to people you hardly know or may not know at all? One reason may be what Cutrona and Russell (1990: 332) refer to as a sixth form of social support: supporting others gives people the *feeling that they are needed*. Helping others online may give people a sense of efficacy (Kollock, 1999). Offering support to others now may lead to receiving support should you ever go looking for it in the future (Kollock, 1999). Being a skilled provider of resources can also increase people's status and prestige within online groups (Matzat, 2004).

Shared identities

The sense of shared space, rituals of shared practices, and exchange of social support all contribute to a feeling of community in digital environments. Shared identities are also important. These include personalities and roles assumed by individuals. Identities also include a shared sense of who "we" are that may be pre-existing or develop within a group. Many regulars take on specific roles. Some of the most common roles are "local experts, answer people, conversationalists, fans, discussion artists, flame warriors, and trolls" (Welser, Gleave, Fischer, & Smith, 2007). People assume roles by enacting consistent and systematic behaviors that serve a particular function. In a music group I frequented, there was a fan known for regularly hunting down and sharing photographs of the band. In r.a.t.s., one woman took on the role of welcome-wagon, greeting all new contributors with an enthusiastic response designed to encourage them to continue participating, a role seen also in The Bronze, where one contributor posted the "shout out" to new posters each morning. In the community of fans of Swedish music, a particularly powerful and recognizable identity was that of mp3 blogger, and the few who claim this role gain status amongst the fans, as well as with the musicians, labels, and others professionally involved with Swedish independent music (Baym, 2007; Baym & Burnett, 2009).

Welser and his colleagues (2007) were interested in whether they could identify people who play roles within Usenet communities from structural information alone. Based on a sample of almost 6,000 messages from three different newsgroups, they determined that several roles could be identified from metadata. "Answer people" frequently responded yet never initiated, while "discussion people" both initiated and responded. Furthermore, there was very little communication amongst the individuals in the threads to which "answer people" contributed, while there was a great deal amongst participants in "discussion people's" threads. They conclude that roles have "behavioral and structural 'signatures'" (Welser et al., 2007). From the point of view of regular participants, these structural signatures are less visible than the fact that the answer person is a regular, one who can be counted on to provide informational support when a new participant asks for it.

The most common role in most, if not all, online communities is that of "lurker," the person who reads but never posts. The Scandinavian music newszine, It's a Trap!, that served as a hub of sorts for that fan community, had a message board. Of the 30,000 people who looked at that board each month, fewer than 100 ever left comments or contributed. Most who do post to an online group do so rarely. In r.a.t.s., more than half who posted did so only once, while the top 10 percent of posters wrote half of all messages (Baym, 2000). Hansen et al. (2007) found that the top 4 percent of the CSS-L mailing list wrote half of the messages. As Crawford (2011) has noted, lurking can be better understood as listening, and, seen through that lens, a valuable mode of participation in online communities. Though one might argue that some speak far too much, few would argue that the quality of online discourse would be higher if everyone who read a message responded to it.

Given the prevalence of this silent majority, Preece, Nonnecke, and Andrews (2004) investigated the reasons for silence. Their survey of a sample from 375 online groups found no differences between lurkers and posters in terms of age, gender, education, or employment. They did find that lurkers were less likely to read the group because they sought answers and less likely to feel they attained the benefits from group membership that they expected, felt a lower sense of group belonging, and respected the other participants less than did the posters. Ironically, posters were more likely to consider lurkers part of the community than were lurkers themselves. The vast majority of lurkers had not intended to read without posting from the outset (only 13.2 percent did). Their silence was motivated by a variety of reasons which Preece et al. (2004) collapse into five. First, many lurkers felt they were already getting what they needed from the group without contributing their own messages. Some felt they needed to get to know the group better. For instance, they may not have felt they knew enough about the group's norms or the topic of discussion, or may have felt shy. Several indicated that they believed they were contributing to the well-being of the community by staying silent when they had nothing to offer. Technical problems with posting were a fourth reason for lurking. Some simply couldn't make the software work or did not know how to post their own messages. Finally, people indicated that they lurked because they did not like the group's dynamics, perhaps because the participants seemed different from themselves, or because they feared aggressive responses.

Groups sometimes develop a sense of themselves as a group, a social identity or schema of who they are that is shared amongst them (Tajfel & Turner, 1986) and which contributes to the feeling of community. These group identities foster ingroup norms and resistance or opposition to outgroups (Spears & Lea, 1992). This is very striking in the case of pro-ana groups, and is also seen in the extreme body modification groups, but is common elsewhere as well. Groups may develop names for themselves, such as those in the Buffy fan group who referred to themselves as "Bronzers." As I showed in *Tune In, Log On* (Baym, 2000), the soap fans in r.a.t.s. defined themselves as intelligent and witty people, primarily women, who loved soap operas, and who had rich, rewarding lives. This was a response to the dominant stereotype of soap opera fans as lazy, stupid women who watched because they had nothing useful to do with their time. This group identity was rarely made explicit, and only stated outright in response to trolls who attacked that self-image, as seen in this excerpt from a post responding to one such flame:

> What do I know? I've only got a suma cum laude BA degree, an MS in chemistry, and in a few more than a few more months, a PHD in X-ray crystallography (that's structural bio-physical chemistry). You say you are well read, Mark? Let's discuss Sartre, Kuhn, Locke, Tolstoy, quantum vs. classical mechanics, cloning, new advances in immunosuppression and drug design, Montessori, James (Henry or William), Kierkegaard, Friedman, Piaget, classical or modern theatre, the pros and cons of recycling, the deterioration of the ozone layer, global warming, James Bay, the Alaskan wilderness crisis, hiking/climbing/ camping, cycling, gourmet cooking, fitness and nutrition, or any other topic in which you may feel adept. Feel free to reply in French, German, or Spanish. Chinese or Japanese, I admit, will take me a little longer to handle.

People may also join groups because they already share a social identity. Many online groups are designed for people who share a race or ethnicity, a profession, or another affiliation. Many social network sites too are designed for specific social identities such as BlackPlanet for African-Americans, Jake for gay professional men, Ravelry for knitting enthusiasts, or FanNation for sports fans (although these sites may have trouble staying in business – several mentioned in the first edition of this book have since folded). Geography also influences the groups and social networks people join. Americans and many Europeans may flock to Facebook, but in China it is Weibo where people congregate online, and, at least as of this writing, Line is wildly popular in Japan.

Interpersonal relationships

Online groups provide contexts for forming one-on-one relationships, which the next two chapters will consider in more detail. These friendships and sometimes romances are made visible to the group when members post reports of having met or spent time with one another

(Baym, 1995). The visible pairs of connections that form are important contributors to the sense of connectivity that Rheingold (1993: 5)
invoked when he famously described virtual communities as "social
aggregations that emerge from the Net when enough people carry on
those public discussions long enough, with sufficient human feeling,
to form webs of personal relationships." Interpersonal pairs provide
a social mesh that underlies and helps to connect the broader web of
interconnection within the group more closely.

Networks

Thus far, I've focused mostly on groups which have clear boundaries
– they are located at one website or have the same mailing address.
Messages go to all members. One-on-one communication is backstage,
conducted through private channels such as private messaging or
chat. Since the early 2000s, SNSs have become increasingly popular,
staking out a middle ground between private dyadic encounters and
tightly bounded group interactions. Wellman (e.g. 1988; Wellman,
Quan-Haase, Boase, Chen, Hampton, & de Diaz, 2003) argues that a
crucial social transformation of late modernism is a shift away from
tightly bounded communities toward increasing "*networked individualism*" in which each person sits at the center of his or her own
personal community.

Social network sites are designed to afford organization and
access to such personalized communities. Ellison and boyd (2013:
158) defined a social network site as a "networked communication
platform in which participants (1) have uniquely identifiable profiles
that consist of user-supplied content, content provided by other users,
and/or system-level data; (2) can publicly articulate connections that
can be viewed and traversed by others; and (3) can consume, produce,
and/or interact with streams of user-generated content provided by
their connections on the site." In SNSs, messages are only seen by
people tied to a user's individualized network, which is a tiny subset
of all users. The only messages available to all users are those sent
by the sites themselves. To the extent that members of different
people's social networks overlap and are internally organized, they
may constitute groups, but social networks are egocentric and no

two will be identical. Thus, no two SNS users will have access to the same set of people or messages, giving them each an experience of the site that is individualized yet overlapping with others. User innovations such as hashtags on Twitter can help to increase the overlap.

Just as individuals organize themselves into networks online, so too do groups. Recent years have seen groups increasingly distributing themselves through the internet in interconnected webs of websites, blogs, SNSs, and other platforms. I call this *networked collectivism*, meaning that groups of people now network throughout the internet and related mobile media, and in-person communication, creating a shared but distributed group identity. The fans of Swedish independent music, for example, organized themselves into clusters on music-based SNSs, blogs, news sites, other SNSs, sites developed around individual bands, and regular nights in local music venues (Baym, 2007).

This development has empowered members of these communities to share more kinds of media with one another, and to interact in a wider variety of ways, but also challenges many of the qualities that can make these groups cohere into something more than the sum of their parts (Baym, 2007). When there is no single shared environment, the metaphor of space quickly unravels. Communities organized through multiple sites do not feel like places. Shared practices are less likely to develop when groups are spread throughout sites, especially since each site is embedded in contexts that bring with them their own communicative traditions. Norms about what constitutes appropriate behavior in comments on YouTube videos may be quite different from in fan websites. In-jokes and jargon are hard to sustain when there are many places to be inside and outside at once. The resources exchanged in supportive interactions may have to be deployed repeatedly to reach all community members, and people who hang out in some of the online spaces but not all may miss them, while those who hang out in all of them may encounter too much repetition. Identities are also harder to develop. People may frequent and play roles in some interrelated sites but not others, with the consequence that a crowd of regulars who contribute in predictable ways may be harder to find or discern. A sense of group identity may be difficult to build. Interpersonal relationships may not be as visible to others, meaning that, although they are valuable to those in the relationships, their existence may be less valuable for the coherence of the group as a whole (Baym, 2007).

Engagement with place-based community

Critics often view the widespread use of online media and social network sites as a threat to geographical community. People are said to be engaging their screens rather than one another (e.g. Turkle, 2011). I turn now to whether and to what extent participation in digital interaction affects engagement with one's geographical community.

One of the defining qualities of communication technologies from their beginnings in bone scratchings is that they rupture the otherwise-mandatory connection between message delivery and shared space. The ability to communicate in the absence of shared space in real time invokes fears of separation from physical reality, hence Gergen's (2002) concern about "floating worlds," Meyrowitz's (1985) worries about "no sense of place," and 100-year-old arguments that the telephone would lead to a lost sense of place (Fischer, 1992). As we lose connection to space, do we also become detached from those nearby whose social support comprised communities of old and on whose interconnections civil society depends?

Testing this is not easy. Most of the data that we have about the impacts of digital media on people's local connections comes from surveys. Many of these divide users into categories based on whether or not they use the internet, how much they use it in comparison to one another, or how long they have been using it. There are serious theoretical problems with these strategies. They assume that simply using the internet or using it more than others may cause effects, regardless of how it is used (Campbell & Kwak, 2011; Jung et al., 2001). More sophisticated measures attempt to distinguish different kinds and contexts of internet use. Hampton, Lee, and Her (2011), for instance, use multiple measures including whether participants use the internet or not, whether they use it frequently from home or from work, and whether they used Instant Messenger, blogged, shared digital photos, or used social networking services.

It's not surprising, given the range of measures, that the results of studies are mixed. As a whole, though, they do not support the dystopian critique that time spent online detracts from social participation offline (Boulianne, 2009). The roles of the internet in civic and political engagement are vast and well beyond the scope of this book (see, e.g., Dahlgren, 2005, 2009; Hartelius, 2005), so consider what follows to be a cursory look.

Civic engagement

People are civically engaged when they act in ways that address "social and/or community issues that are not political by nature but, nevertheless, are conducive to the collective well-being" (Gil de Zúñiga & Valenzuela, 2011: 399). One way to assess civic engagement is to ask people how many of their neighbors they know. Katz and Rice (2002) compared people who had used the internet recently to non-users of the internet and found that recent users knew the fewest, while non-users were most likely to know them all. On the other hand, in a study of a suburb of Toronto built to be wired from the ground up, Hampton and Wellman (2003) found that those who had the high-speed access when they moved in had three times the local connections and communicated more with neighbors both online and offline. They also stayed in touch more with long-distance friends and relatives who continued to provide them social support that the non-wired residents did not have (Wellman et al., 2003). Hampton, Lee, and Her (2011) found that, on average, people who used social network sites knew fewer neighbors than those who did not, but they also had more diverse social networks.

When the internet is used to connect neighbors, it can enhance their connections to one another and to their communities. There are more than 10,000 neighborhood groups in Yahoo!'s group directories, one of many sites that offer neighbors the means to connect (Hampton, 2010). In a study of a neighborhood email list in Israel, Mesch and Levanon (2003) found that the list increased the size of people's local networks and extended their participation in the community. In his "I-Neighbors" project, Hampton (2010) provided all online Americans with the means to create online groups for their neighborhoods and then studied those groups. People created over 6,000 neighborhoods, although 80 percent only attracted 1 or 2 participants. But 28 percent of the most active neighborhoods were disadvantaged communities. People used these groups to organize local activities such as cleaning up the yards of elderly neighbors. Hampton concluded that the internet has the potential to increase the collective efficacy of those who are economically and structurally disadvantaged. However, it seems evident from these studies that simply providing a means of connection does not ensure that people take it up in ways that empower their communities.

In choosing the decline of bowling leagues to epitomize the decline of community in American life, Putnam (1995, 2000) emphasized engagement in clubs and organizations as a means of assessing civic engagement. Several surveys have looked at the relationship between internet use and engagement with clubs and volunteer organizations in the United States and Canada (Cole, 2000; Gil de Zúñiga & Valenzuela, 2011; Hampton, Lee, & Her, 2011; Katz & Aspden, 1997; Katz & Rice, 2002). Though differences are small, these studies find that internet and social network site users spend more time with such civic associations. How people use a medium matters more than whether or not they do; those who use the internet for "information acquisition and community building" are more likely to be civically engaged than those who use it for "entertainment and diversion" (Gil de Zúñiga & Valenzuela, 2011: 401). In one of the few studies looking at mobile phone use and civic engagement, Campbell and Kwak (2009) polled a stratified sample of Americans chosen to reflect their representativeness vis-à-vis census data. People who used mobile phones to exchange information and opinions were more likely to "do volunteer work, work on a community project, contribute money to a social group or cause, go to a community or neighborhood meeting, and [work] on behalf of a social group or cause." Echoing the discussion from chapter 1 about the importance of skill in understanding issues of access, Campbell and Kwak found that using the mobile phone for civic purposes was more likely when people were comfortable with the technology. Designing technologies for ease of use is important in enabling their use for civic purposes.

One can argue that the increases in public wifi and mobile media mean that people are less engaged with their physical environments and hence less likely to engage the diverse people found in public realms. In an observational and interview study of four public parks with wifi in two countries (the USA and Canada), Hampton, Livio, and Sessions (2010) found that wifi users did pay less attention to their surroundings. They kept their heads down and hence closed themselves off to interaction with others in the park. However, when asked, 28 percent of them said that they had met a stranger in that park, and most were actively engaged with other people through their wifi connections.

Complaints about screen-obsession are often cast in contrast to a past in which people spent more time engaged in face-to-face communication, at least in public space. In an ambitious study designed to examine this, Hampton, Sessions-Goulet, and Albanesius (2014) filmed the same public places in Boston, New York City, and Philadelphia as did sociologist William H. Whyte in 1978–79. They found that people in 2008–10 were less likely to be alone than their historical counterparts. They also found that there were more women in public, and that cross-sex pairings were more common now. Despite the common perception that everyone stares at their phone these days, the highest mobile phone usage they found was 9.68 percent in one New York City park, and the average was considerably lower. With the exception of those on the steps of the Metropolitan Museum of Art, most people they observed using a mobile phone were alone. In short, people are more likely to be with others in public than they used to be and, when they aren't, a small percentage of them look at their phones. This hardly suggests a withdrawal from public life.

People who know one another use locative media – applications and features designed to help people find each other in space. Dodgeball (Humphreys, 2007) was an early example of the ground now covered by Foursquare/Swarm, Facebook places, and specialty networks like Grindr (Cassidy, 2013). Such networks can be used to meet potential romantic partners and friends (Cassidy, 2013). Less sociably, they are also used at times to avoid bumping into people you know (Humphreys, 2010).

In times of crisis such as natural disasters, warfare, or social turmoil, people create "hashtag publics" to share information and to offer and organize support (Agarwal, Bennett, Johnson, & Walker, 2014; Bruns & Burgess, 2011; Potts, 2014). These loose collections of people organize through use of a common hashtag, usually on Twitter, though supplemented through other platforms. Monroy-Hernández, boyd, Kiciman, De Choudhury, and Counts (2013) analyzed an enormous corpus of tweets using hashtags associated with the narcowars in Mexico to map patterns of tweets onto local events and locations. They also interviewed residents who had made the potentially dangerous choice to serve as their community's primary warning system. The Mexican government and news media have been intimidated into silence, they argue, leaving local communities dependent on volunteers on social media who share real-time information on violence. This example of citizen journalism speaks to the innovative and important ways people use social media to support their local environments and to engage one another civically. Similarly, automotive enthusiasts in Kazakhstan, for whom explicit political engagement is risky, organize online and off in ways that blur boundaries between civics and politics (Shklovski & Valtysson, 2012).

Political engagement

The example of Mexican women who tweet crimes in their streets that government and journalists are afraid to mention might seem evidence enough that use of the internet does not simply displace real political engagement. Nonetheless, critics (e.g. Morozov, 2009) warn that the kind of activities that have political influence may be replaced by "slacktivism," in which reading political blogs, signing online petitions, sending emails, sharing links, and clicking Like buttons provides an ineffective substitute for effective action (Christensen, 2011).

As we saw in chapter 2, concerns about authenticity and pittings of technologically mediated practices against seemingly more-embodied ones are endemic to the reception of new media. Some evidence suggests that people who use digital media may be more likely to be politically engaged offline than those who do not. Internet users have been found to be more likely than non-users to engage in political activities, read magazines and newspapers, attend to campaign coverage in TV shows and interviews, and, perhaps most importantly, vote (Boulianne, 2009; Katz & Rice, 2002). Campbell and Kwak (2011) found that when people used their mobile phones to discuss and exchange opinions on issues, they were also more likely to "attend a political meeting, rally, or speech, circulate a petition for a candidate or issue, and to contact a public official or political party."

A 2012 survey of Americans (Brenner & Smith, 2013) found that 66 percent of American adults who use social networking sites have used them to "engage in a range of activities around political or social issues," such as posting content related to political/social topics or encouraging others to vote. Those who did this online, like those who did this offline, were considerably more affluent and educated than those who did not. Brenner and Smith found that people who used the SNS politically were "also likely to be engaged in other forms of political and civic activity that occur somewhere other than social networking sites." The survey found that 53 percent of American adults who engage with political or social issues on SNSs regularly talk about politics or public affairs with others in person, by phone, or by letter; 63 percent involved themselves directly in political activities or groups; and 53 percent used offline channels to speak out on political issues. These percentages are considerably higher than they are among adults as a whole.

These trends seem to have some international generalizability, although, as we will see soon, it is complex. Time on Facebook didn't itself correlate with political participation in a study of university students in Hong Kong (Tang & Lee, 2013), but people on Facebook who had more diverse networks, more direct connections to political actors, and were exposed to more political information on Facebook, were more likely to have participated in political activities. Similarly, Chileans who used Facebook for news and socializing were more likely to take part in political protests, in contrast to those who used Facebook for self-expression (Valenzuela, Arriagada, & Scherman, 2012).

New media are being used in many novel ways to engage people in political processes. This is particularly evident in protest movements such as those that comprised the Arab Spring and Occupy.

The internet and mobile media serve as information conduits (e.g. Christensen, 2011) that can change the dynamics of domestic protests. In this regard they are not unlike the taverns of the Middle Ages where people pooled information and let off steam (Briggs & Burke, 2009). Political information shared online can serve as a mirror – reflecting a nation back to its citizens in a new way – or as a window – setting a nation's policies within an international context of which people may not have been previously aware (Bailard, 2012). As Bailard found in a field experiment in Tanzania, internet use can "alter the cost–benefit calculus of political behavior by expanding the range of information individuals have regarding their government's actual performance" (Bailard, 2012: 341). In that study, those people assigned to an internet group were more likely to question the fairness of an election than people in a control group who had not used the internet during or after the elections.

Information distribution can also take the form of culture jamming (Lievrouw, 2011) in which people playfully remix materials in order to convey social messages. The example of Pepper Spray Cop, a meme in which people took a photograph of a police officer spraying protesting students with pepper spray and superimposed him on countless other scenes (Milner, 2012), is one example of how humorous remix was used to build support for the students in this case and for protesters in the United States at that time (including Occupy) more generally.

When information is shared through online channels, it can serve many different functions. It can spread shared grievances, draw international attention to domestic plights, broaden the appeal of social movements, and facilitate new connections between people and organizations (Howard & Parks, 2012; Lim, 2012). Social media exchanges do not necessarily mobilize people to take to the streets to demand change. For instance, online interaction functioned as a safety valve for Chinese bloggers when they discussed issues already covered in the country's newspapers, but as a pressure cooker when those same bloggers discussed topics the mainstream media ignored (Hassid, 2012). As Papacharissi and Oliveira (2012: 280) put it, social media "provide a form of emotional release that simultaneously invigorates and exhausts tension ... depending on context, these affective attachments create feelings of community that may either reflexively drive a movement, and/or capture users in a state of engaged passivity." Furthermore, just as social media allow individuals and groups who are unhappy with their governments to find and connect with each other, it allows those governments to find and intimidate them. In Azerbaijan, for instance, the government has actively used social media to spread misinformation and to intimidate government critics into silence (Pearce & Kendzior, 2012). Even in the most visible cases of people taking to the streets, such as the Tahrir Square protests in Egypt, the role of the internet and mobile media was deeply interwoven with face-to-face communication and other media. Tufekci and Wilson (2012) interviewed 1,200 people at Tahrir Square during the protest. Half had first heard of the protests face-to-face, followed by via Facebook. Once at the protest, 82 percent of protesters used phones for communicating about the protests, and almost everyone who had a Facebook or Twitter account used those platforms to report on the protests. A quarter of them used Facebook to disseminate pictures and videos they had taken.

Even if one grants that political activity online can get people into the street, there is a concern that political interaction through new media serves to polarize rather than facilitating discussion across diverse viewpoints. This is in keeping with the critique that online communities are homogeneous and limit exposure to diversity. Gergen (2008) speculates that people are increasingly engaged in "monadic clusters," small groups that affirm one another's perspective and lead people away from political action. Anyone reading opposing political blogs cannot help but be struck by the sense of parallel worlds, in which the same events have completely different and irreconcilable meanings. Campbell and Kwak (2009) found that the monadic cluster effect holds best when people are in small diverse social networks. When communication happens in a small social circle of people who disagree, individuals are more apt to opt out of political discussion and engagement rather than risk the peace.

In recent studies, Keith Hampton and his collaborators have shown that social network sites can lead to more diverse social networks rather than more homogeneous ones (e.g. Hampton, 2011; Hampton, Lee, & Her, 2011). Gil de Zúñiga and Valenzuela (2011) also found that social network users had more diverse ties and, as a result of having more interaction with weak ties, were more engaged citizens. Pew data (Rainie & Smith, 2012) show that nearly 40 percent of Facebook users have learned their friends have different politics than they thought, and 73 percent only sometimes, or never, agree with the political views their Facebook friends express.

The many complex ways in which engagement in digital interaction impacts civic and political life are not yet clear. New media are used to spread information, to connect people and groups, to support existing communities of activists, to mobilize new people to become engaged, to motivate already engaged people to become more engaged, and to shape and foment opinion. Perhaps most of all, they "reinforce participation in existing foci of activity" (Hampton, Lee, & Her, 2011: 1045) and serve as a "technology and space for expanding and sustaining the networks upon which social movements depend" (Lim, 2012: 234). The effect of the internet relative to other motivations for political (in)action is small, but generally positive. Far from floating, new media are part of a "hybrid complex system of social awareness" (Papacharissi & Oliveira, 2012).

Summary

In closing this chapter, let's return to the key concepts and theoretical perspectives identified in the first two chapters. New technologies offer many affordances that influence what happens through and because of them. Their combination of speed, interactivity, and reach allow people to come together around shared interests, transcending local communities in ways that may be personally empowering but potentially polarizing. Asynchronous platforms in particular offer people access to like-minded others and support, whether those others are online simultaneously or not. Synchronous or near-synchronous platforms like Twitter, combined with broad reach and replicability, can enable swift grassroots organizing. Minimal social cues in some online groups can open doors for people to make riskier self-disclosures, and hence to gain more social support, but may also contribute to polarization, as people may feel less pressured to find peaceful middle grounds. Mobility can help new media be concretely tied to location even as people move around, and hence support local civic engagement and social movements.

Technological determinism might predict either that these combinations of features usher in a new era in which people substitute simulated communities for real ones, or that they are democratizing, empowering people to participate and increasing civic engagement. Social constructivism would focus on the social forces that influence community online and off, including the social identities of people who participate, the motivations that inspire their online actions, and the social norms they develop around how to behave and what counts as skill and competence. Social shaping and domestication approaches would do as this chapter has, looking at both the technological factors and the social ones that combine unpredictably to create practices and outcomes that have not yet cohered into clear consequences. What does seem clear at this point is that new media do not offer inauthentic simulations that detract from or substitute for real engagement. As we will continue to see in the remaining chapters, what happens through mediation is interwoven, not juxtaposed, with everything else.

5
New relationships, new selves?

Tom was a sweet and thoughtful guy who took my class about online interaction in the mid 1990s. In one paper, he explored what would happen if he represented himself in different ways on America Online. He created one profile as an absurdly stereotypically sexy young woman. Within hours of logging in as "Busty," he had received dozens of personal messages inviting him backstage for some quick cybersex. It was his first experience of the receiving end of sexism and, though it wasn't hard for some of us to see it coming, it left him aghast. Some months later, he decided he was ready to find committed romance. His friend advised him that the best strategy was to log onto America Online and search for women in the city who were online and shared his interests, then send them a private message. He took the advice, combined it with the lesson he had learned as Busty ("treat women as people"), and quickly fell into an exchange of messages with a woman who lived nearby but whom he'd never met. The chat progressed so well that, within a couple of hours, she gave him her phone number and told him to call. He called immediately and they spoke on the phone for an hour before she suggested that they meet for dinner that night. She brought friends, just in case he turned out to be a psychokiller. He wasn't, their chemistry was undeniable, and by day's end they were en route to their eventual marriage. Though they had met in person the same day they met online, when her family attended his graduation ceremony, one commented, "Wow, you really were a graduate student!" Because they had met online, some in her family still doubted his honesty.

Tom's story encapsulates the utopian potential the internet holds for our relationships – we can meet new people and form rewarding new relationships – as well as the common concerns that the people we meet online cannot be trusted and may even be dangerous. Busty could be Tom. Tom could be a fraud or even a killer. This could be an episode of *Catfish*. When the telegraph took off, operators working in telegraph offices soon found that the time between customers was well spent using the technology to chat with telegraph operators in other offices in the network. As Standage (1998) recounts, this led to the formation of new relationships, many of which were regarded with suspicion by others. In chapter 2, we saw that, throughout the history of electronic communication, some have celebrated the ability to form new relationships across time and space, but others have seen it as enabling communication between people who should not be forming relationships and as offering pale substitutes for authentic connection. The internet has been heralded for its potential to bridge divides and create meaningful new connections, but more often accused of leading people to lie about themselves, making victims of women and children, or taking people away from the relationships they should be having with their families and communities.

Initially, most of the focus in both the popular imagination and internet scholarship was on the development of new relationships between strangers who met through the internet. In this chapter and the next, we will look at the processes of forming, developing, maintaining, and ending relationships through the internet. This chapter focuses on meeting, presenting ourselves to, and forming impressions of other people online. After discussing how and why people form new relationships through the internet, I turn to the topic of identity. We look at the questions mediated communication raises for identity, particularly what happens when bodies are not visible. We look at the kinds of cues people use to represent themselves as individuals and as members of social groups, as well as how impressions are shaped by forces outside an individual's control. The chapter closes with a brief consideration of how self-understandings and behaviors can change through online experiences of identity.

New relationships online

As shared location has lost its status as a prerequisite for first meeting, the range of potential relational partners is bigger than at any previous point in history. In many cases, relationships emerge naturally out of the online communities we discussed in the previous chapter. In the soap opera discussion forum I studied, rec.arts.tv.soaps (r.a.t.s.), friendships developed in the course of talking about soap operas and the tangents that discussion prompted. Participants often described the group as "a bunch of close friends" (Baym, 2000). This was typical for newsgroups. In the early 1990s, Parks and Floyd (1996) sampled 24 Usenet newsgroups and then emailed a survey to a sampling of people who had posted to each group. They found that 60.7 percent of respondents had established a personal relationship of some sort through the group. In a follow-up survey of MOO participants, Parks and Roberts (1998) found that so many respondents had formed personal relationships through MOOs that there weren't enough people left over to use for comparison.

Although people mainly use social network sites (SNSs) to maintain existing relationships (as we'll cover in the next chapter), they are also used to form new relationships (e.g. Tosun, 2012). Haythornthwaite (2002) coined the term "latent tie" to refer to potential relationships that are structurally enabled but have not been activated. Friends of friends on Facebook are a good example of latent ties. By making friends' lists visible and, in some cases, offering automated recommendations of latent ties, the architecture of social network sites facilitates the conversion of latent ties to acquaintanceships (Ellison et al., 2007).

People may also seek new romantic or sexual partners through dating sites. Match making is not new to digital media. Newspapers have long hosted classified ads for those seeking romance and, in alternative publications, playmates. When media become "marriage market intermediaries" they blur interpersonal and mass communication (Adelman & Ahuvia, 1991). Ideologies of romanticism, in which true love arises out of unpredictable moments of serendipitous fate, are pitted against ideologies of social exchange in which finding love through media seems more of a business transaction than destiny and people are reduced to dehumanizing lists of attributes (Adelman & Ahuvia, 1991). For people who use these sites, the time they spend building their profile can indeed feel more like work than romance if not rewarded with successful offline encounters (Cassidy, 2013).

Once stigmatized, online dating has rapidly become normalized. A random-sample survey of Americans (Smith & Dugan, 2013) found that in the United States 5 percent of all committed relationships and marriages – 11 percent of those started in the last ten years – began online. 38 percent of single US adults have used online dating sites or mobile dating apps. The poll shows that a modest majority of Americans agree that online dating is a good way to meet people and can allow people to find better matches, but those who have tried it have also had bad experiences. And though the number is lower than a decade ago, a fifth of Americans still think online dating is for the desperate.

There are many reasons the internet can serve as an appealing environment for forming new relationships. Regardless of medium, people are intrinsically motivated to reduce their uncertainty about others and find affinities with them (Walther, 1992). Walther (1992) proposed the Social Information Processing (SIP) model to explain relational development online. In his 1992 piece and in Walther et al. (1994: 465), he argued that, because people need to reduce uncertainty, in online contexts they "adapt their linguistic and textual behaviors to the solicitation and presentation of socially revealing, relational behavior." The longer the interaction lasts or the more expectation the participants have of continued interaction, the truer this is (Walther et al., 1994). When people are in a discussion forum based on common interest, there is a presumption of similarity which can make potential partners seem more attractive. Similarity functions as a form of propinquity (Baker, 2008). In online forums and groups, we bump into the people who share our interests rather than those who happen to be in the same physical location. This leads to connections that might not otherwise form. In SNSs such as Facebook, on the other hand, new connections are usually formed with people within existing social circles. The internet also lowers the social risk of communicating, as we will return to later in this chapter. We saw this, for example, in chapter 4's discussion of McKenna and Bargh's (1998) work on newsgroups for homosexuals. Just as people spill their secrets to strangers seated beside them on airplanes, anonymity online makes some people more willing to disclose, and fosters new relationship formation.

Given these advantages of new media, one could imagine a world in which they are wholeheartedly embraced as a wonderful opportunity. But shared location has been intrinsic to our understandings of how relationships start and their place in our personal networks for millennia. We are most likely to form relationships with those with whom we get the chance to interact, and, without communication technology, those are the people who are most likely to be in the same place at the same time. In substituting interest or other factors for place, mediated meeting challenges much of what we've taken for granted in forming relationships for most of human history.

Mediated meeting also challenges understandings of relationship building, because we are used to assessing people and doing much of the work of getting closer nonverbally. We often size people up and decide whether or not to talk to them based on how they look. At least in romantic relationships, people may be most motivated to pursue connections with those whose level of physical attractiveness matches their own, a phenomenon known as the "matching hypothesis" (Berscheid, Dion, Hatfield, & Walster, 1971). In online contexts, we may be unaware of what our communication partner really looks like, or may not find out until well into the relationship. Once a relationship has begun, nonverbal cues are important in its development. We smile, make eye contact, stand closer and touch to signal attraction and deepen our bonds (e.g. Knapp, 1983). How then can we form relationships in the absence of such nonverbal messages? And what are the consequences of doing so?

One answer, as we saw in the third chapter, is that even text-based new media afford many ways to express emotion. We use emoticons to signal friendliness, punctuation and capitalization to insert feeling, informal language and talk-like phonetic spellings to create an air of conversationality. Emojis enliven countless texts, tweets, and captions. Multimedia platforms let us share video and engage in real-time video chat. We use language to talk about our feelings. Socioemotional communication may be easier face-to-face, but it is common and successful in digital media as well. In one of his SIP studies, Walther (1994) conducted experiments online with groups who had never met. They were told either that this was a one-shot meeting or that they would be interacting again in the future. When people expected to interact again they were more likely to express immediacy and affection, similarity and depth, trust and composure.

Another reason for societal discomfort with formation of online relationships is that they may be between people who would not have formed relationships offline. People meeting online are more likely to form relationships that blur the social boundaries between groups and hence challenge social norms of appropriateness. New media make it easier to have "pure relationships," in which the relationship is its own reward instead of serving a useful function in maintaining the social order (Clark, 1998; Giddens, 1993). Standage (1998) wrote of then-shocking interracial relationships that emerged through the telegraph, as well as of romances formed without parental consent and over parental objections. One couple was even married by telegraph in distant locations to avoid the marriage the bride's father had planned for her. Though her father challenged the marriage's authenticity, its legitimacy was upheld by the courts.

Cross-sex friendships are more common online. Offline, these relationships are generally seen as a threat to the social order (e.g. Rawlins, 1992). In English they are described with the term "just friends," betraying the cultural definition of such relationships as something less than would be expected of a man and a woman. Parks and Roberts (1998) found far more cross-sex friendships in MOOs than face-to-face. In a survey of users of the international music-oriented SNS Last.fm, I asked people to describe a random on-site friendship. Relationships on Last.fm were as likely to be cross-sex as same-sex, making the former more common on Last.fm than offline (Baym & Ledbetter, 2009). In a survey of nearly 1,000 Israeli teens, Mesch and Talmud (2006) also found more cross-sex relationships between online than offline friends.

Relationships that transcend age barriers may also be more common online (Mesch & Talmud, 2006), although we did not find this to be the case on Last.fm (Baym & Ledbetter, 2009). People in their forties and teenagers who share guild membership in online role-playing games may become friends; people who share musical taste may connect without even knowing one another's age in music-oriented sites and groups; television fans may bond over shows regardless of age. When cross-sex and cross-age friends interact online, they are less likely to face the pressures of others' (and, for some, their own) suspicions than they are face-to-face. These relationships may thus be easier to create and maintain online than off.

Identity

Without doubt, the issues that shake people the most about forming relationships online center on identity. When people's bodies aren't visible, will they lie about who they are? Can they be known? Can they be trusted? Alternatively, might some be liberated? People in Western cultures often think of the self as a set of essential truths that can be revealed through communication. However, identities are always social. They are made, displayed, and reshaped through interaction. Identities are personal to the extent that they distinguish us from other people. Personal identity refers to the aspects of our selves that distinguish us from others. This includes things like values, traits, tastes, and biographies. Though this may seem completely individual, it is shaped through social observations of, comparisons to, interactions with, and feedback from others. Social identity refers to the aspects of our selves that define us as group members. Some of these are involuntary – our ethnicities, sex, sexual orientation, nationalities, and the like – while others are affiliations of choice.

Disembodied identities

Many scholars have noted that digital media, especially the internet, disrupt the notion held dear in many cultures that each body gets one self (e.g. Stone, 1995). Digital media seem to separate selves from bodies, leading to disembodied identities that exist only in actions and words. The affordances of new media open up new possibilities for exploring and representing ourselves and others. Yet it turns out that, with some significant exceptions, most people, most of the time, use new media to act in ways mostly consistent with their embodied selves. Many academic reports in the early 1990s focused on Multi-User Domains (MUDs) and MOOs in which much of the point was to play with identity. However, observational research showed that, even in those environments where people could self-present as anything from a monster to a six-pack of beer, most people did not take advantage of disembodiment to create fantastic or radically deceptive selves (Curtis, 1997). Many people expect others to be deceptive in less fanciful ways online, masking motivations or distorting facts to manipulate others. As we will see below, what constitutes deception is complex, and even when people are deceptive online, there are many ways they can be and are called out. Furthermore, self-representations are just one source of information about others in networked environments.

The disembodied identities presented online can also be multiple. On Spotify and Last.fm, for instance, I am popgurl, a self-representation I took great pains to keep separate from Nancy Baym for some time before publicly claiming her. In the fan board discussing my favorite band, I used my cat's name, not because I didn't want the others in the group to know who I am, but because I didn't want that fangirl to show up when people search for this scholar. A search for Nancy Baym will turn up my academic persona on my website, and a more well-rounded if trite self-presentation on Twitter. All of these are genuine parts of me, but online they are segmented into separate spaces. My son, well socialized by educators to believe it's dangerous to reveal under-aged status or identifying information online, maintains several different online identities with different ages, locations, and names (Waning Gibbous is my favorite).

Such multiplicity is enhanced on the internet, but it is nothing new. It was Shakespeare who wrote that "all the world's a stage," recognizing that all of our social encounters involve playing roles designed to suit the interactants and the context. Identity scholars such as Goffman (1959) have long argued that the self plays multiple roles in everyday life and cannot be understood adequately as a single unified entity. Rather than there being One True Self, variations of which are inherently false, contemporary scholars have come to see the self as flexible and multiple, taking different incarnations in different situations. Finkenauer, Engels, Meeus, and Oosterwegel (2002: 28), for instance, defined identity as representing "the aspect of the self that is accessible and salient in a particular context and that interacts with the environment." Turkle (1996: 14) used the metaphor of windows. If you think of a computer screen, an internet user may have multiple windows open. In one, he is playing a warlock in a role-playing game; in another he is chatting with his best friend in another town; in a third, he is working on homework; in yet another, he's drafting an email to his parents; and in a fifth, he's in a chat room pretending to be a woman. "Windows have become a powerful metaphor for thinking about the self as a multiple, distributed system," Turkle writes; "The self is no longer simply playing different roles in different settings at different times. The life practice of windows is that of a decentered self that exists in many worlds, that plays many roles at the same time." Now the embodied self, as one of Turkle's interviewees put it, may be "just one more window." Nonetheless, we do expect people's identities to have some degree of coherence and internal consistency. Representing one's self too differently across contexts may be seen as inauthentic, and potentially damaging to both your self and your relationships, even amongst digitally savvy youth (Davis, 2012).

Bodies usually anchor multiplicity and flexibility and are often seen as key to knowing individuals. They are also important in determining whether someone's actions are valid, and in holding them accountable for what they do (Stone, 1995). When there's no body attached to behavior, the authenticity of behavior becomes less clear. It took a nineteenth-century court to determine that the marriage ceremony conducted via telegraph counted as real despite the lack of co-presence (Standage, 1998). Consider the example of the "cyberaffairs" we saw cited repeatedly in the advice columns of the American 1990s as one of the internet's worst relational consequences. For the letter writers, there was no question such relationships were affronts to their marriages, but whether they constitute adultery is less clear. Divorce courts increasingly deliberate cases in which one partner has been accused of "adultery" for an "affair" carried on through the verbal description of sex acts with a partner online. Most of us may feel betrayed were this to happen in our relationships, but does a sex act count as a sex act without bodies? Can it be adultery if they never physically touched? The problem of what kinds of realities are warranted by online behaviors are by no means limited to sex. What about when an avatar "steals" a digital object in an online role-playing game? Is that really theft? Can the person playing the stealing avatar be held accountable in real-world courts of law (a question addressed in Charles Stross's 2007 novel *Halting State*, in which authorities were initially reluctant to intervene in a bank robbery conducted within a role-playing game)? What if they make what can be read as threats in Facebook status updates or tweets? Does that count as adequate evidence for firing or criminal conviction? We don't yet have clear strategies to think through the actions of personas that may be distinct from those in the bodies that type those behaviors.

Disembodied audiences

Identities are invoked and created in particular contexts for particular audiences. Just as the people performing identities online are disembodied, so too are their audiences. People get less information about their audiences through mediated communication than they would in embodied encounters (Baym & boyd, 2012). If you are sending a private message to your best friend, you have a clear sense of audience. But if you have several hundred connections on Facebook or followers on Twitter, you can't hold each in mind while crafting a message, even if you could know which of them might actually see it. When people construct online messages, they rely on an imagined audience, the "mental conceptualization of the people with whom we are communicating" (Litt, 2012: 331). Our picture of the imagined audience is influenced by structural factors (including social roles, social contexts, audience activity, site features and services) and individual agency (social skills, motivations, internet skills) (Litt, 2012). Imagining an audience is a way to bound what is in fact potentially limitless (Marwick & boyd, 2010).

That audiences online are not always known leads to worries about privacy. As Marwick and boyd (2014) explain, most understandings of privacy – as an individual problem of whether or not to share information about one's self – are ill suited to networked environments where the real problems concern control over how information flows. Privacy is about controlling access to information and the integrity of the contexts in which information was shared, not secrecy (Nissenbaum, 2010; Solove, 2007). Although it is commonly assumed that young people are especially lax about privacy, in fact they have many strategies – some quite clever – for maintaining privacy while being public (Marwick & boyd, 2014). For instance, one teenager interviewed by Marwick and boyd de-activated her Facebook account every time she closed the window. Another deleted all the comments on her profile after she read them, and all those she had left on others' profiles a couple of days after posting them. Many kept dual accounts – one for friends, another for adults. Some spoke in code, a practice Marwick and boyd (2014) call "social stenography" – quoting movie lines they know their parents will read as cheerful but friends will correctly identify as expressions of unhappiness. As this last example points out, from the teen perspective, the scary audiences are not potentially dangerous strangers, but the far more power-ful and significantly more real parents. In contrast to adults, most American teenagers change their Facebook privacy settings (Madden et al., 2013). If all of this sounds like a lot of work, it's because it is. Continuously having to imagine and manage who gets what informa-tion, what should be private and what can be public, requires ongoing effort (Marwick, 2012).

Furthermore, there is often a gap between imagined and actual audiences. The internet makes it hard to visualize the breadth of our exposure (Solove, 2007). Because information is stored and replicable, it can travel to audiences for whom it was never intended. Because it is often searchable, it can be accessed by people with no understanding of the context in which it was created. A message on Twitter meant for a subset of followers may later be read by potential employers. A pathetic letter from a scorned lover can become an international joke. There are also "silent listeners" (Stutzman, Gross, & Acquisti, 2012), like the companies that own the platforms on which people represent themselves, the advertisers to whom those companies sell personal information, and third-party apps that tap personal information about all of a user's contacts. Much of their activities may be benign, but we simply cannot know whom the information we share online may eventually reach.

The flipside of privacy is publicness (Baym & boyd, 2012). Communicating online to unknown and disembodied audiences is a way to build a public identity, often in service of "self-branding" (Marwick, 2012). People may be just as concerned with building public identities as with hiding private ones. The "micro-celebrities" Senft (2008) analyzed used social media to build audiences for themselves, a phenomenon that has grown enormously with the rise of YouTube, Twitter, and Instagram. Self-branding is often seen as being in contrast with authenticity. The Twitter users Marwick and boyd interviewed (2010) who said they wrote for themselves were rejecting self-branding and the very idea of having an audience. Yet, being authentic is itself a marketing strategy (Banet-Weiser, 2012; Baym, 2013; Marwick, 2013). Being public, in short, is not always bad. It can often be desirable and, in some fields, necessary.

Online, the audiences we present ourselves to are collapsed (boyd & Heer, 2006). The musicians I have interviewed (Baym, 2012) address social media audiences that include fans, friends, peers, families, and those managing their careers as well as haters and stalkers. Madden and colleagues (2013) found that the Facebook friends of teens include people they know from school (98 percent), members of their extended families (91 percent), friends not at their schools (89 percent), siblings (76 percent), parents (70 percent), people they have not met in person (33 percent), teachers and coaches (30 percent), as well as celebrities, musicians, and athletes (30 percent). Lim, Vadrevu, Chan, and Basnyat (2012) interviewed Singaporean youth in trouble with the legal system. They found that these kids had to maintain Facebook profiles that simultaneously made themselves look exceptional for members of other gangs, showed appropriate deference for other members of their own gangs, and yet stayed below the radar of the justice system workers who also had access to their profiles. Navigating these multiple audiences through one profile while maintaining a sense and appearance of consistency is challenging (Baym, 2012; Davis, 2012; Marwick & boyd, 2010). Privacy is one problem, but so too are propriety, utility, and impression management (Stutzman & Hartzog, 2013). One consequence can be that efforts to manage an impression for one audience may be "construed as embellishments, distortions, or dishonesties when viewed by others" (DeAndrea & Walther, 2011: 806).

Identity cues

Our ability to construct an online self-representation – whether authentic, fanciful, or manipulative – is limited and enabled by the communicative tools, or affordances, a platform makes available and our skill at strategically managing them. In this section, we'll look at the sources of information there are about people online. We begin with self-presentation, looking at how people construct personal and social identities and considering the evidence regarding honesty. We'll then turn to sources of information a person can't control, such as other people and the platforms themselves.

Self-presentation

Different kinds of sites and media provide different cues that people use to construct personal identity. Some early text-based sites offered all kinds of fanciful ways to do this. In Farside MUD, a fantasy environment, high-level players could purchase genitalia in order to make their avatars sexually mature (Ito, 1997). In graphic role-playing games, identities are often created through costumes, weapons, and levels of skill. The role-playing game Runescape, which my sons spent their middle childhood playing, requires a considerable investment of time and a high level of competence to build an identity by collecting the right clothes and weapons and constructing an impressive in-game dwelling. The opportunities for identity play available in Second Life are limited only by imagination and facility with their programming language. Not all digital environments are so creative, but all provide us with options for self-presentation. On mailing lists and web boards, our signature files, choices of name, and even our domain names become important markers of who we are.

The most important identity signal may be one's name. Most email providers, web boards, blogs, and SNSs allow users to select any name. Mark Zuckerberg, Facebook's founder, who must never have read Goffman, has stated that having multiple identities reflects a lack of integrity (Kirkpatrick, 2010), hence his platform requires real names. One analysis of 4,540 Facebook profiles of students at Carnegie Mellon University (USA) (Gross & Acquisti, 2005) found that 89 percent of user names seemed to be real. Only 8 percent were clearly false and just 3 percent partial. However, Facebook is not good at recognizing which names are real and which are not. "If this rule is being followed," jokes Baron (2008: 82), "then Karl Marx,

Anne Boleyn, and Kermit the Frog are alive and well." Google's SNS, Google+, began by requiring real names and quickly ran into protest from people who resented not being able to sign up by the nicknames by which they were known or who felt unsafe using their real name in a public environment. This conflict, known as the "nymwars," eventually led Google to relent. Korea's Cyworld, on the other hand, allows people to pick pseudonyms only after their identity has been verified and "the site's search functions are able to validate the name, date of birth, and gender of other users" (Kim & Yun, 2007). On other sites, like Instagram, Tumblr, or Last.fm, it is unusual to see a real name, and the names chosen can send many different social messages.

In textual media, the use of written language is a far more powerful force in making impressions than it is when people interact body-to-body. While physically attractive people may be the ones who get noticed at a party, it's often the articulate, insightful, and witty ones who know how to spell who gain notice at the online equivalent. In a study of humor on Facebook profiles of college students in Kansas, Pennington and Hall (2013) found that humor was displayed through talk about relationships and mundane life events, pop culture references, self-mockery, and funny moments from everyday life. Language is also our primary tool for telling others about ourselves. As we'll discuss in the next chapter, self-disclosure is indispensable in turning strangers into relational partners and maintaining ongoing relationships.

Most SNSs partially engineer self-presentation by providing predetermined sets of categories through which to build identities. Though the categories vary, most provide slots for demographic information including age, place of residence, and general interests. Lampe, Ellison, and Steinfeld (2007) used automated data collection to gather profile information from all available profiles on their university's Facebook system and found that, on average, users filled in 59 percent of fields available to them. Gross and Acquisti (2005) found that 98.5 percent of their university's Facebook users disclosed their full birthdates. General-interest categorizations encourage users to construct themselves in part by identifying with popular culture. The early SNS, Friendster, offered five categories (general interests, music, movies, television, and books) which were also used on MySpace, Facebook, and Orkut (Liu, 2007). This kind of categorization of the self began in online dating sites (Fiore & Donath, 2005), the assumption being that people who share such tastes are likely to be interpersonally compatible and hence good prospects for relational success. On Last. fm, we found that friends were more likely than not to share musical taste, but the extent to which a Last.fm relationship was motivated by the other person's taste in music and a shared musical history did not predict how developed their relationship was (Baym & Ledbetter, 2009). Taste lists also provide a way to perform our individuality by differentiating ourselves from others (Liu, 2007). Liu (2007) examined 127,477 MySpace profiles and found that "on average, MySpace users tended to differentiate themselves from their friends, rather than identifying with their friends' tastes." However, as Parks (2011) notes, almost all MySpace profiles were unused, reminding us that taste differentiation – at least outside of Facebook – may be a marginal practice.

The images we associate with ourselves, including our photographs and avatars, are also important identity cues. Facebook profile pictures – usually of one's self – may change to indicate life changes, as when a Tanzanian college student goes abroad (Uimonen, 2013) or a new parent uses a baby picture. On Last.fm, in contrast, avatar pictures rarely depict the users, just as users rarely use real names. In a study looking at teen chat profiles, Kapedzic and Herring (2011) found that girls' profile pictures tended toward seductive poses, gazes, and clothing while boys' pictures featured a wider range of behavior at a greater distance from the viewer. The appeal of profile pictures alone may lead to the initiation of new relationships, as Last.fm users told me when I asked them about how they came to friend the people they did (Baym & Ledbetter, 2009).

Because self-presentations are constrained by the cues a medium makes available, people's technological competence in cue manipulation is particularly important. In the case of a website, for example, we need to know how to make the blank slate into something meaningful. Knowledge of language and spelling matters, but so too does facility with code and design. In a content analysis of 1,000 homepages from four different networks, Papacharissi (2002) found that many people tried to display an image of technological competence. Facebook's standardized profile template lessened this need (another factor in its success), but, nonetheless, people continue to form identities in part by demonstrating design savvy. For example, when Facebook introduced the profile header photo, some people quickly figured out how to artistically integrate their profile and header photos.

The fears about honesty with which this chapter began might lead people to expect that given anonymity and tools to manipulate self-presentation, people would lie. Usually when people think of deception, they mean stating falsehoods in an effort to make others believe things known to be untrue. In general, research does not support the idea that lean media make people lie. In r.a.t.s., group norms encouraged honest self-presentation (Baym, 2000). Though people may have tinkered with their self-presentations around the edges, only one person, who insisted he was the nephew of the fictional soap opera character Aunt Phoebe, was discernibly deceptive during my three years in the site. New users with anonymous usernames were regularly asked to share their real names and a little about themselves so we could get to know them better. In-depth interviews with a small sample of users of chat rooms (Henderson & Gilding, 2004) showed that the interviewees focused on the continuities rather than the differences between online and offline relationships, and described high rates of honest self-disclosure in both.

Whether anonymous or identifiable, people seem at least as likely to be more honest online than off. Reduced social cues make it easier to lie, but separation, time lags, and sparse cues also remove social pressures that make lying seem a good idea. When we can't be seen and can easily log off and change screen names, we don't have to face the consequences of disclosures gone wrong. When the people with whom we're interacting online don't know any of the same people that we do offline and we are using a fake name, word won't get around (McKenna et al., 2002). The sense of safety in anonymous sites may be important for honest self-expression. This can also be important for those who are socially anxious and lonely or who have stigmatized identities. McKenna and her collaborators (2002) emailed a survey to every fifth poster in a sample of 20 Usenet newsgroups. They found that people who were socially anxious or lonely were more likely to feel they could express their real selves online, and this was positively correlated with developing relationships online that led to other media and offline meetings. The Turkish undergraduate students who tested highest for feeling they could express their "true self" on the internet in Tosun's (2012) study were more likely to use Facebook to establish new relationships. Even when interacting with those who know us, the ability to write out one's thoughts and not have to face the other immediately can lead to more honesty. Americans report being more honest with loved ones through email than face-to-face (Rainie, Lenhart, Fox, Spooner, & Horrigan, 2000).

It would be as naive to imagine that people do not deceive online as it is to think everyone is always honest offline. With the rare and well-publicized exception, however, most lies told are minor strategic manipulations rather than malevolent falsehoods. Self-representations on SNSs are "selective and carefully managed but not false" (Gentile, Twenge, Freeman, & Campbell, 2012: 1929). In part, as we will see in the next section, this is because people get called out by their peers and castigated when they are too deceptive (Cover, 2012; Hall & Pennington, 2012). On SNS profiles and websites, people may claim to like things they don't, or omit embarrassing true favorites, in order to create a public image in line with what they think others find attractive (Liu, Maes, & Davenport, 2006). On Last.fm, people routinely turn off the site's recording and display of their current listening when they are streaming artists inconsistent with the image they wish to project. They may also play cool artists on repeat when they are away in order to appear to like what they do not.

Whitty and Gavin (2001) trained their students to conduct interviews with people who regularly used the internet in their study of online relational development. These 60 interviews showed that people were worried about honesty, and with good reason. Men and women offered different reasons for deception. Women who lied generally did so for safety reasons. The men rarely reported that rationale; they were, however, more likely to report that the internet's anonymity made them feel more able to disclose honestly. Whitty and Gavin conclude that "the ideals that are important in traditional relationships, such as trust, honesty, and commitment, are equally important online" (2001: 630).

Ellison, Heino, and Gibbs (2006) interviewed people who used a large online dating site. They found that people were generally truthful, but many exaggerated socially appealing qualities, claiming to weigh less than they really did, to be taller than they really were, or to be nonsmokers. Some posted photos from when they were younger. Toma and Hancock (2010) found in interviews with 80 users of four different dating sites that less physically attractive daters were more likely to post self-enhancing photographs and to lie in their verbal descriptions of their own attractiveness. Yet people building profiles in dating sites understood that they had to be credible and sought to manage the tension between that and the need to make themselves appear attractive enough to raise interest (Ellison et al., 2006).

Sometimes being deceptive is about presenting one's ideal self more than a fictitious one. As one blogger (2birds1blog, 2008) wrote about choosing her SNS profile image:

> As a girl, I choose my facebook photo primarily by how unrealistically attractive I look in it. It's narcissistic, but you can't deny that you do the same thing. I'm not going to lie, sometimes when I'm getting ready to go out, I'll evaluate whether or not I'm lookin' "Facebook-worthy" that night. In other instances I'll even attend certain events just because I think I'll get a cute Facebook pic out of it. Overall, it's accepted that girls use their Facebook pic as an outlet to display their "Oh my Gawd I look HAWT!" pictures.

When people lied in dating sites, saying they were thin or a nonsmoker, they sometimes genuinely believed that by the time they met the person they sought they would have lost weight or quit smoking (Ellison et al., 2006). Since dating sites by design are oriented toward future rather than current interaction, daters may perceive a "license to lie" as the time between now and the eventual meeting can be used to create the self presented in the profile (Ellison, Hancock, & Toma, 2012). A profile may represent a promise more than an accurate current description (2012). People are also limited in their self-knowledge and what they believe to be true about themselves may not be seen in them by others, a phenomenon Ellison et al. (2006) referred to as the "foggy mirror." People may also understand that they have multiple selves, and argue that what may seem like misrepresentation is merely another true aspect of their selves (Ellison et al., 2011). Complicating the picture further, people may lie because they have heard so much discourse about the dangers of meeting people online that they feel compelled to protect themselves by lying about who they are; hence, Whitty and Gavin's (2001) finding that women may lie about where they live, or my son's use of fake identities in his online activity. Teens and children are often taught by parents and other significant adults never to reveal their names, phone numbers, addresses, or any other identifying information online, essentially instructing them to lie. In a random-sample survey of American parents of children aged 10–14, for instance, boyd, Hargittai, Schultz, and Palfrey (2011) found that two-thirds of parents whose children had started Facebook accounts before the entry age of 13 had actually helped their kids create the accounts in knowing violation of what they saw as stupid Terms of Service from Facebook rather than federal law.

In addition to the cues we "give" others about our personal and social identities, we also "give off" cues inadvertently (Goffman, 1959). The ways we behave can be more informative than the content of our messages. As I wrote this paragraph I was "followed" by a new person on Twitter. His self-description said he could get me 16,000 Twitter followers in 90 days through an automated process. He had 4 followers. Even if I were out to collect as many followers as possible, I'd have had to go with the information given off over that given. Cues given off become highly informative in sparse-cue situations (Ellison et al., 2006), so that, for example, poor spelling, which would never be relevant in most early face-to-face encounters, comes to be a highly significant marker of identity in textual media. Ellison, Hancock, and Toma (2012) found that profiles of people who admitted to misrepresenting themselves on dating sites gave off linguistic deception cues, including more negations and fewer self-references. However, student judges did not use these cues in assessing trustworthiness. Cues given off can also work for us: Brand, Bonatsos, D'Orazio, and DeShong (2012) found that daters whose profile pictures were ranked as more attractive also wrote profile text that gave off confidence, enhancing their attractiveness, even to research participants who did not see the photos.

Thus far I've been discussing the social cues to personal identity. We also present social identities online. Everyone's identity is entwined with those of others. We build self-representations by linking to others, whether by initiating or accepting connection requests on SNSs (Cover, 2012) or by using links on websites, blogs, signature files, and elsewhere that send messages about who we are and with whom we seek to be affiliated. These links serve as elements of our representation, and the behavior of and impressions left by those others become elements that shape how we are perceived. In an analysis of homepages, Wynn and Katz (1998) found that identities constructed through homepages were richly contextualized in offline social groups through self-descriptions, implied audiences, and links to websites of other people and groups.

As is the case with personal identities, different platforms provide differing cues for building shared social and cultural identities. Whether, and how, a user can construct a racial identity will vary considerably from site to site. In her analysis of BlackPlanet.com, Byrne (2007) reports that, until 2005, members' only choices for racial identification were Black, Asian, Latino, Native American, and White. Following Nakamura (2002), she argues this "forces users into dominant notions of race," leaving little room for intercultural diversity or intraracial identities. Other SNSs, such as MySpace, Last.fm, or Facebook, do not provide any category for race. Twitter offers no official means of creating racialized social identities, but people have used hashtags and language style to create racialized identities, as we saw in chapter 3 (Brock, 2012; Florini, 2013).

Like race, nationality can be a charged identity category. We saw in chapter 3 that nations vary dramatically in the extent to which they are represented online, and that English-speaking nations are disproportionately present. When platforms bridge cultures, people may choose to make their national identities apparent as a means of differentiating themselves from others. Miller and Slater's (2000) interviews with Trinidadians about their internet use described Trinis as often surprised to realize that the strangers they met from other countries online had not heard of their country. They responded by seeking to represent Trinidad as part of their own identities online, acting as nationalistic selves. They filled their homepages with links to official Trini sites, and, as we discussed in chapter 3, replicated norms of the Trini speech community in their online interactions. Tanzanian students may use Tanzanian-themed Facebook profile pictures, especially when they are studying abroad (Uimonen, 2013).

On-site cultures emerge around national identities, and platforms differ in whether and how they foreground it. Last.fm used to display all users' nationality if they'd selected it from a drop-down list of options, leading to some distress from people such as Scots, some of whom self-identified as residents not of the United Kingdom (which was provided in the drop-down menu), but of Scotland (which was not). The most striking example of this is Orkut (Fragoso, 2006). Orkut, owned by Google, launched as a US-based SNS in 2004. People could join only when invited by an existing member. Within a short time, Brazilians outnumbered every other country's members, a phenomenon which usually has been attributed to Brazilians' purported sociable and outgoing nature, an explanation which is surely inadequate (2006). People on Orkut began to construct their identities in terms of nationalism, leading to intense conflicts that were often grounded in language wars as Portuguese speakers colonized what had been English-language discussion groups.

Race, nationality, and other social identities can be given off through cues such as the taste selections on one's profile or the interests one displays. Our vocabulary choices may reveal our age or nationality. It's not hard, for instance, to spot the British on Twitter when they use terms such as "bollocks." Tastes and interests are shaped by socioeconomic factors, including money, class, and education, as well as by age and locational cohorts (Bourdieu, 1984; Liu, 2007). Digital identity cues are "signals of social position in an information based society" (Donath, 2007).

Social Identity Theory of Deindividuation Effects, or the SIDE model, seeks to explain under what circumstances people online will favor their personal or their social identities. SIDE proposes that this is influenced by affordances, such as anonymity, which interact with social context, and social understandings of the self (e.g. Spears & Lea, 1992). In a series of experiments manipulating the extent to which people in online groups were connected and given varying amounts of information that served to anonymize, individualize, or invoke social identities for participants, Lea, Spears, and their collaborators (e.g. Lea & Spears, 1991) found that, when people have access to individualizing cues, they are more likely to differentiate themselves from one another. In anonymous contexts, however, people are more likely to stereotype and conform to group norms, experiencing more of a sense of "we" and less a sense of "me." This stereotyping extends to self-perceptions and behaviors (Postmes & Baym, 2005). Thus, for instance, fans of University of Kansas athletics (the Jayhawks) participating in online forums where their status as a Jayhawk is foregrounded over individualizing social cues are likely to engage in behaviors such as saying nasty things about rivals University of Missouri (the Tigers) and all those affiliated with them. The same individuals, participating in groups that emphasize their individualized identities or shared social identity as Midwestern college students, might be less likely to present themselves as Jayhawks or Tigers and, as a result, the two groups might get along just fine.

The influence of others

The cues we provide are far from the only information available about us online. Others may post information about us, tag us in photographs, link to us, and discuss us, and all of these uncontrollable bits of information about our identities may be visible to others whether we wish they were or not. Content posted by others may contribute disproportionately to one's image because it may be seen as less biased by a desire to look good (Walther et al., 2008).

Our SNS friends affect our identities. Since most SNSs display friend lists, everyone's connections are visible to at least some others. When links to others require acceptance, as is the case in many SNSs, the sheer number of links a person has can be a status marker or liability (boyd, 2006; Fono and Raynes-Goldie, 2006). Donath and boyd (2004: 72) were among the first to note that displaying one's connections carries potential risk to one's reputation, writing that "Seeing someone within the context of their connections provides the viewer with information about them. Social status, political beliefs, musical taste, etc., may be inferred from the company one keeps."

On SNSs our friends' names, words, and even looks can influence others' impressions of us. Walther et al. (2008) had one group evaluate the attractiveness of people's photos. They then created fake

Facebook profiles to display photos of friends with varying degrees of attractiveness and had another set of subjects evaluate the profiles. The same people were rated as more attractive when they had better-looking Facebook friends. Dutch high school students studied by Antheunis and Schouten (2011) were also seen as more attractive when they had more attractive friends. Utz (2010) found that people were judged as being more communally oriented when their friends had extraverted profile pictures.

SNS contacts can also affect one's image by writing on one's "wall" or "shoutbox" (Walther et al., 2008), tagging photographs with one's name, and commenting on content one has uploaded. Cover (2012) argues that on SNSs, friends police others' self-presentations, commenting when they see behaviors that seem to breach the coherence of their identities.

Friends are not the only people with the power to shape a person's online image and identity. The internet offers many ways to discuss people who are not friends, and those discussions may be searchable. Daniel Solove (2007) has written extensively on the problems of reputation online. As he explains it, reputation is one of our most cherished possessions, yet it is bestowed by others. Gossip and shaming are mechanisms that societies use to keep behaviors in line and let others know who can and cannot be trusted. In this regard, these practices serve useful social functions. However, online anyone can create messages that are stored, replicable, and have broad reach. Thus the internet transforms the nature and effects of gossip, making it more permanent and widespread, yet less discriminating in its audience. There are new kinds and degrees of shaming and harm now. Even people who violate social norms can be shamed in ways far disproportionate to their transgressions. Online there is no due process and, what's worse, self-appointed norm enforcers can be mean, can make mistakes, and can take on qualities of vigilante mobs. People can also be dishonest, spreading gossip and shaming others out of self-interest and to distort judgments rather than to make them more accurate. It is increasingly difficult to escape past mistakes or lies that have been told about us. Online reputations have become so important that companies have arisen to assess them and clean them up and, in 2014, Europe passed a "Right to be Forgotten" law, forcing

Google to take down links to – for example – coverage of crimes for which people had served their sentence, upon request. Yet such take-down technological solutions have an inevitable whack-a-mole quality that seems destined to fail.

Online identities do not simply depend on the information that is available. They also depend on the ability of observers to interpret them. In most encounters online, others will have fairly limited cues with which to interpret us, and may or may not make of them the meanings we had intended. Social psychologists have described as "cognitive misers" people who try to get as much information as possible out of as few cues as they can. In mediated environments, where there are so many blanks to fill in, people make more out of others' small cues than they might face-to-face (Ellison et al., 2006).

Some research has explored how accurately people can assess others' personalities from their SNS profiles. As we saw, parents of teens on SNSs may not know how to read their social steno-graphic messages. Using Stone's (1995) concept of warranting, Hall, Pennington, and Leuders (2013) pose three ways of understanding online identity cues – Can a cue be manipulated? Is it seen as useful and actually used in understanding others? Most importantly, does it give accurate information about what it is taken to represent? This last kind of cue they call a "diagnostic warrant." For example, how are we to interpret the number of friends a person has? It is a cue that can be manipulated, it is seen as useful and used, but what can it really tell us about someone? Lee, Moore, Park, and Park (2012) found that the number of Facebook friends was tied to extraversion and affinity seeking. However, people with low self-esteem who were highly self-conscious engaged in "compensatory friending," meaning that they too could have high friend counts. People use different cues to assess different qualities. Judgements of social orientation and extraversion, for instance, are more likely to rely on photographs than on text (Van der Heide, D'Angelo, & Shumaker, 2012).

Hall and colleagues (2013) conducted a "lens model" analysis of Facebook profiles – having profile-holders fill out a series of psychological scales to gain one measure of their personalities, content-analyzing their profiles for evidence of personality traits, having strangers rate their profiles for evidence of those traits, and then comparing the three. They identified 53 cues people used in forming impressions. The more diagnostic warrants people used, the more accurate their impressions (2013). They found that extraversion could be assessed; conscientiousness was somewhat diagnosable, though not as strongly; agreeableness was easy to identify; but neuroticism was not (2013). Humorous orientation was also easy to judge accurately. Contrary to what theory would predict, most cues people thought had warrant value were self-generated, rather than other-oriented (2013). This suggests that the cues people use may not be the most diagnostic, and that some people may be better at cue-use than others. Indeed, as Hall and Pennington (2012) argue, some people are simply better at forming accurate impressions of others online.

The influence of platforms

In this section we'll look more closely at how platforms shape identities through design and norms. Technological design and affordances have been shown to influence deception. Hancock, Thom-Santelli, and Ritchie (2004) had students keep a communication diary in which they recorded all of their efforts to mislead someone for seven days. They found that, on average, people told 6.11 lies a day. Deception rates were highest on the telephone, followed by face-to-face communication. Email had the most honesty. They suggest this is because people realize they are less likely to get caught when using synchronous media that are neither stored nor replicable.

Platforms can also affect self-representation by determining which information is available to whom by default. Consider, for example, how Facebook's design has changed since it started. Once featuring only interlinked profiles, over the years it has added the newsfeed, replaced the "about me" box with specific fields for adding likes, added the ability to share other people's posts, developed apps that can provide information about you from other sites (such as what songs you listened to on Spotify or what film character the latest quiz says you are), provided the ability to check other people in to places and tag them in photographs, and created "Timelines." In a follow-up to Gross and Acquisti (2005), Stutzman, Gross, and Acquisti (2012) tracked the changes in Facebook privacy policies and platform architecture between 2005 and 2011 and the privacy behaviors of the same Carnegie Mellon account holders. They found that, although people locked down their own privacy settings more and more, the way the system structure changed (for instance, shifting taste preferences from listing them in a section of the profile to liking public shared pages) meant that people were making more information public.

The introduction of Facebook's Timeline in 2011 similarly made material that had been created for and shared with friends at particular moments in historical time easily accessible for everyone with current access to the profile. Thus material posted years earlier became easily available to Facebook friends made years later. This public archiving of the self makes the changes, inconsistencies, and incoherence of our selves over time easily visible (Cover, 2012). "Facebook's tendency to make information visible in unforeseen ways" (Cassidy, 2013: 177) poses difficult challenges for people seeking to manage their identities. Thus, even though Facebook seems to have highly granular privacy controls, it still poses large risks to privacy, when it displays information to unforeseen others.

Platforms also shape identities via the norms they push, and those that emerge through the processes described in chapter 4. Ottoni and collaborators (2014) compared the linguistic features of profiles on Pinterest and Twitter for 23,000 target users who had signed up for Pinterest using Twitter accounts. Most people used similar language across sites, and language across users within a site was quite similar, indicating site norms. Some users did use different language on each site, and, in those cases, that language still conformed to the linguistic norms of the platform (2014).

Twitter has developed to have norms of authenticity and of self-branding (Baym, 2013; Marwick & boyd, 2010). By building in and foregrounding popularity metrics such as the number of followers and retweets (Baym, 2013; Marwick, 2013), Twitter instructs "wannabes in the art of entrepreneurialism, self-promotion, and careful self-editing" (Marwick, 2013). Dating sites too have norms that shape presentation. Ellison, Hancock, and Toma found (2012) that users share an expectation that everyone on these sites embellishes their profiles, and this is used to justify self-misrepresentation and euphemism. The algorithmic filters of dating sites also led to misrepresentation. Ellison et al. (2006) found that one reason people lied about their ages in dating site profiles was to avoid being screened out in searches that clustered search results into systemically prede-termined age ranges.

In his (2013) Ph.D. thesis, Cassidy analyzed profile pages on Facebook and Gaydar and interviewed focus groups of young gay men in Brisbane, Australia. He found that Facebook's structure and norms allowed them to construct their homosexuality as the banal part of their everyday lives they understood it to be, while Gaydar pushed them into a hypersexualized gay male identity with which they did not identify. The language of the site, its ads, competitions, promotions, and images construct a body-focused gay male identity that prefers hook-ups to committed relationships. This representation of gay masculinity as promiscuous combined with Gaydar's "digital infrastructure that organizes user profiles around penis size, sexual fetishes and the like," did not resonate with the users he interviewed, most of whom wanted committed relationships (Cassidy, 2013: 92). As a result, these men omitted information about their sexuality from Gaydar profiles. Paradoxically, although they understood their own reasons for omitting such information, when they saw the same absences in others' profiles, they read the omissions as deception.

People who use platforms are usually aware of what they see on their own and others' profiles, but unaware of site algorithms that filter what they and their friends do and do not see (Hamilton, Karahalios, Sandvig, & Eslami, 2014). Sites such as Facebook rely on ever-changing algorithms that weight dozens of variables in determin-ing what should go in a person's news feed. In the summer of 2014, a series of events made the power of algorithms and those who control them particularly salient. A study published in PNAS (Kramer, Guillory, & Hancock, 2014) revealed that, for a short time, some Facebook users had their algorithms weighted to omit posts with negative emotion words from their feeds while others had algorithms weighted to omit posts with positive emotion words. They found a slight increase in positive word use from the former and in negative words from the latter, which they took to be indicative of emotional contagion. At the least, the study demonstrates that people conform to the social norms they see within platforms. It also caused an international public furor. Also that summer, the dating site OKCupid revealed that it too used experiments in order to help them improve their matching algorithms, proudly announcing "We Experiment on Human Beings!" (Rudder, 2014). In this experiment, some people were paired with "bad" matches and others had elements of their profile (pictures or text fields) removed when they were presented to others. Together, these studies demonstrate both that our feeds are shaped by algorithms, and that those algorithms are shaped by people whose interests may not always overlap with those of the site's users.

Self-perception

Thus far, this chapter has presented identity as something performed for, created by, and interpreted by others. Identities people create and have created for them online can also feed back into people's self-concepts, for better and for worse (Boellstorff, 2008; Uimonen, 2013). In this final section, I briefly consider how online identity can lead to new – or at least changed – selves. For some people, blogging and using SNSs is motivated partly by a desire to find their own voices (Chen, 2012) or make themselves coherent (Cover, 2012). Testing out honest self-disclosure and expressing one's "real" self online can be empowering and liberating. Practicing skills such as assertiveness can help people to work through issues involving control and mastery, gain competence, and find a comfort which they can then transfer to their embodied encounters. This is especially so when they receive positive feedback for their online expressions of identity (Chen, 2012; Jung, Song, & Vorderer, 2012; McKenna & Bargh, 1998; Myers, 1987b; Turkle, 1996, 1997).

This feedback loop can reshape self-concepts, leading to more actions that are in line with the self a person constructed online (Walther et al., 2011). The socially anxious people McKenna et al. (2002) studied formed new close relationships through the internet and reported less loneliness and greater ease making friends offline two years later. On the other hand, the cohort of young men who sought friendship and love on Gaydar, discussed in Cassidy (2013), felt estranged and alienated from what they perceived as the gay community, shaped in large part by Gaydar's stereotypical representation of gay masculinity. Though Gaydar made it easier to navigate their city as gay men, it led to a form of self-loathing with long histories of queer experience (2013). The rise of visible social media metrics such as followers, friends, likes, retweets, subscribers, shares, and so on can easily become a measure of self-worth, as anyone who has ever felt a twinge of joy at receiving a lot of likes should attest (Banet-Weiser, 2012; Marwick, 2013).

Summary

When people meet online, it raises questions about whether they are honest about who they are, and, hence, whether they and the relationships they create can be trusted. However, we have seen that online identities are created through complex socio-technical processes. People offer information about themselves, others offer information about them, sites filter what information which people see. Though it may seem that we can be anyone we want to be online, in fact the procedures through which information about us is generated, stored, replicated, and made accessible are impossible to control. At best, they might be managed.

That technological affordances influence self-presentations does not mean that they determine them. Indeed, the same affordances can have opposite effects for different people in different circumstances. Some may feel free to lie, while others may feel free to be more honest. Most people, in most cases, seem to err on the side of truthfulness, especially when they are linked to other people and social identities through their self-representations, although they may manipulate their self-presentations strategically. Self-presentations can be supported or countered by information about the people to whom we are connected or who write about us, as well as by site designs and algorithms that direct and filter who sees what about us. Looking at the evidence, there's no compelling reason to assume that people who meet online are inherently less able or willing to represent themselves as they understand themselves to be than they are when they meet in unmediated contexts. People may lie online, but, then, face-to-face communication has never been a guarantor of truth, as people whose married lovers have sworn they were single or intended to leave their spouses will quickly tell you. The flip side of our fear of online deception is our gullibility in believing that vision prevents us from falling for lies.

The identity foundations on which new relationships are built can be every bit as sturdy online as off. As SIP argued, when people interact online with others over time, they become more likely to solicit and present "socially revealing, relational behavior" (Walther et al., 1994: 465), leading new acquaintances who pursue relationships to fairly accurate understandings of one another's identities. Over time, impressions formed through online interaction become increasingly similar to those formed face-to-face (Walther & Burgoon, 1992). When people meet online, they may need to make a leap of faith in deciding they know each other well enough to trust each other (Henderson & Gilding, 2004). However, believing that you know and can trust someone else always requires a leap of faith, no matter how you meet.

6

Digital media in everyday relationships

I had been reading, teaching, and conducting research about online relationship formation for many years before I ever formed a close friendship online. Then I met and came to know Markus, a younger male Swedish graphic designer and musician whom I met through email. In late 2004, I spent a lot of time listening to two CDs by an obscure Swedish pop band. I sent them this email (which included my home address and a link to my university website) in appreciation:

> Hello,
> You are my reward for adolescent individuality. Here is why.
> I went to high school in Urbana Illinois in the late 1970s/early 1980s. One of my friends was [*the person who owned the label on which the band's recordings had been released*]. I had multicolored hair and listened to the Kinks, the Buzzcocks, Sparks, and all kinds of other bands he'd never heard of. Everyone thought I was really weird. He didn't. We talked about music. A lot. I like to think I sparked what was until then his latent audiophile gene (I think he'd agree, although he overtook me within a very short time). He grew up to create [*their label*]. I grew up to have too little to do with all that music I still love. And now, 20+ years later, he brings me you. Life can be so sweet.
> Thanks for [your record]. It's making my winter so much more fun. I'll be bopping around Northern Europe this summer, maybe you'll play some shows and I'll get to see you.
> I hope you have a wonderful 2005.

The band member who happened to be their tech guy, Markus, wrote back quickly saying my email had made his day. A few days later, I wrote back. A week or so later, he wrote back. We began a correspondence that at times involved multiple emails every day for weeks, and rarely went more than two weeks between contacts. We exchanged more than 2,500 emails in four years. We've vacationed together with our families. He loves that he gets to make an appearance in this chapter, and when I told him I was doing a second edition he asked not to be deleted. Had we lived in the same town, we probably would have met. But, as we saw in the last chapter, our age and sex differences would likely have stood in the way of forming a close friendship, as would my lack of Swedish and his shyness with conversational English.

Markus and I illustrate how the internet has enabled fans and bands to become friends, a process that was integral to the growth of MySpace (boyd & Ellison, 2007) and is seen throughout the internet (Baym, 2012). Our relationship and its development also demonstrate most of the patterns and issues seen in relational development that begins online. The first part of this chapter continues last chapter's discussion of meeting online to examine how people like Markus and me, who meet via the internet, develop their relationships. We'll begin by addressing the early stages of relationships, the way communication changes as they develop and strengthen, and we'll look at the question of how relationships that begin online compare to those started face-to-face.

The second part of this chapter comes at the topic from the other side, asking how digital media fit into the landscape of interpersonal communication. We'll see that people tend to add media as they grow closer and look at the roles different media play in relational maintenance. In chapter 4, we asked whether internet use affected civic and political engagement. Here we'll address what effects the use of the internet has on people's social engagement. I'll also identify some of the main influences on which communication media people use when. The chapter closes by considering some of the ways relational media use remains an object of dispute, as different people and different groups develop different norms of appropriateness.

Building relationships with people we meet online

When Jeff Cole surveyed Americans in 2000, people knew an average of 3.1 people online whom they had never met in person. In 2012, that figure had jumped to 11.1 (Cole, 2013). The number of friendships formed online that resulted in face-to-face relationships rose from 0.7 to 3 (2013). Most relationships that start online do not become

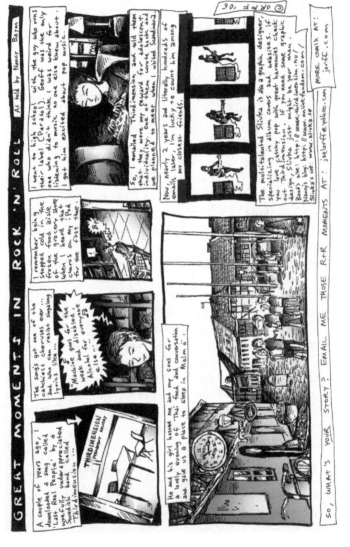

Cartoon 6.1 Joel Orff

intimate, just as most people who meet face-to-face are unlikely to ever become more than distant acquaintances. Of the countless people I've met online, very few have made their way into my inner circle through the internet. Most have either drifted away completely or remained on the far peripheries of my social world. Others have become acquaintances.

Most interpersonal relationships are weak ties (Granovetter, 1973), limited in the range of activities, thoughts, and feelings partners exchange. The internet helps us have more specialized and intermittent contacts with more people. Like Markus and me, many – though by no means most – people have formed at least one enduring strong tie through digital media. Strong ties are those that encourage frequent, companionable contact. They are voluntary, reciprocal, supportive of partners' needs, and they create long-term contact (Haythornthwaite, 2005).

We form relationships by communicating. Our messages are the tool with which we build and tinker with our connections, and the mirror through which we see them. Most relational communication is implicit. Unless there are problems, we rarely discuss the correct label for our relationship, how close we are, and what obligations and responsibilities we owe each other (Watzlawick, Beavin, & Jackson, 1967). For the most part, we show each other these things through *how* we communicate with each other. As we move from strangers to relational partners, we communicate more often, and our communication takes on consistent patterns. Once a relationship is established, every interaction serves as an opportunity to reaffirm it by behaving just as we always do, to end it by saying something that cannot be repaired, or to negotiate it by communicating a little differently from our norm.

Early idealization

When people meet online, especially in media with few identity cues, they often seem to like one another more than they would if they had met in person. This phenomenon of "hyperpersonal communication" (Walther, 1996) was first documented in experiments comparing groups of students who worked on projects together in person or remotely via text-based online discussion. It has since been affirmed in naturalistic studies (e.g. Henderson & Gilding, 2004; McKenna et al., 2002) and developed further. I had taught this concept for years, but was still taken aback as I watched it happen to me with Markus. Even knowing the reasons (which I'll cover just below) that I might be driven to find him unrealistically attractive, I still found myself knowingly exaggerating his appeal. My husband, appropriately confident of my affections, even took to jokingly referring to him as my "Swedish boyfriend."

There are several reasons we might like the people we meet online more than those we meet offline, at least early on. Hyperpersonal communication stems from a mix of media affordances and how message senders and receivers interpret one another and behave. As we saw in the last chapter, sparse cues leave a great deal of room for presenting the self and imagining the other. When, as they often do, online relationships form because of shared interests or common experiences, it is easy to imagine other shared qualities not yet discussed. When we decide that someone has appeals such as humor, good response time, or writing style (Baker, 2008), it is easy to fill in the blanks about their other traits with ideals. Markus's facility with words, cleverness, and status as a member of a band I really liked led me to assume much more about him than those qualities could reveal. Although some of those early assumptions were right, others were not. It turned out, for instance, that, although we have overlapping musical taste, our taste is more different than similar.

Walther also argued that we might appear more attractive to others in online meetings because sparse cues give us more control over our messages, letting us be more selective in what we reveal and when. My first email to Markus, as you can see above, was extremely selective in which pieces of my autobiography I chose to foreground. Walther suggested that reduced-cue environments allow people to focus more on message production. This might lead to their creating better messages, presenting a self online that really is more attractive. In the last chapter we saw that people who receive validation for their online self-presentations are likely to become more like the selves they present. This also plays a role in hyperpersonal communication. As people receive positive feedback for some messages (like self-disclosure), they are likely to do more of those messages, fine-tuning their responses so that they become more attractive communicators (Walther, 2011).

Asynchronous media allow people to revise. I reread and rewrote many of the emails I sent Markus when we were first getting to know each other. Other times, though, synchronous media may be more powerful. In an interview study with people in Second Life support groups, Green-Hamann et al. (2011: 486) found it was synchronicity and rich cues that enhanced members' sense of intimacy, writing "an attractive avatar who sits nearby, stays after a meeting to chat privately and is online and available at other times, can stimulate a hyperpersonal relationship in a way that an asynchronous text-based comment in a discussion forum may not."

Another reason for hyperpersonal communication is hinted at in Ellen Ullman's (1997) tale of meeting a new man online. She and he exchanged emails filled with literary passages and dreams. But when they finally met, they realized they could only "speak in emails." In retrospect, she saw that part of the attraction had been the anticipation of hearing from him and, ultimately, of meeting. The very title of the film *You've Got Mail* speaks to the excitement of anticipation in online relationships.

Relational development

As once-weak ties develop and strengthen, communication patterns change to reflect and build the evolving relationship. One way in which communication changes as people get closer is that our discussions span a wider range of topics, which we address at greater depth. We also become increasingly direct about our feelings, and come to trust each other with our personal confidences. From the start, Markus and I disclosed about our past, our attitudes, music, where we lived, and how we spent our days. Over time, we had broadened the topic range so much that, when we met in person six months after the first emails, he was surprised that I did not know his parents' careers.

Self-disclosure is one of the most powerful communication practices we have for building a relationship, although it can backfire if one shares too much too soon or shares something the other person finds unappealing. Relationship theorists have described relationship formation as a process of "social penetration" in which people grow closer by revealing ever-deeper aspects of themselves, peeling back the layers of an onion until they reach the core of intimacy (Altman & Taylor, 1973). This approach has been critiqued for envisioning the self as a static entity with multiple layers rather than the ever-shifting dynamic and flexible set of constructions depicted in the last chapter, but it remains the case that we can't get to know one another well and build trust without self-disclosure.

In a clever experiment, Jiang, Bazarova, and Hancock (2011) had a research participant meet a confederate either face-to-face or through computer-mediated communication. The confederates were trained to offer differing amounts of self-disclosure. After the interaction, participants were asked to rate their sense of intimacy with the other. Confirming hyperpersonal communication theory, they found that self-disclosure led to more intimacy online than in face-to-face contexts. They were able to show that the reason for this difference was that, in the online environment, people were more likely to attribute the confederates' self-disclosure to interpersonal motivations. In other words, when people interpret self-disclosure as an effort to increase closeness, it does.

As relationships strengthen, we also become more interdependent, influencing one another's behaviors, thoughts, and feelings, which is reflected in and enacted through communication. We become better able to predict what each other will say and do. We come to know one another's communication styles, so that we can read between the lines of one another's messages. We may use secret terms or words and phrases with private connotations or give one another nicknames. Markus and I, for instance, fell into the habit of beginning our emails with an ever-changing array of silly affectionate greetings (e.g. Hello handsome, Hola guapa). We introduce our partners to other friends and our families, and we are willing to expend effort to ensure that the relationship endures (Parks, 2006; Parks & Floyd, 1996).

At the start of chapter 5, we saw Tom and his eventual wife go from internet to telephone to dinner at the same table in a day. It is not always this fast, but as relationships that begin online develop, they tend to add other media in a predictable pattern. Often beginning in public discussion, online partners add private one-on-one interaction via messaging, email, or chat. As relationships continue to develop online, without giving up those means of communication, pairs begin to include texting and the telephone. Once they've spoken on the phone, odds that a pair will meet in person increase (McKenna et al., 2002). In our survey of friends on Last.fm, 47 percent said they had never met. Of those, most were interested in meeting: 60 percent said they would meet if it were convenient, 13 percent were split between being willing to make plans to meet and already having made such plans. However, 27 percent of respondents said they were not interested in meeting their Last.fm friend. The more media we use together, the more access we grant each other to our lives and the more interdependent we become.

Markus and I share a fondness for the written word, and went from email to snail mail. Six weeks after we first met, he sent me a hard-to-find single with an otherwise unreleased song I'd asked him for. With it, he included a letter. Though I doubt he thought it through, his letter, the first handwritten tangible marker of our relationship, contained his first deep disclosures. In it he shared his sadness at the recent unexpected loss of his girlfriend's father (a disclosure which also served to show me the depth of his connection to her) and his fears of his parents' and his own mortality. A few months later, when my travels took me to northern Europe, we used email to plan our meeting. When I got to Europe, Markus and I began text messaging on our mobile phones (the text message he sent me was, embarrassingly, the first one I'd ever received – I had to read the manual and fumble my way through a typo-ridden response). Not until the day we met did we talk on the telephone. How was our first meeting? Awkward. There were long silences. Markus felt nervous and lost confidence in his English. But I met (and was smitten by) his girlfriend, he met my sons and carried the little one around town on his shoulders, and the reservoir of knowledge and affection we had built carried us through. We've seen one another many times since. Writing remains our primary mode of interaction, but being together now feels easy and familiar.

Comparing online to offline relationships

As we develop relationships that begin online, we add media that offer a wider range of social cues. Any limits on those relationships that could be attributed to sparse cues become increasingly irrelevant. Nonetheless, people often think of "online" and "offline" relationships as different and try to compare them. Some studies have found friendships that begin face-to-face to be slightly more developed (Chan & Cheng, 2004; Mesch & Talmud, 2006; Parks & Roberts, 1998), with partners who met online spending less time together, engaging in fewer shared activities, and – in some studies (e.g. Mesch & Talmud, 2006) but not others (Parks & Roberts, 1998) – engaging in less discussion of personal problems and romantic relationships. The one important exception seems to be that cross-sex friendships that began online (like mine and Markus's) may be of higher quality than same-sex friendships, in contrast to those relationships that began offline (Chan & Cheng, 2004).

Longitudinal studies that follow online friendships over time do not show meaningful differences between them and offline friendships. Chan and Cheng (2004) found that the differences between online and offline friendships increased within the first year but then diminished, and the relationships converged over time. They speculate that online friendships are more tentative in early stages, but after six months to a year grow quickly and become more like offline friendships (2004). McKenna et al. (2002) also tracked friendship pairs over time and found that online relationships lasted well over two years, comparing favorably with offline relationships. After two years, 71 percent of romantic relationships and 75 percent of all relationships begun online were still going. Most had grown closer and stronger.

Michael Rabby (2007) compared four groups of relationships – those that began and remained online, those that began online and moved to being primarily maintained face-to-face, those that began face-to-face and remained there, and those that began face-to-face and moved to being primarily maintained online. Rabby found that the degree of commitment people had to their relationship was far more important than the means of communication in determining the kinds and amounts of relational maintenance behaviors people

used. He did find that those he called the "virtuals," who only communicated online, used fewer relational maintenance strategies than
others, but those differences "were sometimes not significant," and
virtuals' commitment levels were often "still relatively high" (Rabby,
2007: 333).

In the end, then, people can and do develop meaningful personal
relationships online. Many of them remain weak and specialized,
used to exchange resources around a fairly narrow set of topics of
shared interest. These relationships make important contributions
to people's lives, especially when they allow people to interact about
interests and concerns that their close relational partners do not
share. Pairs who do become closer interact through multiple media,
eventually making the influence of the internet difficult to conceptually distinguish from the many other influences on their partnership.
Reduced cues may be an issue in early stages of relationships, or in
those that never have any prospect of going beyond initial encounters,
but over time people can reveal themselves to one another verbally
and nonverbally until they form understandings of one another as
rich as, or richer than, those they hold of people they meet in any
other way.

Mediated relational maintenance

"Online" relationships turn into "offline" ones much less often than
"offline" friendships turn into "online" ones. The rise of SNSs, which
are used primarily to replicate connections that exist offline rather
than to build new ones (boyd & Ellison, 2007), has cast this phenomenon into the spotlight. One out of every seven people (1.23 billion) on
earth now use Facebook monthly, mostly to connect with people they
already know. But taking offline ties online is a practice as old as the
internet. An American random-sample telephone survey in the late
1990s, for instance, found that 41 percent of the reasons offered for
home use of the internet had to do with supporting and maintaining
meaningful relationships (Stafford, Kline, & Dimmick, 1999).

Relational maintenance behaviors

Relationships are maintained through communication that demonstrates ongoing attention to the relationship. The primary purpose of SNSs is to maintain personal relationships, especially those with friends (Ellison, Vitak, Gray, & Lampe, 2014). Madden and colleagues (2013) found that 98 percent of US teens who use Facebook are friends with people they already know from school. A study of almost all the Facebook users at Texas A&M (Mayer & Puller, 2007) showed that only 0.4 percent met online. Relationship maintenance, rather than relational creation, has also been found to be a primary motive for using Cyworld (Choi, 2006) and MySpace (boyd, 2006). Though people were far less likely to already know one another on Last.fm than were pairs in these studies, Baym and Ledbetter (2009) still found that over half (52.9 percent) knew each other before becoming Last.fm friends.

Although people in close relationships use SNSs with each other, most relationships maintained via SNSs are weak. Baron (2008) found that students reported an average of 72 "real" friends in their 229 Facebook friends, a 1:3 ratio almost identical to Ellison, Steinfeld, and Lampe's (2009) result. Ledbetter and I (Baym & Ledbetter, 2009) found that, while a few people reported close relationships on Last. fm, on average Last.fm friends rated their relationships just below the midpoint on measures of relational development. The range of relationship types included amongst Last.fm friends included everything from strangers who had since decided they didn't like one another to lifelong best-friends, family members, and romantic partners. Weak ties connected through SNSs can grow into stronger ones through SNS use. Craig and Wright (2012) had students focus on a relationship in which they communicate frequently and primarily through Facebook. They found that when those people thought they had similar attitudes to one another, they found one another more socially attractive and, as a result, engaged in broader and deeper self-disclosure, increasing the interdependence and predictability of the relationship.

The vast majority of people connected through SNSs never interact with most of their "friends." In their analysis of 362 million messages on Facebook, Golder et al. (2007) found that only 15.1 percent of friends ever exchanged messages. Baron (2008) found that 60 percent of Facebook users wrote on others' walls either never or less than once a week. In their analysis of over 200,000 MySpace messages, Gilbert, Karahalios, and Sandvig (2008) found that 43.5 percent of friends never commented on one another's profiles, and only 4 percent ever exchanged ten or more comments.

When people do interact with each other, they often engage in "Facebook Relational Maintenance Behaviors" (Ellison et al., 2014) such as responding to good or bad news, giving advice when requested, posting birthday greetings, and answering questions. SNSs are also useful for organizing joint activities on the fly (Humphreys, 2007; Ling, 2004), especially when they are well integrated with mobile devices. As we saw in the last chapter, in some cases SNSs allow emotionally riskier exchanges than people would brave face-to-face. Larsen's (2007) work on Arto.dk shows that participants, in particular adolescent girls, often leave emotionally effusive messages proclaiming their love and admiration for one another on each other's profiles, a form of communication out of keeping with Danish norms. Kim and Yun's (2007) research likewise suggests that, for Koreans, who may avoid negative emotional communication face-to-face, Cyworld can offer a venue for such communication, with one informant reporting that she had "been able to save many relationships thanks to my minihompy [profile]" (2007).

Much of what people do on SNSs is "share." Many platforms instruct users to "share your life" and equate "sharing" with "caring" (John, 2013a). Indeed, linking to information you think others will find interesting or enjoy is a major motivation for Facebook use (Baek et al., 2011). Though disclosing or posting a link on Facebook can feel very interpersonal, it is central to the economic models of SNSs (John, 2013a), which rely on building detailed models of users, which they sell for targeted advertising. When people click, comment, or otherwise show attention to one another on an SNS, they are contributing data about themselves that Facebook and other sites use to shape what information they will see next. Every time you post on someone's wall, click like, or otherwise display attention in ways a friend can see, ever-changing algorithms use that information to reshape your feed.

These past actions shape what is displayed each time you view the site (Ellison et al., 2014). The success of Facebook and other SNSs as relationship maintenance tools comes from their wide but selective reach: people can communicate with multiple weak ties simultaneously. Equally, if not more importantly, people can share photographs. As of this writing, Facebook is the world's largest photo-sharing site. Even without direct interaction, simply having access to one another's updates on an SNS may facilitate a sense of connection (e.g. Humphreys, 2007). Several of the friends who took our Last.fm survey mentioned the sense of connection they maintained with the other as one of the benefits they received from maintaining a relationship on the site. Baron (2008: 85) cites a respondent who describes it as "a way of maintaining a friendship without having to make any effort whatsoever."

Along with social networks, texting and phone calls are also extremely important relational maintenance media, especially in close relationships. If SNSs allow us to connect with broader circles of people than we could possibly sustain relationships with face-to-face, mobile phones do the opposite, tying those already close ever more tightly together. The affordances of the mobile telephone – it is small, portable, and can be used relatively quickly and discreetly in a wide variety of circumstances – enhance its usefulness in close relationships. Brief calls between people who see one another regularly can activate emotional bonds, enacting and reinforcing closeness (Licoppe & Heurtin, 2002). Mobile communication devices also allow people to micro-coordinate their actions, for example calling to ask whether to stop and buy milk on the way home, suggesting a spur-of-the-moment get-together, or telling someone you're running late (Ling, 2004; Ling & Yttri, 2002). Acquaintances may offer "weak invitations" to one another through FourSquare check-ins (Licoppe & Legout, 2014). For teens – who, as we have seen, may be particularly enmeshed in mobile phone networks with their peers – this micro-coordination can become hypercoordination, to the extent that they may feel left out of their social circles if deprived of their mobile phones for even a short time (Ling & Yttri, 2002), a feeling I've seen displayed by many adults as well.

The continuous relational accessibility enabled by mobile phones keeps local peers and family more interdependent, but can also come to feel overwhelming and imprisoning. Duran et al. (2011) found that romantic partners who were having more tensions between independence and connection were more likely to experience conflict over not calling and texting enough, phone calls from members of the opposite sex, and not answering when the other called. Those who were dissatisfied with phone use in the romantic relationship were less satisfied with the time spent with their partner and more likely to feel their freedom was restricted (2011). Jeff Hall and I (Hall & Baym, 2012) showed that, for people who are close, this heightened dialectical tension between connection and independence emerged as a result of using the phone together. Using the mobile phone for either texting or phoning created expectations of phone use in the relationship. These mobile maintenance expectations simultaneously brought pairs closer together, increasing their solidarity, and made them feel overdependent and hence entrapped. The effects of the phone on close relationships are thus simultaneously positive and negative. These tensions between independence and control, privacy and surveillance, also play out between kids and their parents, as parents often perceive new media as a means of controlling and sur- veilling their children, while the children view new media as a means of achieving independence and privacy (Horst, 2010).

In long-distance relationships, video chat platforms can be espe- cially important in relational maintenance (Madianou & Miller, 2012a, 2012b; Neustaedter & Greenberg, 2012): 40 percent of transnational communication happens through Skype (Harper, Bird, Zimmerman, & Murphy, 2013), some of which is business, but much of which is interpersonal, often familial. There are also more and more niche networking apps to sustain personal relationships, from the very popular WhatsApp, acquired by Facebook in 2013, to "micro-social networking apps" like Couple and Avocado which connect only two people. O'Hara, Massimi, Harper, Rubens, and Morris (2014) draw on Simmel to argue that these applications are part of how people "dwell" together, integrating a sense of co-presence throughout their daily experience.

Multiplexity

The kind of dwelling O'Hara et al. (2014) describe is one in which any particular medium – WhatsApp, Skype, Facebook, a phone call – flows with all the others into one complex lifeworld. Most relationships are characterized by "media multiplexity," meaning that they are conducted through more than one medium, and that closer relationships use more media (Haythornthwaite, 2005). When we shift from a media perspective to a relational perspective, instead of asking how media affect relationships, we ask how people communicate in their relationships (Caughlin & Sharabi, 2013). What range of media do they use? When and how do they work together or interfere? In this section, we'll see how media fit together into a whole and how the choice of medium comes to have important meanings in its own right.

In one of my studies of media use in college student relationships, 496 college students assessed the extent to which they used the internet in their social circles (Baym, Zhang, & Lin, 2004). The majority of their interpersonal internet communication was within pairs who also spoke on the telephone or face-to-face. We also asked them to estimate what percentage of total interaction in a specific relationship was conducted through each medium and found that this had no bearing on how close or satisfying they perceived that relationship to be (Baym, Zhang, Kunkel, Lin, & Ledbetter, 2007). They were also asked to report on their most recent significant voluntary social interaction online, face-to-face, or on the telephone (Baym et al., 2004). Despite their tendency to rank media in the order that we saw in the opening quotations in chapter 3, across random interactions, the statistical differences in quality amongst media were few and slight. The telephone was perceived as equal in quality to face-to-face conversation. Online interaction (primarily email) was perceived as slightly lower quality, but the difference was very small – a quarter of a point on a five-point scale – and a very small percentage of total variation in quality was accounted for by medium. By far the most influential predictor of the quality of an interaction turned out to be the relationship type. People in close relationships had high-quality interactions regardless of the medium through which they interacted.

In a related study, 51 students kept a diary of all their voluntary social interactions for several days (Baym et al., 2004). Only 1 of the 51 reported having only face-to-face interactions or internet interactions during the reported days. In contrast, 32 people (64 percent) reported conducting interactions face-to-face, on the phone, and online; 13 people reported no significant internet interactions; 6 people reported no significant telephone calls; 2 did not report any face-to-face conversations. There were nearly as many internet interactions as there were telephone interactions, but most interactions were face-to-face. This is in keeping with previous studies finding that the internet is used on a par with the telephone in personal relationships (Dimmick, Kline, & Stafford, 2000; Flanagin & Metzger, 2001; Stafford et al., 1999).

I came at this from a different angle in a later study, starting with friendship pairs on Last.fm and asking what other media they used (Baym & Ledbetter, 2009). One of our goals was to explore the diversity of ways people engage one another online as well as offline. Although almost a third said Last.fm was the only way they communicated in this relationship, on average the pairs reported using between two and three other ways of interacting with each other. Many of the pairs also used Instant Messaging (42 percent), other websites (34.7 percent), and email (31.3 percent). A third of the pairs said they also communicated face-to-face. Of those who had ever met face to face, 60 percent said they saw one another "regularly" or "all the time"; 23.6 percent used the telephone and 21.3 percent texted; 1 pair in 20 even used the postal service. In subsequent work, Ledbetter (2009b) showed that, within same-sex friendship, each medium a pair used uniquely contributed to interdependence and was in some ways interchangeable with any other as a means of sustaining interdependence.

When people use different media within a relationship, those media may be more or less integrated. When they are integrated, people continue conversations begun in one medium in another (Caughlin & Sharabi, 2013). People may also segment their communication, limiting some kinds of interactions to some media, or feel anxious when they switch between media (such as from texting to calling). Caughlin and Sharabi (2013) found that close pairs had more mediated communication and more integrated communication. Pairs who had difficulty transitioning between media or who communicated only via technology were less close or satisfied (2013).

People divide their media use within a relationship based in part on their goals for that interaction. Neustaedter and Greenberg (2012) studied frequent and regular use of video chat in long-distance romantic relationships. The couples used video to achieve the sense of everyday dwelling that O'Hara et al. (2014) discuss. Partners left video chat open ritualistically to hang out, eat together, watch TV together, or watch each other fall asleep. But to say good morning and check in throughout the day they used texting or Instant Messaging. To share stories and funny items they ran across, they used email. For deep conversations, they often preferred the telephone. Kissing and sex, not surprisingly, worked best in person, although mock-kissing on video chat had its charms.

Media's symbolic value

When people can choose between many different media, which ones they use becomes significant in itself. I once remarked to a friend that I had received a text message from a long-distance colleague we both like very much. "Oh!" she replied, somewhat excited for me, "I didn't realize you two had a texting relationship!" Madianou and Miller (2012a, 2012b) call this kind of multimedia context "polymedia." In polymedia, we do not simply choose a medium. Media unite to become a single integrated structure of affordances that we exploit in order to manage emotions and relationships. The negotiation over which affordances to exploit "often becomes the message itself" (Madianou & Miller, 2012b: 173). "Email," as they put it, "is not simply email; it is defined relationally as also not a letter, not a text message and not a conversation via webcam; which, in turn, is not a phone call" (2012b: 175).

In their rich comparative ethnography of communication between migrants from Trinidad and the Philippines and their families who had remained at home, Madianou and Miller found that at first new media are used much like old media (the kind of "remediation" we covered in the first chapter). Over time, they come to have their own resonance and possibilities, enabling new kinds of meanings and relationships. For instance, grandparents and toddlers are able to have long-distance relationships that were never before possible because toddlers can connect with video chat but not phone calls. Certain kinds of media come to seem appropriate for certain kinds of relationships, particular relationships find configurations of media use that work for them, and individuals develop idiosyncratic interpretations of media. Madianou and Miller argue that polymedia creates a new kind of social and moral responsibility. It is no longer enough to send the right message, we must do it through the right medium.

This idea has also been explored by Larson (2010) and Gershon (2010). Larson focused on communication modes in early courtship amongst college students. In early stages of relationships, when uncertainty was high, media choice was fraught. The choice of medium could be enough to signal both interest and disinterest. One young woman explained that she knew the man she was seeing was "genuinely interested instead of just being a guy trying to hook up" because he "actually called just to talk." Texting sent its own signals and needed careful management too. Texting too much, too soon, or texting again before receiving a reply were seen as signs of desperation. Gershon refers to the beliefs about the symbolic value of particular media as "media ideologies." Having a satisfying relationship depends in part on understanding each other's media ideologies and practices so partners can interpret one another correctly.

The end and aftermath of relationships

As social media have connected people in more persistent ways, inevitably they have also become means of ending relationships and raised issues about how to handle the aftermath of relationships that end either by choice or death. Gershon (2010) interviewed undergraduate students about breaking up. Most of the time, breaking up was a process that happened across media. People might begin in one medium and switch to one with more social distance when they began to fight. They shared a sense that breaking up in a way others could see (such as through Facebook posts) was inappropriate. This seems to be a message American kids learn young (Pascoe, 2010). One of my son's friends in seventh grade dumped his girlfriend on Facebook, thus demonstrating to their entire social network that he was, as my son put it, "a jerk," and leading them to ostracize him.

After breaking up, some people may stop using a medium entirely in order to avoid another person. Others worry about how their messages on a site will be read by their ex-partner or stalk their former partners' profiles in efforts to better understand the reasons for the breakup (Gershon, 2010). Some may even do what *New York Times* reporter Nick Bilton (2014) did after his divorce and stay up all night deleting every reminder of the relationship from their profiles. Media can also help us negotiate the world after a breakup. A recent divorcee I know used Swarm to see where her ex checked in, enabling her to avoid accidental encounters.

Unfriending also happens on social network sites. Most platforms make this hard to see. No one gets an announcement that they have been unfriended; they only notice if they happen to seek a person out and find access denied or if they notice their friend count has dropped and investigate further. Bevan et al. (2012) found that this kind of unfriending can be depressing, leading to rumination, especially when people know who unfriended them and think it was because of something they did on Facebook.

People's profiles may remain on SNSs or new ones may be created for them on memorial sites even after death. Facebook faced a great deal of heat for recommending that users "reconnect" with friends they had not communicated with in some time, not realizing those friends had passed. People use the profiles of friends who have passed to continue talking to the dead person, sharing memories of the deceased with others, and maintaining their ongoing bonds with the person who is gone (Marwick & Ellison, 2012). Yet questions of who maintains a profile (or memorial page) after death are very much unsettled, and, especially in public memorial pages, people may spend time after losing a loved one policing the comments from "grief tourists" and "trolls" (Marwick & Ellison, 2012). These can be especially awful when a person has committed suicide (Leonard & Toller, 2012).

Influences on media use in relationships

We have seen that relationships use multiple media to sustain themselves and that media choice carries relational messages. In this section we will look at some of the factors that shape which media people choose. These include individual differences, culture, age, relationship type and relationship stage, and gender.

People have different personality traits, and they also have different attitudes toward media. Some have looked at the effects of the "Big Five" personality traits – extraversion, agreeableness, openness, conscientiousness, and narcissism – on SNS use. A large survey of Australians found Facebook users were more extraverted and less conscientious than non-users, and that non-users were more shy and socially lonely (Ryan & Xenos, 2011). Muscanell and Guadagno (2012) found that extraversion, agreeableness, openness, and conscientiousness predicted SNS behaviors, but narcissism didn't, which may surprise those convinced social media use is inherently narcissistic. Highly sociable people seem to communicate via any medium they can. A study of Japanese youth found that those with more social skills used more mobile voice and PC email and less mobile texting (Ishii, 2006).

People with social anxiety may prefer media with fewer cues (McKenna et al., 2002). Ledbetter (2009a) developed a measure of "Online Communication Attitude" to assess how individuals feel about using online media to self-disclose and connect socially. The scale also measures apprehension, concern about miscommunication, and ease of use. He used a modified version of this scale to assess people's attitudes toward maintaining relationships through Xbox Live (Ledbetter & Kuznekoff, 2011). In a study of same-sex friends, he found that the more comfortable people were with self-disclosure online, the less communicatively competent they reported themselves to be, the more they communicated with their friend through all online media, and the less they communicated with that friend face-to-face (Ledbetter, 2009a). Xbox players who had strongly positive attitudes toward using the platform for social connection did more relationship maintenance online and interacted less often offline (Ledbetter & Kuznekoff, 2011).

Relational media use is also shaped by the demands of cultural contexts, peer groups, and age. Baron and Hård af Segerstad (2010) compared mobile phone use in Sweden, the United States, and Japan, and found that some of the differences in public media use could be explained by cultural norms. In Japan, for example, where there is an expectation of public quiet in places such as subways and sidewalks, text messaging is used far more often than in the other two countries. Although texting is almost ubiquitous now, young people text most. Ling (2010) analyzed texting behavior of a large Norwegian population over time, which allowed him to separate age effect from cohort effect. He found texting peaked in the late teens and early twenties, a life stage when people are busy cultivating friends and working out their social lives (2010). In the United States, Cole (2013) found that texting was seen as critical to relationship maintenance for most people under 24 but only a third of people over 45.

Finnish teenagers have highly ritualized ways of using mobile phones that demonstrate how different media use can be in different peer groups (Kasesniemi & Rautiainen, 2002). Text messaging is pervasive amongst teens where it serves to solidify their peer culture. Although these text messages, or SMSs, are ephemeral, these teenagers collected them, writing them down in notebooks specially designed and marketed for this purpose. Text messages became objects to be compared, traded, and composed with friends.

How far from one another people live is also an important influence on which media we use. Locally, face-to-face and telephone calls seem to predominate, although more recent research would surely show the importance of texting and SNSs in these relationships too. Chen, Boase, and Wellman (2002) and Quan-Haase, Wellman, Witte, and Hampton (2002) found that, internationally, the telephone was the medium most used in local relationships. Amongst college students, local relationships were most likely to use face-to-face conversation, followed by the telephone (Baym et al., 2004), a difference which can likely be attributed to the differences between living on a residential campus and the kinds of lifestyles more likely encompassed by these other scholars' international online sample. Our students reported using the internet in just over a third of all local relationships (2004).

In long-distance relationships, the telephone does not seem to have the same functionality. Survey studies in the early 2000s found that email was the predominant means of keeping in touch across long-distance time-zone differences (Dimmick et al., 2000). In distant relationships, Quan-Haase et al. (2002) found that 49 percent of all social contact with kin was conducted online, while 62 percent of interactions with friends used the internet. Dimmick et al.'s (2000) research revealed that email was considered superior to the telephone for such communication; nearly half reported using the long-distance telephone less now that they were online. Our students' internet interactions were more likely to be long-distance than local, and their long-distance interactions were more likely to be online than on the telephone (Baym et al., 2004).

Relationship type is also important in shaping media use. People seem more likely to use the internet to communicate with friends than with family. In a large international survey, Chen et al. (2002) found that email was used more with friends than with relatives. Quan-Haase et al. (2002), using the same data, found that email and face-to-face conversation were equally frequent amongst nearby friends. Email was less frequent with local family, however. Houser et al. (2012) found that relatives use more email than friends or significant others, and friends communicate more via social networking sites than do relatives or romantic partners. We saw in chapters 4 and 5 that cross-sex friendships seem more likely to be built and sustained online than off. Ledbetter et al. (2011) found that cross-sex friends did less everyday communication with one another than same-sex friends on the phone and face-to-face, but the same amount online.

Relational intimacy is also important. The more intimate the relationships of the American college students I studied, the more likely they were to use face-to-face conversations and telephone calls. Their internet use neither increased nor decreased with relational closeness. On the other hand, Last.fm friends' responses to open-ended questions asking why they befriended one another revealed that, for many of them, part of a close relationship was bringing the other person along to any medium they discovered. The symbolic impact of media choice is especially significant when people are negotiating relational intimacy. Sarch's (1993) study of telephone use in dating relationships showed that relationships could be measured in terms of how often the two spoke on the phone, for how long, and, perhaps most importantly, whether the calls resulted in plans to see one another. The appeal of the phone at that time was that it is a low-cue medium. The advent of even lower-cue media, particularly texting, have changed early courtship. Larson (2010) identified four types of courtship relationships – hanging out, just talking, dating, and hooking up. Only people who were dating used phone calls. Early in the relationship it was hard to decide which medium to use, as people were concerned with protecting their face and not appearing desperate. For these reasons they often start with asynchronous media like texting which increase control and allow the other to respond in their own time (Caughlin & Sharabi, 2013; Larson, 2010; Pascoe, 2010). As a courtship develops, moving to the telephone becomes a turning point symbolizing greater seriousness and commitment (Larson, 2010). Relational closeness can also be symbolized with Facebook wall posts or changing relationship status on Facebook (Larson, 2010; Pascoe, 2010). Making a new relationship visible online elicits peer support and approval, but can be problematic for the same reasons. Such updates may be negotiated between a couple offline first (Pascoe, 2010).

Cultural contexts that define appropriate behavior for different relational stages also shape media use and its meanings. In dating relationships amongst young Palestinian people in Israel in the early 2000s, for instance (Hijazi-Omari & Ribak, 2008), young men presented mobile phones to young women as a sign of their relational commitment. The telephones, which, like the romances themselves, had to be kept secret from the women's parents, required networks of friends to safeguard them and also shaped preferences for what telephones should look like (small and unremarkable in appearance). A tether to the man on the one hand and a resistance of the parents on the other, the phone freed young women from their fathers and mothers (although the maneuvers required to keep it secret from them continued to demonstrate parental authority) but situated them under greater control by their boyfriends. Traditions such as these may be short-lived, however, as, within a few short years, Palestinian norms around mobile phones had changed so that parents were buying mobile phones for their teenage daughters.

As these examples show, relational media use can be a way to symbolize and enact our gender roles as men and women (Hijazi-Omari & Ribak, 2008; Ling, 2004; Sarch, 1993). Gender is, not surprisingly, another influence on how and which media are used. In general, women do more everyday talk through social media and the telephone (Ledbetter et al., 2011; Muscanell & Guadagno, 2012). Men are more likely to use SNSs to find dates, network for careers, make new friends, and play games. Women post more photographs and public messages, private messages and make more friend requests (Muscanell & Guadagno, 2012).

Effects of internet use on other relationships

"Okay," you might say, "valuable new relationships form online and everyday relationships use all kinds of media, but it's still true that we spend too much time online and looking at our phones and that damages our other relationships." This is one of the core issues we saw raised in the public discourse in chapter 2 as well as the central thesis of Turkle's best-selling *Alone Together* (2011). Do new communication technologies undermine or replace face-to-face relationships? Just as critics cautioned that digital communities would replace locally grounded communities, the internet and mobile media raise fears that digital media lead us to substitute shallow relationships for authentic personal connections. Instead of being present with those who share our physical environments, we may become separated, isolated, and never more than partially anywhere.

Some early studies found that internet users spend less time with family and friends. Katz and Rice (2002) found that people who had used the internet recently were more likely to have been away from their homes, and Cole (2000) found that, compared to non-users, internet users socialized slightly less with household members. Nie, Hillygus, and Erbring (2002) quantified that each minute online takes away 20 seconds with family members, 7 seconds with friends, 11 seconds with colleagues, and adds 45 seconds of time spent alone. Yet in a 2012 survey of North Americans, "more than ten times the percentage of users said going online increased their contact with friends than said it decreased their contact; more than eight times as many said contact increased with members of their family" (Cole, 2013: 110).

The introduction of communication technology into relational life has problems, and we'll turn to them soon, but making us less communicative with others does not seem to be one of them. My work with college students (Baym et al., 2004) and Last.fm (Baym &

Ledbetter, 2009) showed that media use and face-to-face communication were positively correlated. The more students reported using the internet to maintain their social relationships, the more likely they were to use face-to-face conversations, telephone calls, and mail. Last. fm friends' use of any one medium positively predicted use of all the others, with especially strong associations between face-to-face interaction and telephone calls, texting and telephone calls, telephone calls and IM, and texting and IM. Others have found this too. A diary study by Copher, Kanfer, and Walker (2002) had American community leaders keep records of all interactions that went beyond a greeting for one week. When they compared heavy to light email users, they found that heavy email users also used proportionately more face-to-face communication for personal interactions than light users. Heavy emailers also had "greater numbers and percentages of communications, time spent communicating, and [communication partners] than light email users" across media (Copher et al., 2002: 274). Matei and Ball-Rokeach (2002) compared internet users in diverse neighborhoods in Los Angeles. They found that people who had more social ties in their local communities were more likely to use the internet in order to meet new people. They concluded that "belongers belong everywhere." In the Japanese context, Ishii (2006) found that the youth who used more email widened their social circles to include more distant friends.

Studies that look at all internet use, rather than just relational internet use, also show that internet users are generally more social than non-users. Hampton, Sessions, and Her (2011) found that internet users are 55 percent more likely than non-users to have a non-kin confidant. In a 2000 poll, the Pew Internet and American Life Project found that 72 percent of internet users, including longtime and heavy users, reported having visited with family or friends "yesterday" while only 61 percent of non-users did. Robinson, Kestnbaum, Neustadtl, and Alvarez (2002) conducted a random-sample survey of the American population and walked them through the last 24 hours of their lives in 15-minute increments. Internet users reported spending three times as long attending social events and reported significantly more conversation than non-users. Internet users also slept less, spent less time on personal hygiene, and had more free time, giving some indications of what might really be displaced by time spent online.

People also use the internet together. Cole (2000) found that 47 percent of internet users report spending some time each week using the internet with family members. An observational study of children's computer use at home (Orleans & Laney, 2000) found that the internet provides many opportunities for children to interact. Online materials served as a topic for conversation; children searched online for commonly valued items together; they found opportunities for social experimentation together; and the internet allowed them to demonstrate esteemed knowledge and skills. Though I must admit that in my own home there are times when familial computer use has detracted from family together time, I also value the hours of brotherly bonding my sons have spent side by side – sometimes in the same chair – in front of the screen playing a game or showing one another their coolest new find. Fathers often game with their children (Horst, 2010).

The presence of communication technologies during face-to-face encounters can be problematic, though, and people are deeply divided as to how and whether these technologies can be incorporated into body-to-body conversation without becoming intrusions. Nearly half (48 percent) of Americans say they are sometimes or often ignored because their partner spends too much time online (Cole, 2013). Mobile phones, with their ever-handy appeal, are a greater problem. Work on the mobile phone, especially Lee Humphreys's (2005), shows the nuance with which we reorganize our interactions when someone makes or takes a call during a face-to-face conversation. Using Goffman's (1963, 1971) terms, she describes phone calls as making "withs" into "singles" and shows how people singled by telephone calls accommodate the situation by looking elsewhere, engaging in other activities, walking ahead, or listening in. As many as 92 percent of Americans have felt ignored because their partner is on their mobile device (Cole, 2013).

Whether a person's communication technology use is harmful to a relationship depends in large measure on how the other person interprets it. Ahlstrom, Lundberg, Zabriskie, Eggett, and Lindsay (2012) surveyed couples in which only one person played massively multiplayer online role-playing games, and couples where both did, though one more than the other. How the spouse who gamed less felt about the gaming was key to marital satisfaction. More than half of the people in only-one-gamer couples said they argued about gaming, and more than 70 percent of gamers and more of their partners said gaming had negative effects on their marriage. But in couples where both gamed, only a third reported quarreling, half said they usually spoke positively about gaming, and about 75 percent said the effect of gaming on the relationship was positive (the authors did warn against being in the same guild or clan).

To summarize, relationships are built and sustained through many media – including face-to-face communication – that offer an enormous range of affordances and fit together into a unified if complicated system. Deciding which to use when can be a loaded choice; media send hints of relational significance that may or may not be intended. Media use is influenced by many factors. It is ever more important for relational partners to find normative behaviors and moral orders for technology use upon which they can agree. In this chapter's final section, we turn briefly to some areas of ongoing normative upheaval.

Uncertain norms

As technologies are domesticated, they move from being completely novel to routine. For this to happen, as I argued in chapter 2, people have to get beyond the utopian and dystopian reactions to wrestle with messy nuances. This book has shown that many of those nuances are shaking out into order already. Others, like the question of when it's appropriate to take or make a mobile phone call, are far from resolved, even within particular couples (Duran et al., 2011). In closing this chapter, we'll look at three sets of issues around digital communication technologies that show us still in a process of making sense of these media. First, I'll address disagreements over when media use is appropriate. I'll turn then to the question of what a "friend" is when three-quarters of SNS friends aren't "real." Finally, we'll look at the question of how much information is too much.

When is it appropriate?

To say that the internet is used locally is not to say that everyone thinks it always should be or agrees on how it should be. A few years ago I conducted focus-group interviews with college students to explore their sentiments about using the internet in their local personal relationships (Baym, 2005). Though my university was not noted for the diversity of the student body, these students' attitudes ranged widely, showing just how unsettled and potentially relationally problematic the topic could be. The students disagreed about whether it was appropriate to end a romantic relationship with an email or on IM or to use the internet as a means of confronting friends who had offended you when you were last together. Some loved the internet for ending relationships – especially women – while others were horrified at the thought. Most thought it was not a good way to handle conflict, but others explained that, since they anger easily, they would understand why their friend had chosen that medium, or that they were glad their friend had a means of raising an issue they didn't feel able to confront in person. At least one indicated that, were she confronted via the internet, she would consider it a sign of such disrespect that it would be grounds for ending the friendship.

Hall, Miltner, and I (Hall, Baym, & Miltner, 2014) looked at how a close relational partner's use of the mobile phone in their presence affected relational quality. What we found was that it depended in subtle ways on whether the behavior was public, semipublic, or private, but that, overall, it did not matter whether their partner followed what they agreed were the established social norms. What was important was following idiosyncratic norms. Those who felt that both they and their partner lived up to their personal standards were content, regardless of whether or not they lived up to societal standards. We concluded that there are many standards for what counts as appropriate, and that we should be wary of making judgements about the quality of others' relationships based on our own media ideologies.

What's a "friend?"

Another area in which we see disagreement is the practice of "friend-ing" in SNSs. If "friend" in an SNS doesn't mean what it means offline, or rather, if people one would introduce or consider as a "real" friend offline are only a subset of the people under that umbrella on an SNS, then there is potential for conflict over what it means to be a "friend" and who does and doesn't get included.

Many scholars of friendship have noted the ambiguity of personal connections (e.g. Parks, 2006; Rawlins, 1992). Online, as well as off, "the very term 'friendship' is both vague and symbolically charged and may denote many different types of relationship" (Kendall, 2002: 141). Partners within the same relationship may differ in how they categorize it. In SNSs, the technical necessity of labeling connections enhances this ambiguity. Pairs may differ on what kind of relation-ship their "friendship" represents (Fono & Raynes-Goldie, 2006); people may be held to account for the behaviors of "friends" they barely know (boyd & Heer, 2006; Donath & boyd, 2004); people may not be sure or disagree about what obligations such links entail (Kim & Yun, 2007). Sheer's (2011) survey of Hong Kong teens found that it was easy for them to define which of their MSN friends were stran-gers or close friends, but harder to define which were "friends."

Ambiguity can lead to conflict. Speaking of the term "friend" in LiveJournal, Fono and Raynes-Goldie (2006) say its "reflexivity and multiplicity of meaning causes much of the social anxiety, conflict and misunderstanding." In Cyworld, where the Korean kinship term "ilchon" is used, similar problems arise. "The ilchon metaphor," wrote Kim and Yun (2007), "created varying levels of relational ten-sions, depending on the degree of intimacy that the word ilchon connoted to users." When there are variants of labels available, that too can cause problems. One of boyd's (2006) teenage interviewees described MySpace's "Top 8" feature, which allowed people to list eight of their friends above all the others, as "psychological warfare." Musicians I interviewed had fans who took social media friendships to entail obligations the musicians did not intend.

How much information?

The 2008 word of the year, as decided by the editors of Webster's *World Dictionary*, was "overshare," meaning too much self-disclosure. In a YouTube video, the chief editor explains they chose it not just because it functions as both noun and verb, but because it reflected an important trend in public communication. "Some people use it disparagingly, they don't like oversharing," he explained; "Other people think oversharing is good. And sometimes there's a generational shift in how people look at this practice and therefore view the world." The cultural turmoil regarding how much disclosure is appropriate to whom under what circumstances, and its flip side, how much privacy must be protected, is indeed intense. Many online forums now use the acronym "TMI" for "Too Much Information," indicating both how routinized "over"-disclosure has become and how uncertain its appropriateness remains.

One element of the urge to disclose is, as we have discussed many times, the limits on cues, which can make it easier to be honest and make negative social repercussions of such honesty seem more distant and less likely. Another is the problem of disembodied and collapsed audiences as we discussed in chapter 5. As we saw there, people may imagine a different audience than all those whom they reach. Messages posted to an entire network may not be meant for everyone in that network. One person's TMI is another person's interesting insight or opportunity to offer support or solidarity. When personal information about us is accessed by viewers we did not imagine as part of our audience, the results can be embarrassing or life-altering. Information posted in SNSs has resulted in lost jobs, revoked visas, imprisonment, and tarnished reputations (Snyder, Carpenter, & Slauson, 2006).

The public mobile phone conversation is another example of a new communication practice that has unsettled the norms about disclosure. Many who object to having to overhear half of a telephone call seem particularly incensed when that call is personal. I vividly remember an elevator ride years ago with a student who was on the phone explaining her debt and asking for money. Most of the time the speakers seem not to care that they are being overheard, expecting, as

Goffman (1971) put it, that unintended audiences will provide "civil inattention" by pretending not to notice.

Summary

The questions around relationships and new media cannot be answered with utopian or dystopian oversimplifications, nor can they be understood as direct consequences either of technology or of the people who use it. Technological affordances intersect with personal, social, and cultural influences in ways that lead to media use meaning different things to different people in different relationships at different times. The very existence of interactive media that connect people across space gives rise to new connections. Again we see that the amount of cues in a medium influence its use and perception in new relationships. Sparse cues may lead to overestimating one another's appeal early in relationships, and, in long-standing ones, they may lead to conflict. As relationships develop, we seek media that offer more cues to enrich our ties. As our ties become enriched, we seek multiple media through which to interact. Media blend together into polymedia environments.

Qualities of media affect what we can use them to do in relationships. The size, portability, and discreetness of mobile phones makes them ideal for maintaining contact with loved ones, but can disrupt conversations with co-present partners. Asynchronous media that transcend space, such as texting and SNSs, lend themselves to long-distance relational maintenance, yet also have local uses. The ease of relational creation and maintenance online allows people to expand their circles to maintain and include more weak ties, but can also serve to support strong ties.

Social influences are also essential in shaping how we use new media, with whom, and for what purposes. Relationship stage is a factor. Early in relationships, we stick to the media in which we started or to safer low-cue media. As relationships progress, we expand into others. Personality matters. Shy and anxious people may prefer online media, while those who are sociable to begin with may gravitate toward any medium that allows more opportunities to interact with others. Culture matters. Our national norms about behavior shape whether and when we text or call, and likely shape other media use as well. Peer group, age, and gender norms influence which behaviors we engage in and what we take for normal.

Over time it has become more normal in many cultures for people to meet and begin relationships online, but the norms that guide which media people use when and for what purposes are still unclear. Disagreements about appropriate partners for mediated encounters, the boundaries and expectations of online relationships, and the topics of mediated interaction have relational implications. People can't take for granted that the people with whom they have relationships share their attitudes. Figuring out when and how to use media to communicate with each other is part of figuring out what it means to relate well to others. Individuals have to find their own comfort levels in different media. Relational partners have to negotiate how they will use media with one another and what that says about their relationship, lest it lead to conflict. As societies, we will surely reach an operational consensus on these matters. But by then, there will be a new medium, and the process will begin again.

Conclusion: the myth of cyberspace

For those who vividly remember life without them, the internet and the mobile phone can still seem like they came out of nowhere and took over our lives. Those who grew up with them as part of their daily environments don't get what the fuss is about and may not reflect critically on their use. There will be new communication technologies which today's children will find extraordinary and theirs will find mundane. This book was written for those who see the technologies it discusses as new and different, those who take them for granted, and those who will be thinking through technologies not yet invented.

When we first encounter interactive media yet to come, it will be almost entirely through the filters of communication. Our peers will talk about them. They will start turning up in news stories, movies, and television shows. We'll see ads for them. Maybe some of the people we know will use them. The topics these discourses stress, the tales they tell, and the impressions they pass along will be shaped by cultural forces far deeper and more powerful than a new machine or kind of interface. We all need to be savvy interpreters of the messages in popular media and interactions instead of taking them at face value.

The tendency is to think about new technologies deterministically, asking what they do to us, and whether that is good or bad. Thus we see concerns that mediated communication damages our ability to have face-to-face conversations, degrades language, undermines our connections to our communities and families, and replaces meaningful relationships with shallow substitutions. These perspectives co-exist in uneasy tensions with more optimistic scenarios in which mediation leads to closer families, more engaged citizens, more resources, and larger, better-connected social networks. Determinism can be recognized from its causal construction. The media are positioned as cause; the people are positioned as changed.

Yet people are adaptive, innovative, and influential in determining what technology is and will become. We use technology to suit our own aims, and developers redesign and innovate to provide people with better ways to do the things they didn't expect us to do. Computers were never envisioned as an interpersonal medium. Based on features alone, at first blush they seemed poorly positioned to become one. But, once networked, people took advantage of the affordances they did offer to make them into a social resource. Our drive to be social and find means of connecting with one another has been a guiding force in the internet's transformation from military and scientific network to staple of everyday life.

In 1984, William Gibson published *Neuromancer*, a futuristic computer-oriented science fiction novel in which he developed his neologism "cyberspace." He described it like this (ellipses in original):

> Cyberspace. A consensual hallucination experienced daily by billions of legitimate operators, in every nation, by children being taught mathematical concepts ... A graphic representation of data abstracted from the banks of every computer in the human system. Unthinkable complexity. Line of light ranged in the nonspace of the mind, clusters and constellations of data. Like city lights, receding. (Gibson, 1984/2000: 51)

Gibson depicted his fictional cyberspace as a hallucinated "nonspace" like a never-ending city. The transition from real world to cyberspace, when you "hit the switch, was instantaneous" (Gibson, 1984/2000: 55). For the book's protagonist, Case, a "cyberspace cowboy," cyberspace offered "the bodiless exultation" that gave him a reason to live (1984/2000: 5–6). Though relatively few of the people who talk about new media have read *Neuromancer*, Gibson's prescient envisioning remains timely and influential. Throughout this book, we have seen many instances in which mediated interaction is treated as a "hallucination," bodiless, unreal, and seductive in its modern offering of the pioneering freedom of reinvention enjoyed by the cowboys of American mythos.

Deterministic orientations toward digital communication are often built on this sense of mediated communication as apart and different from real, embodied face-to-face interaction. Determinism is built on juxtaposing the online with the offline, comparing, contrasting, and looking for clear lines of influence. Yet, as we have seen throughout this book, the idea that these are separate realms does not hold up to scrutiny. There may be fantasy realms where people use the internet to create selves with no bearing on their offline selves though, on close examination, even there the lines bleed. People do use the internet to create false identities. But these are the exceptions, not the norm. Taken as a whole, mediated communication is not a space, it is a set of tools people use to connect, each with meanings that depend on the others and which can only be understood as deeply embedded in and influenced by the daily realities of embodied life.

Machines do have effects. The seven key concepts outlined in the introduction describe the primary affordances offered by digital media and devices, which reverberate throughout their use and consequences. Digital media vary in the extent to which they are interactive, storable, replicable, mobile, and how many people they can reach. They differ in whether they demand that people interact simultaneously or whether there can be time lags between messages. They offer widely varying ranges of social cues which, as we've seen, can affect self-presentation, honesty, relational development, and relational maintenance. Without the communication technologies we have now, we could not sustain the mobile and dispersed social and professional networks which many people take for granted. Just as we need critical tools for understanding the messages about new media, we need conceptual tools to look concretely at the qualities of a medium, consider how those qualities have played out in previous innovations, and understand how they are modified or expanded in combination in new media. Platforms also have effects. Their formats, algorithms, and business models shape their relational affordances and hence our relationships. As more of our relational communication moves into commercial spaces where the accountability is to stock holders rather than users and the data traces of our interactions become assets to be bought and sold in ways we can't control, we should be ever more attentive to and critical of their practices.

People also have effects on our personal connections. We need to understand the social dynamics into which technologies are introduced and in which they play out. Technologies do not arise from blank slates. They are first developed and deployed in social and cultural contexts. As adapters or non-adapters, throughout history, we come to media with social agendas, social commitments, and deeply ingrained social practices that are largely replicated and enacted through new technologies. We have seen this in the ways that relational contexts, gender, nationality, and group identities influence mediated behaviors and perceptions.

If we see digital connections as part and parcel of our everyday lives and social contexts, it's hard to see them as agents of radical relational transformation, either utopian or dystopian. There are no doors where we can check our personal, social, cultural, and historical identities and world views before entering. We are not free to create entirely new kinds of communication, selves, relationships, groups, networks, or worlds. Nor are we forced into an alternative world of shallow simulations of inauthentic message exchange that take us farther from one another. Digital media aren't saving us or ruining us. They aren't reinventing us. But they are changing the ways we relate to others and ourselves in countless, pervasive ways. We stay in touch with more people for longer and across greater distances. We find and share supportive resources we could never access before. We create groups and relationships that cross boundaries we could rarely span before. In some cases, we wander into bad circumstances we would have been better off without. In others we find new opportunities.

To ask whether mediated communication is as good as unmediated interaction, or whether online relationships are as good as unmediated relationships, is to miss the point. It is not a question of either/or, of one vs. the other. It's a question of who's communicating, for what purposes, in what contexts, and what their expectations are. There are circumstances in which mediated interaction is preferable to face-to-face interaction, circumstances in which it is worse, and others when it's interchangeable. When people need more than mediation can provide, their use of the internet and telephones does not stop them from getting it. They just step away from the machines and get together, often using machines to coordinate that togetherness.

The research evidence and most of our personal experiences show that new media are not cyberspaces juxtaposed with the offline. My hope is that what eventually makes this book dated will be its evocation of a time when "online" and "offline" were still talked about in contrast to one another. But the history of new communication technologies suggests that the tendency to compare mediation to embodiment and look for the influence of the former upon the latter runs deep and will endure. New forms of mediation are disruptive in consistent ways throughout history. They evoke long-standing opposing tensions, or dialectics (Baxter & Montgomery, 2007). By transcending space, they enable us to connect with people who are not physically with us. Our bodies can be in one environment, yet our thoughts, feelings, and selves with someone elsewhere, positioning the body against the mind in a dualism that philosophers have been mulling for centuries. The tension between autonomy and interdependence, our desire to be left alone to be free to do what we like and our desire to need and be needed by others is exacerbated when new forms of technology allow both more control over one's own schedule and interactions and more continuous interconnection and accountability in our relationships. In all of our relationships, we need to find balances between how much we tell about, and how much we keep to, ourselves. When new media collapse and expand our audiences, this challenge inherent in personal connections is amplified. When technologies afford us new capabilities, which we then depend on machines to attain, we must ask where the boundary lies between the people and their machines. In the digital age, just as at the dawn of writing, media evoke questions about what it means to be authentically human.

New media for personal connection make the social norms we take for granted visible and offer opportunities for changing them. This is hardly new to the digital age. Social norms have been diversifying and changing since they first appeared millennia ago, and will continue to evolve as long as there are people. Our need to sort through social evolution will continue, and technologies will remain opportune vehicles for triggering this reflection. I have emphasized the social shaping approach to understanding technology, recognizing that the machines have affordances that can push us in some directions rather than others, and that people have long- and short-term cultural, situational, and personal trajectories that shape the development, uses, and consequences of technologies. This means that people have power. We can shape our personal connections through the ways we choose to understand and use embodied interaction, old media, and new media. The norms for appropriate use of communication media are in a continuous state of development. By being conscientious and aware of what media offer, what choices we make with them, and what consequences those choices have for us, we can intervene in and influence the process of norm development in our own relationships, our peer and familial groups, and our cultures. We can shape the contexts in which new media are developed and deployed.

The discourses around technology and the findings of research into its use and consequences tell us that, millennia after the inventions of the first communication technologies, we remain oriented toward preserving the authenticity of human connection and of ourselves. We develop and appropriate technologies as means of fostering meaningful personal connection. Along the way there are diversions, distractions, disasters, and delights. What kinds of connections we foster with what kinds of people evolves. Like everyone who's come before us, we don't know what the future holds for our relationships. But when I look at how quickly and effectively people took over networks of digital signals that were never meant for sociability in the service of our need to connect, I am optimistic that we will navigate our way through innovation without losing hold of one another.

References

2birds1blog (2008) *The Twenty Male Poses of Facebook*. (Online) Available at www.2birds1blog.com/2008/04/20-male-poses-of-facebook.html (accessed September 10, 2013).

Aakhus, M. & Rumsey, E. (2010) Crafting supportive communication online: a communication design analysis of conflict in an online support group. *Journal of Applied Communication Research* 38(1), 65–84.

Abbate, J. (1999) *Inventing the Internet*. Cambridge, MA: MIT Press.

Adelman, M. & Ahuvia, A. (1991) Mediated channels for mate seeking: a solution to involuntary singlehood? *Critical Studies in Mass Communication* 8, 273–89.

Agarwal, S. D., Bennett, W. L., Johnson, C. N., & Walker, S. (2014) A model of crowd-enabled organization: theory and methods for understanding the role of Twitter in the Occupy protests. *International Journal of Communication* 8, 646–72.

Ahlstrom, M., Lundberg, N. R., Zabriskie, R., Eggett, D., & Lindsay, G. B. (2012) Me, my spouse, and my avatar: the relationship between marital satisfaction and playing Massively Multiplayer Online Role-Playing Games (MMORPGs). *Journal of Leisure Research* 44(1), 1–22.

Albury, K., Crawford, K., Byron, P., & Mathews, B. (2013) *Young People and Sexting in Australia: Ethics, Representation and the Law*. (Online) Available at www.cci.edu.au/sites/default/files/Young_People_And_Sexting_Final. pdf.

Alper, M. (2013) War on Instagram: framing mobile photography apps in embedded photojournalism. *New Media & Society* (Advance Online Publication). Available at http://nms.sagepub.com/content/early/ 2013/09/16/1461444813504265.full.pdf+html (accessed August 27, 2014).

Altman, I. & Taylor, D. A. (1973) *Social Penetration: The Development of Interpersonal Relationships*. New York: Holt, Rinehart & Winston.

Andersen, P. & Guerrero, L. (1998) Principles of communication and emotion in social interaction. In P. Andersen & L. Guerrero (eds.)

Handbook of Communication and Emotion: Research, Theory, Applications, and Contexts. San Diego, CA: Academic Press, pp. 49–99.

Anderson, J. Q. (2005) *Imagining the Internet.* Lanham, MA: Rowman & Littlefield.

Antheunis, M. L. & Schouten, A. P. (2011) The effects of other-generated and system-generated cues on adolescents' perceived attractiveness on social networking sites. *Journal of Computer-Mediated Communication* 16(3), 391–406.

Baek, K., Holton, A., Harp, D., & Yaschur, C. (2011) The links that bind: uncovering novel motivations for linking on Facebook. *Computers in Human Behavior* 27(6), 2243–8.

Bailard, C. S. (2012) A field experiment on the internet's effect in an African election: savvier citizens, disaffected voters, or both? *Journal of Communication* 62(2), 330–44.

Baker, A. (2008) Down the rabbit hole: the role of place in the initiation and development of online relationships. In A. Barak (ed.) *Psychological Aspects of Cyberspace: Theory, Research, Applications.* New York: Cambridge University Press, pp. 163–84.

Banet-Weiser, S. (2004) Surfin' the net: children, parental obsolescence, and citizenship. In M. Sturken, D. Thomas, & S. J. Ball-Rokeach (eds.) *Technological Visions: The Hopes and Fears that Shape New Technologies.* Philadelphia, PA: Temple University Press, pp. 270–92.

—(2012) *Authentic™: The Politics of Ambivalence in a Brand Culture.* New York: New York University Press.

Baron, N. S. (1984) Computer mediated communication as a force in language change. *Visible Language* 18(2), 118–41.

—(1998) Letters by phone or speech by other means: the linguistics of email. *Language and Communication* 18, 133–70.

—(2000) *Alphabet to Email: How Written English Evolved and Where It's Heading.* London: Routledge.

—(2008) *Always On: Language in an Online and Mobile World.* New York: Oxford University Press.

Baron, N. S. & Hård af Segerstad, Y. (2010) Cross-cultural patterns in mobile phone use: public space and reachability in Sweden, the US, and Japan. *New Media & Society* 12(1), 13–34.

Baron, N. S. & Ling, R. (2003) IM and SMS: a linguistic comparison. Paper presented at Association of Internet Researchers Conference: Internet Research 4.0. Toronto, October.

Bartle, R. (2004) *Designing Virtual Worlds.* Berkeley, CA: New Riders Publishing.

Baxter, L. & Montgomery, B. (2007) *Relating: Dialogues and Dialectics*. New York: Guilford Press.

Baym, N. K. (1995) The performance of humor in computer-mediated communication. *Journal of Computer-Mediated Communication* 1(2). (Online) Available at http://onlinelibrary.wiley.com/doi/10.1111/j.1083-6101.1995.tb00327.x/full.

—(1996) Agreement and disagreement in a computer-mediated group. *Research on Language and Social Interaction* 29, 315–46.

—(2000) *Tune In, Log On: Soaps, Fandom, and Online Community*. Thousand Oaks, CA: Sage.

—(2005) Online communication in close relationships: revealing what surveys obscure. In M. Consalvo & M. Allen (eds.) *Internet Research Annual* Volume II. Berlin: Peter Lang, pp. 51–62.

—(2007) The new shape of online community: the example of Swedish independent music fandom. *First Monday* 12(8). (Online) Available at http://firstmonday.org/ojs/index.php/fm/article/view/1978/1853.

—(2012) Fans or friends? Seeing social media audiences as musicians do. *Participations: Journal of Audience & Reception Studies* 9(2), 286–316.

—(2013) The perils and pleasures of tweeting with fans. In K. Weller, A. Bruns, J. Burgess, M. Mahrt, & C. Puschmann (eds.) *Twitter and Society*. New York: Peter Lang, pp. 221–36.

Baym, N. K. & boyd, d. (2012) Socially mediated publicness: an introduction. *Journal of Broadcasting & Electronic Media* 56(3), 320–9.

Baym, N. K. & Burnett, R. (2009) Amateur experts: international fan labour in Swedish independent music. *International Journal of Cultural Studies* 12(5), 433–49.

Baym, N. K. & Ledbetter, A. (2009) Tunes that bind? Predicting friendship strength in a music-based social network. *Information, Community, & Society* 12(3), 408–27.

Baym, N. K., Zhang, Y. B., Kunkel, A., Lin, M.-C., & Ledbetter, A. (2007) Relational quality and media use. *New Media & Society* 9(5), 735–52.

Baym, N. K., Zhang, Y. B., & Lin, M. (2004) Social interactions across media: interpersonal communication on the internet, telephone, and face to face. *New Media & Society* 6(3), 299–318.

Benjamin, W. (2009 [1935]) *The Work of Art in the Age of Mechanical Reproduction*. New York: Classic Books America.

Bermudez, E. (2009) Death of blogger mom's daughter prompts outpouring from Internet community. *Los Angeles Times*, April 12. (Online) Available at http://articles.latimes.com/2009/apr/12/local/me-sickgirl12.

Berscheid, E., Dion, K., Hatfield, E., & Walster, G. W. (1971) Physical attractiveness and dating choice, a test of the matching hypothesis. *Journal of Experimental Social Psychology* 7, 173–89.

Bevan, J. L., Pfyl, J., & Barclay, B. (2012) Negative emotional and cognitive responses to being unfriended on Facebook: an exploratory study. *Computers in Human Behavior* 28(4), 1458–64.

Bijker, W. E., Hughes, T. P., & Pinch, T. J. (1987) *The Social Construction of Technological Systems: New Directions in the Sociology and History of Technology.* Cambridge, MA: MIT Press.

Bijker, W. E. & Law, J. (1992) *Shaping Technology / Building Society: Studies in Sociotechnical Change.* Cambridge, MA: MIT Press.

Bilton, N. (2014) Tangled web of memories lingers after a breakup. *The New York Times,* July 9. (Online) Available at www.nytimes.com/2014/07/10/fashion/on-social-media-memories-linger-after-a-breakup.html?_r=0.

Boddy, W. (2004) *New Media and Popular Imagination: Launching Radio, Television, and Digital Media in the United States.* Oxford: Oxford University Press.

Boellstorff, T. (2008) *Coming of Age in Second Life: An Anthropologist Explores the Virtually Human.* Princeton, NJ: Princeton University Press.

Bordbar, F. (2010) Gender, identity, and language use: a case of Tehrani teenage bloggers' virtual speech community. *International Journal of Language Studies* 4(2), 119–38.

Boulianne, S. (2009) Does internet use affect engagement? A meta-analysis of research. *Political Communication* 26(2), 193–211.

Bourdieu, P. (1984) *Distinction: A Social Critique of the Judgement of Taste.* London: Routledge.

boyd, d. (2006) Friends, friendsters, and MySpace top 8: writing community into being on social network sites. *First Monday* 11(12). (Online) Available at http://firstmonday.org/ojs/index.php/fm/article/view/1418/1336.

boyd, d. & Ellison, N. B. (2007) Social network sites: definition, history, and scholarship. *Journal of Computer-Mediated Communication* 13(1). (Online) Available at http://onlinelibrary.wiley.com/doi/10.1111/j.1083-6101.2007.00393.x/full (accessed September 10, 2013).

boyd, d., Hargittai, E., Schultz, J., & Palfrey, J. (2011) Why parents help their children lie to Facebook about age: unintended consequences of the "Children's Online Privacy Protection Act." *First Monday.* (Online) Available at http://journals.uic.edu/ojs/index.php/fm/article/view/3850/3075.

boyd, d. & Heer, J. (2006) Profiles as conversation: networked identity performance on Friendster. In *Proceedings of Thirty-Ninth Hawai'i*

International Conference on System Sciences. Los Alamitos, CA: IEEE Press.

Brand, R. J., Bonatsos, A., D'Orazio, R., & DeShong, H. (2012) What is beautiful is good, even online: correlations between photo attractiveness and text attractiveness in men's online dating profiles. *Computers in Human Behavior* 28(1), 166–70.

Brenner, J. & Smith, A. (2013) 72% of online adults are social networking site users. *Pew Internet & American Life Project.* (Online) Available at www.pewinternet.org/files/old-media//Files/Reports/2013/PIP_Social_networking_sites_update_PDF.pdf.

Briggs, A. & Burke, P. (2009) *A Social History of the Media: From Gutenberg to the Internet.* Malden, MA: Polity.

Brock, A. (2012) From the blackhand side: Twitter as a cultural conversation. *Journal of Broadcasting & Electronic Media* 56(4), 529–49.

Bruns, A. & Burgess, J. (2011) The use of Twitter hashtags in the formation of ad hoc publics. Paper presented at the 6th European Consortium for Political Research General Conference. Reykjavik, August.

Burgess, J. (2006) Hearing ordinary voices: cultural studies, vernacular creativity and digital storytelling. *Continuum: Journal of Media and Cultural Studies* 20(2), 201–14.

Burgess, J. & Baym, N. K. (2014) Web history and popular memory. Paper presented at the International Communication Association Conference. Seattle, WA, May.

Burgess, J. & Green, J. (2009) *YouTube: Online Video and Participatory Culture.* Cambridge: Polity.

Burleson, B. R. & Kunkel, A. (2006) Revisiting the different cultures thesis: an assessment of sex differences and similarities in supportive communication. In K. Dindia & D. Canary (eds.) *Sex Differences and Similarities in Communication*, 2nd edn. Mahwah, NJ: Lawrence Erlbaum, pp. 135–55.

Burleson, B. R. & MacGeorge, E. L. (2002) Supportive communication. In M. L. Knapp & J. A. Daly (eds.) *Handbook of Interpersonal Communication* 3rd edn. Thousand Oaks, CA: Sage, pp. 374–424.

Byrne, D. N. (2007) Public discourse, community concerns, and civic engagement: exploring black social networking traditions on BlackPlanet.com. *Journal of Computer-Mediated Communication* 13(1). (Online) Available at http://onlinelibrary.wiley.com/doi/10.1111/j.1083-6101.2007.00398.x/full.

Campbell, S. W. & Kwak, N. (2009) Political involvement in "mobilized" society: the interactive relationships among mobile communication, social network characteristics, and political life. Paper presented at

International Communication Association Pre-conference, Mobile.

Campbell, S. & Kwak, N. (2011) Political involvement in "mobilized" society: the interactive relationships among mobile communication, network characteristics, and political participation. *Journal of Communication* 61(6), 1005–24.

Campbell, S. & Russo, R. (2003) The social construction of mobile telephony: an application of the social influence model to perceptions and uses of mobile phones within personal communication networks. *Communication Monographs* 70, 317–34.

Carnevale, P. & Probst, T. M. (1997) Conflict on the internet. In S. Kiesler (ed.) *Culture of the Internet*. Mahwah, NJ: Lawrence Erlbaum, pp. 233–55.

Carr, N. (2008) Is Google making us stupid? *The Atlantic*, July/August. (Online) Available at www.theatlantic.com/doc/200807/google.

Cassell, J. & Cramer, M. (2007) Hi tech or high risk? Moral panics about girls online. In T. MacPherson (ed.) *Digital Youth, Innovation, and the Unexpected*. The MacArthur Foundation Series on Digital Media and Learning. Cambridge, MA: MIT Press, pp. 53–75.

Cassidy, E. M. (2013) Gay men, social media and self-presentation: managing identities in Gaydar, Facebook and beyond. (Dissertation) Available at http://eprints.qut.edu.au/61773.

Castronova, E. (2004) The price of bodies: a hedonic pricing model of avatar attributes in a synthetic world. *Kyklos* 57(2), 173–96.

Caughlin, J. P. & Sharabi, L. L. (2013) A communicative interdependence perspective of close relationships: the connections between mediated and unmediated interactions matter. *Journal of Communication* 63(5), 873–93.

Chan, D. K. S. & Cheng, G. H. L. (2004) A comparison of offline and online friendship qualities at different stages of relationship development. *Journal of Social and Personal Relationships* 21(3), 305–20.

Chayko, M. (2008) *Portable Communities: The Social Dynamics of Online and Mobile Connectedness*. Albany, NY: SUNY Press.

Chen, G. M. (2012) Why do women write personal blogs? Satisfying needs for self-disclosure and affiliation tell part of the story. *Computers in Human Behavior* 28(1), 171–80.

Chen, W., Boase, J., & Wellman, B. (2002) The global villagers: comparing internet users and uses around the world. In B. Wellman & C. Haythornthwaite (eds.) *The Internet in Everyday Life*. Malden, MA: Blackwell, pp. 74–113.

Cherny, L. (1999) *Conversation and Community: Chat in a Virtual World*. Stanford: CSLI Publications.

Choi, J. H. (2006) Living in Cyworld: contextualising cy-ties in South Korea.

In A. Bruns & J. Jacobs (eds.) *Use of Blogs*. New York: Peter Lang, pp. 173–86.

Christensen, H. S. (2011) Political activities on the internet: slacktivism or political participation by other means? *First Monday* 2(7). (Online) Available at http://firstmonday.org/ojs/index.php/fm/article/view/3336/2767.

Citron, D. K. & Norton, H. (2011) Intermediaries and hate speech: fostering digital citizenship for our information age. *Boston University Law Review* 91, 1435–84.

Clark, L. S. (1998) Dating on the net: teens and the rise of "pure" relationships. In S. Jones (ed.) *Cybersociety 2.0: Revisiting Computer Mediated Communication and Community*. Thousand Oaks, CA: Sage, pp. 159–83.

Cockroft, L. (2009) Facebook "enhances intelligence" but Twitter "diminishes it" claims psychologist. *Telegraph*, September 7. (Online) Available at www.telegraph.co.uk/technology/twitter/6147668/Facebook-enhances-intelligence-but-Twitter-diminishes-it-claims-psychologist.html.

Cohen, S. (1972) *Folk Devils and Moral Panics*. London: MacGibbon and Kee.

Cole, J. (2000) *Surveying the Digital Future*. UCLA Center for Communication Policy. (Online) Available at www.digitalcenter.org/wp-content/uploads/2012/12/2000_digital_future_report_year1.pdf.

—(2013) *Surveying the Digital Future*. USC Annenberg School Center for the Digital Future. (Online) Available at www.digitalcenter.org/wp-content/uploads/2013/06/2013-Report.pdf.

Coleman, J. S. (1988) Social capital in the creation of human capital. *The American Journal of Sociology* 94, S95–S120.

Convince & Convert (2012) 42 percent of consumers complaining in social media expect 60 minute response time. (Online) Available at www.convinceandconvert.com/social-media-research/42-percent-of-consumers-complaining-in-social-media-expect-60-minute-response-time.

Copher, J. I., Kanfer, A. G., & Walker, M. B. (2002) Everyday communication patterns of heavy and light email users. In B. Wellman & C. Haythornthwaite (eds.) *The Internet in Everyday Life*. Malden, MA: Blackwell, pp. 263–90.

Cortese, J. & Seo, M. (2012) The role of social presence in opinion expression during FtF and CMC discussions. *Communication Research Reports* 29(1), 44–53.

Cover, R. (2012) Performing and undoing identity online: social networking, identity theories and the incompatibility of online profiles and friendship regimes. *Convergence* 18(2), 177–93.

Craig, E. & Wright, K. B. (2012) Computer-mediated relational development and maintenance on Facebook. *Communication Research Reports* 29(2), 119–29.

Crawford, K. (2011) Listening not lurking: the neglected form of participation. In H. Grief, L. Hjorth, & A. Lasén (eds.) *Cultures of Participation*. Berlin: Peter Lang, pp. 63–77.

Culnan, M. J. & Markus, M. L. (1987) Information technologies. In F. M. Jablin, L. L. Putnam, H. Roberts, & L. W. Porter (eds.) *Handbook of Organizational Computing: An Interdisciplinary Perspective*. Newbury Park, CA: Sage, pp. 420–43.

Curtis, P. (1997) Mudding: social phenomena in text-based virtual realities. In S. Kiesler (ed.) *Culture of the Internet*. Mahwah, NJ: Lawrence Erlbaum, pp. 121–42.

Cutrona, C. E. & Russell, D. W. (1990) Type of social support and specific stress: toward a theory of optimal matching. In B. R. Sarason, I. G. Sarason, & G. R. Pearce (eds.) *Social Support: An Interactional View*. New York: Wiley, pp. 319–66.

Daft, R. L. & Lengel, R. H. (1984) Information richness: a new approach to managerial behaviour and organizational design. *Research in Organizational Behaviour* 6, 191–233.

Dahlgren, P. (2005) The internet, public spheres, and political communication: dispersion and deliberation. *Political Communication* 22, 147–62.

—(2009) *Media and Political Engagement: Citizens, Communication, and Democracy*. Cambridge: Cambridge University Press.

Danet, B. (1997) Books, letters, documents: the changing aesthetics of texts in late print culture. *Journal of Material Culture* 2(1), 5–38.

—(1998) Text as mask: gender, play and performance on the internet. In S. G. Jones (ed.) *Cybersociety 2.0: Computer-Mediated Communication and Community Revisited*. Thousand Oaks, CA: Sage, pp. 129–58.

—(2001) *Cyberpl@y: Communicating Online*. Oxford: Berg.

Darics, E. (2010) Politeness in computer-mediated discourse of a virtual team. *Journal of Politeness Research* 6(1), 129–50.

Davis, K. (2012) Tensions of identity in a networked era: young people's perspectives on the risks and rewards of online self-expression. *New Media & Society* 14(4), 634–51.

DeAndrea, D. C. & Walther, J. B. (2011) Attributions for inconsistencies between online and offline self-presentations. *Communication Research* 38(6), 805–25.

de Sola Pool, I. (1977) *The Social Impact of the Telephone.* Cambridge, MA: MIT Press.

de Zúñiga, G. & Valenzuela, S. (2010) The mediating path to a stronger citizenship: online and offline networks, weak ties, and civic engagement. *Communication Research* 38(3), 397–421.

Dimmick, J. (2003) *Media Competition and Coexistence: The Theory of the Niche.* Mahwah, NJ: Lawrence Erlbaum Associates.

Dimmick, J., Feaster, J. C., & Ramirez Jr., A. (2011) The niches of interpersonal media: relationships in time and space. *New Media and Society* 8, 1265–82.

Dimmick, J., Kline, S.L., & Stafford, L. (2000) The gratification niches of personal e-mail and the telephone: competition, displacement, and complementarity. *Communication Research* 27(2), 227–48.

Donath, J. (2007) Signals in social supernets. *Journal of Computer-Mediated Communication* 13(1). (Online) Available at http://onlinelibrary.wiley.com/doi/10.1111/j.1083-6101.2007.00394.x/full.

Donath, J. & boyd, d. (2004) Public displays of connection. *BT Technology Journal* 22(4), 71–82.

Douglas, S. (2004 [1999]) *Listening In: Radio and the American Imagination.* Minneapolis, MN: University of Minnesota Press.

Dresner, E. & Herring, S. C. (2010) Functions of the nonverbal in CMC: emoticons and illocutionary force. *Communication Theory* 20(3), 249–68.

Driscoll, K. (2014) Hobbyist inter-networking and the popular internet imaginary: forgotten histories of networked personal computing. (Dissertation) Available at http://digitallibrary.usc.edu/cdm/compoundobject/collection/p15799coll3/id/444362/rec/2.

Dundes, A. (1977) Who are the folk? In W. Bascom (ed.) *Frontiers of Folklore.* Boulder, CO: Westview Press, pp. 17–35.

Duran, R. L., Kelly, L., & Rotaru, T. (2011) Mobile phones in romantic relationships and the dialectic of autonomy versus connection. *Communication Quarterly* 59(1), 19–26.

Ellison, N. & boyd, d. (2013) Sociality through social network sites. In W. Dutton (ed.) *The Oxford Handbook of Internet Studies.* Oxford: Oxford University Press, pp. 151–72.

Ellison, N., Hancock, J. T., & Toma, C. L. (2012) Profile as promise: a framework for conceptualizing veracity in online dating self-presentations. *New Media & Society* 14(1), pp. 45–62.

Ellison, N., Heino, R., & Gibbs, J. (2006) Managing impressions online: self-presentation processes in the online dating environment. *Journal of Computer-Mediated Communication* 11(2). (Online) Available at http://onlinelibrary.wiley.com/doi/10.1111/j.1083-6101.2006.00020.x/full.

Ellison, N., Steinfeld, C., & Lampe, C. (2007) The benefits of Facebook "friends": exploring the relationship between college students' use of online social networks and social capital. *Journal of Computer-Mediated Communication* 12(4). (Online) Available at http://onlinelibrary.wiley.com/doi/10.1111/j.1083-6101.2007.00367.x/full.

—(2009) Connection strategies: relationship formation and maintenance on social network sites. Paper presented at International Communication Association Conference. Chicago, IL, May.

Ellison, N., Vitak, J., Gray, R., & Lampe, C. (2014) Cultivating social resources on social network sites: Facebook relationship maintenance behaviors and their role in social capital. *Journal of Computer-Mediated Communication* 19(4), 855–70.

Facer, K. (2012) After the moral panic? Reframing the debate about child safety online. *Discourse: Studies in the Cultural Politics of Education* 33(3), 397–413.

Fang, I. (2008) *Alphabet to Internet: Mediated Communication in Our Lives.* St. Paul, MN: Rada Press.

Ferrara, K., Brunner, H., & Whittemore, G. (1991) Interactive written discourse as an emergent register. *Written Communication* 8, 8–34.

Finkenauer, C., Engels, R. C. M. E., Meeus, W., & Oosterwegel, A. (2002) Self and identity in early adolescence: the pains and gains of knowing who and what you are. In T. H. Brinthaupt & R. P. Lipka (eds.) *Understanding Early Adolescent Self and Identity: Applications and Interventions.* Albany, NY: SUNY Press, pp. 25–56.

Fiore, A. T. & Donath, J. S. (2005) Homophily in online dating: when do you like someone like yourself? Paper presented at ACM Computer–Human Interaction Conference. Portland, OR.

Fischer, C. S. (1992) *America Calling: A Social History of the Telephone to 1940.* Berkeley, CA: University of California Press.

Flanagin, A. J. & Metzger, M. J. (2001) Internet use in the contemporary media environment. *Human Communication Research* 27, 153–81.

Florini, S. (2013) Tweets, tweeps, and signifyin': communication and cultural performance on "Black Twitter." *Television & New Media* 15(3), 223–37.

Fono, D. & Raynes-Goldie, K. (2006) Hyperfriendship and beyond: friends and social norms on LiveJournal. In M. Consalvo & C. Haythornthwaite (eds.) *Internet Research Annual*, Volume IV: *Selected Papers from the AOIR Conference.* New York: Peter Lang, pp. 91–103.

Fornås, J., Klein, K., Ladendorf, J., Sundén, J., & Sveningsson, M. (2002) Into digital borderlands. In J. Fornås, K. Klein, J. Ladendorf, J. Sunden, & M. Sveningsson (eds.) *Digital Borderlands: Cultural Studies of Identity and Interactivity on the Internet.* New York: Peter Lang, pp. 1–47.

Fortunati, L. (2005) Is body to body communication still the prototype? *The Information Society* 21, 53–61.

Fox, S. & Boyles, J. L. (2012) Disability in the digital age. *Pew Internet & American Life Project.* (Online) Available at www.pewinternet. org/2012/08/06/disability-in-the-digital-age.

Fragoso, S. (2006) WTF, a crazy Brazilian invasion. In F. Sudweeks & H. Hrachovec (eds.) *Proceedings of CATaC 2006.* Murdoch, Australia: Murdoch University Press, pp. 255–74.

Fulk, J. (1993) Social construction of communication technology. *Academy of Management Journal* 36, 921–50.

Fulk, J. & Collins-Jarvis, L. (2001) Wired meetings: technological mediation of organizational gatherings. In F. M. Jablin & L. L. Putnam (eds.) *The New Handbook of Organizational Communication: Advances in Theory, Research and Methods.* Thousand Oaks, CA: Sage, pp. 624–63.

Fulk, J., Steinfield, C. W., Schmitz, J., & Power, J. G. (1987) A social information processing model of media use in organizations. *Communication Research* 14(5), 529–52.

Gentile, B., Twenge, J. M., Freeman, E. C., & Campbell, W. K. (2012) The effect of social networking websites on positive self-views: an experimental investigation. *Computers in Human Behavior* 28(5), 1929–33.

Gergen, K. J. (1991) *The Saturated Self: Dilemmas of Identity in Contemporary Life.* New York: Basic Books.

—(2002) The challenge of absent presence. In J. E. Katz & M. Aakhus (eds.) *Perpetual Contact: Mobile Communication, Private Talk, Public Performance.* Cambridge: Cambridge University Press, pp. 227–41.

—(2008) Mobile communication and the transformation of the democratic process. In J. E. Katz (ed.) *Handbook of Mobile Communication Studies.* Cambridge, MA: MIT Press, pp. 297–310.

Gershon, I. (2010) *The Breakup 2.0: Disconnecting over New Media.* Ithaca, NY: Cornell University Press.

Gibson, J. J. (1977) The theory of affordances. In R. Shaw & J. Bransford (eds.) *Perceiving, Acting and Knowing.* Hillsdale, NJ: Erlbaum, pp. 67–82.

Gibson, W. (1984/2000) *Neuromancer,* ACE edn. New York: The Berkley Publishing Group.

Giddens, A. (1993) *The Transformation of Intimacy.* Palo Alto, CA: Stanford University Press.

Gilbert, E., Karahalios, K., & Sandvig, C. (2008) The network in the garden: an empirical analysis of social media in rural life. Paper presented at CHI 2008 conference. Florence, Italy, April.

Gil de Zúñiga, H. & Valenzuela, S. (2011) The mediating path to a stronger citizenship: online and offline networks, weak ties and civic engagement. *Communication Research* 38(3), 397–421.

Gillespie, T. (2010) The politics of "platforms." *New Media & Society* 12(3), 347–64.

Goffman, E. (1959) *The Presentation of Self in Everyday Life*. Garden City, NY: Doubleday.

—(1963) *Behavior in Public Places: Notes on the Social Organization of Gatherings*. New York: Free Press.

—(1971) *Relations in Public: Microstudies of the Public Order*. New York: Basic Books.

Golder, S. A., Wilkinson, D., & Huberman, B. A. (2007) Rhythms of social interaction: messaging within a massive online network. In C. Steinfield, B. Pentland, M. Ackerman, & N. Contractor (eds.) *Proceedings of Third International Conference on Communities and Technologies*. London: Springer, pp. 41–66.

Goodwin, C. (1981) *Conversational Organization: Interaction between Speakers and Hearers*. New York: Academic Press.

Granovetter, M. S. (1973) The strength of weak ties. *American Journal of Sociology* 78, 1160–80.

Gray, K. (2012) Intersecting oppressions and online communities: examining the experiences of women of color in Xbox Live. *Information, Communication, & Society* 15(3), 411–28.

Green-Hamann, S., Eichhorn, K. C., & Sherblom, J. C. (2011) An exploration of why people participate in *Second Life* social support groups. *Journal of Computer-Mediated Communication* 16(4), 465–91.

Gross, R. & Acquisti, A. (2005) Information revelation and privacy in online social networks. In *Proceedings of the ACM WPES'05*. Alexandria, VA: ACM Press, pp. 71–80.

Gurak, L. L. (1997) *Persuasion and Privacy in Cyberspace: The Online Protests over Lotus MarketPlace and the Clipper Chip*. New Haven, CT: Yale University Press.

—(2001) *Cyberliteracy: Navigating the Internet with Awareness*. New Haven, CT: Yale University Press.

Haas, S. M., Irr, M. E., Jennings, N. A., & Wagner, L. M. (2011) Communicating thin: a grounded model of online negative enabling support groups in the pro-anorexia movement. *New Media & Society* 13(1), 40–57.

Haddon, L. (2006) The contribution of domestication research. *The Information Society* 22(4), 195–204.

Hall, J. A. & Baym, N. K. (2012) Calling and texting (too much): mobile maintenance expectations, (over)dependence, entrapment, and friendship satisfaction. *New Media & Society* 14(2), 316–31.

Hall, J. A., Baym, N. K., & Miltner, K. M. (2014) Put down that phone and talk to me: understanding the roles of mobile phones – norm adherence and similarity in relationships. *Mobile Media & Communication* 2(2), 134–53.

Hall, J. A. & Pennington, N. (2012) What you can really know about someone from their Facebook profile (and where you should look to find out). In C. Cunningham (ed.) *Social Networking and Impression Management*. Lanham, MD: Lexington Books, pp. 247–70.

Hall, J. A., Pennington, N., & Leuders, A. (2013) Impression management and formation on Facebook: a lens model approach. *New Media & Society* 21(4), 460–87.

Hamilton, K., Karahalios, K., Sandvig, C., & Eslami, M. (2014) A path to understanding the effects of algorithm awareness. In *Proceedings of the ACM CHI Conference on Human Factors in Computing Systems*. (Online) Available at http://dl.acm.org/citation.cfm?id=2559206.2578883&coll=D L&dl=ACM&CFID=413711084&CFTOKEN=99840305.

Hampton, K. N. (2010) Internet use and the concentration of disadvantage: glocalization and the urban underclass. *American Behavioral Scientist* 53(8), 1111–32.

Hampton, K. (2011) Comparing bonding and bridging ties for democratic engagement: everyday use of communication technologies within social networks for civic and civil behaviors. *Information, Communication & Society* 14(4), 510–28.

Hampton, K., Lee, C.-J., & Her, E. J. (2011) How new media affords network diversity: direct and mediated access to social capital through participation in local social settings. *New Media & Society* 13(7), 1031–49.

Hampton, K. N., Livio, O., & Sessions, L. (2010) The social life of wireless urban spaces: internet use, social networks, and the public realm. *Journal of Communication* 60(4), 701–22.

Hampton, K. N., Sessions, L., & Her, E. J. (2011) Core networks, social isolation, and new media: how internet and mobile phone use is related to network size and diversity. *Information, Communication & Society* 14(1), 130–55.

Hampton, K. N., Sessions-Goulet, L., & Albanesius, G. (2014) Change in the social life of urban public spaces: the rise of mobile phones and women, and the decline of aloneness over 30 years. *Urban Studies*. (Online) Available at http://usj.sagepub.com/content/early/2014/05/28/004209 8014534905.

Hampton, K. N. & Wellman, B. (2003) Neighboring in Netville: how the internet supports community and social capital in a wired suburb. *City & Community* 2(4), 277–311.

Hancock, J. T., Thom-Santelli, J., & Ritchie, T. (2004) Deception and design: the impact of communication technology on lying behavior. Paper presented at CHI 2004 conference. Vienna, Austria, April.

Hansen, D., Ackerman, M., Resnick, P., & Munson, S. (2007) Virtual community maintenance with a repository. In *Proceedings of ASIS&T 2007*. Milwaukee, WI, pp. 1–20.

Haraway, D. (1990) A manifesto for cyborgs: science, technology, and socialist feminism in the 1980s. In L. J. Nicholson (ed.) *Feminism/ Postmodernism*. London: Routledge, pp. 190–233.

Hård af Segerstad, Y. (2005) Language use in Swedish mobile text messaging. In R. Ling & P. Pederson (eds.) *Mobile Communications: Renegotiations of the Social Sphere*. London: Springer, pp. 313–34.

Hardaker, C. (2010) Trolling in asynchronous computer-mediated communication: from user discussions to academic definitions. *Journal of Politeness Research* 6(2), 215–42.

Hargittai, E. (2002) Second-level digital divide: differences in people's online skills. *First Monday* 7(4). (Online) Available at http://firstmonday.org/ojs/index.php/fm/article/view/942/864for.

Hargittai, E. & Hinnant, A. (2008) Digital inequality: differences in young adults' use of the internet. *Communication Research* 35(5), 602–21.

Harper, R., Bird, C., Zimmerman, T., & Murphy, B. (2013) Dwelling in software: aspects of the felt-life of engineers in large software projects. In *Proceedings of the 13th European Conference on Computer Supported Creative Work*. Paphos, Cyprus, pp. 163–80.

Hartelius, E. (2005) A content-based taxonomy of blogs and the formation of a virtual community. *Kaleidoscope: A Graduate Journal of Qualitative Communication Research* 4, 71–91.

Hassid, J. (2102) Safety valve or pressure cooker: blogs in Chinese political life. *Journal of Communication* 62, 212–30.

Haythornthwaite, C. (2002) Strong, weak, and latent ties and the impact of new media. *Information Society* 18, 385–401.

—(2005) Social networks and internet connectivity effects. *Information, Communication, & Society* 8(2), 125–47.

Haythornthwaite, C. & Wellman, B. (2002) The internet in everyday life: an introduction. In B. Wellman & C. Haythornthwaite (eds.) *The Internet in Everyday Life*. Malden, MA: Blackwell, pp. 3–41.

Helsper, E. & Eynon, R. (2013) Distinct skill pathways to digital engagement. *European Journal of Communication* 28(6), 696–713.

Henderson, S. & Gilding, M. (2004) "I've never clicked this much with anyone in my life": trust and hyperpersonal communication in online friendships. *New Media & Society* 6, 487–506.

Herring, S. (1996) Posting in a different voice: gender and ethics in computer-mediated communication. In C. Ess (ed.) *Philosophical Perspectives on Computer-Mediated Communication*. Albany, NY: SUNY Press, pp. 115–45.

—(2001) Computer-mediated discourse. In D. Schiffrin, D. Tannen, & H. E. Hamilton (eds.) *The Handbook of Discourse Analysis*. Malden, MA: Blackwell, pp. 612–34.

Herring, S. & Danet, B. (2003) Editor's introduction: the multilingual internet. *Journal of Computer-Mediated Communication* 9(1). (Online) Available at http://onlinelibrary.wiley.com/doi/10.1111/j.1083-6101.2003. tb00354.x/full.

Herring, S. C., Paolillo, J. C., Ramos-Vielba, I., et al. (2007) Language networks on LiveJournal. In *Proceedings of the Fortieth Hawaii International Conference on System Sciences*. Los Alamitos, CA. (Online) Available at http://ella.slis.indiana.edu/~herring/hicss07.pdf.

Hijazi-Omari, H. & Ribak, R. (2008) Playing with fire: on the domestication of the mobile phone among Palestinian girls in Israel. *Information, Communication & Society* 11, 149–66.

Hiltz, S. R. & Turoff, M. (1978) *The Network Nation: Human Communication via Computer*. Reading, MA: Addison-Wesley.

Hochman, N. & Manovich, L. (2013) Zooming into an Instagram city: reading the local through social media. *First Monday* 18(7). (Online) Available at http://firstmonday.org/ojs/index.php/fm/article/view/4711/3698.

Hochman, N. & Schwartz, R. (2012) Visualizing Instagram: tracing cultural visual rhythms. In *Proceedings of the International AAAI Conference on Weblogs and Social Media*. (Online) Available at https://www.aaai.org/ocs/index.php/ICWSM/ICWSM12/paper/view/4782/5091.

Horrigan, J. & Rainie, L. (2002) The broadband difference: how online behavior changes with high-speed internet connections. *Pew Internet & American Life Project*. (Online) Available at www.pewinternet. org/Reports/2002/The-Broadband-Difference-How-online-behavior changes-with-highspeed-Internet-connections.aspx.

Horst, H. A. (2010) Families. In M. Ito et al. (eds.) *Hanging Out, Messing Around, and Geeking Out: Kids Living and Learning with New Media*. Cambridge, MA: MIT Press, pp. 149–94.

Houser, M. L., Fleuriet, C., & Estrada, D. (2012) The cyber factor: an analysis of relational maintenance through the use of computer-mediated communication. *Communication Research Reports* 29(1), 34–43.

Howard, P. N. & Parks, M. R. (2012) Social media and political change: capacity, constraint, and consequence. *Journal of Communication* 62, 359–62.

Howard, P. N., Rainie, L., & Jones, S. (2001) Days and nights on the internet: the impact of a diffusing technology. *American Behavioral Scientist* 45(3), 383–404.

Humphreys, L. (2005) Cell phones in public: social interactions in a wireless era. *New Media & Society* 7(6), 810–33.

—(2007) Mobile social networks and social practice: a case study of Dodgeball. *Journal of Computer-Mediated Communication*, 13(1). (Online) Available at http://onlinelibrary.wiley.com/doi/10.1111/j.1083-6101.2007.00399.x/full.

—(2010) Mobile social networks and urban public space. *New Media & Society* 12(5), 763–78.

—(2011) Who's watching whom? A study of interactive technology and surveillance. *Journal of Communication* 61(4), 575–95.

Institut za Etnologiju i Folkloristiku (2004) *Etnografije interneta*. Zagreb: Ibis grafika.

International Telecommunications Union (2013) Measuring the information society. (Online) Available at www.itu.int/en/ITU-D/Statistics/Documents/publications/mis2013/MIS2013_without_Annex_4.pdf.

Internet Safety Technical Task Force (2008) *Enhancing Child Safety & Online Technologies*. Cambridge, MA: Berkman Center for Internet & Society, Harvard University. (Online) Available at http://cyber.law.harvard.edu/pubrelease/isttf.

Ishii, K. (2006) Implications of mobility: the uses of personal communication media in everyday life. *Journal of Communication* 56(2), 346–65.

Ito, M. (1997) Virtually embodied: the reality of fantasy in a multi-user dungeon. In D. Porter (ed.) *Internet Culture*. New York: Routledge, pp. 87–110.

Ito, M., Baumer, S., Bittanti, M., et al. (2010) *Hanging Out, Messing Around, and Geeking Out*. Cambridge, MA: MIT Press.

Jenkins, H. (2006) *Convergence Culture: Where Old and New Media Collide*. New York: New York University Press.

Jiang, L. C., Bazarova, N. N., & Hancock, J. T. (2011) The disclosure–intimacy link in computer-mediated communication: an attributional extension of the hyperpersonal model. *Human Communication Research* 37(1), 58–77.

John, N. A. (2013a) Sharing and Web 2.0: the emergence of a keyword. *New Media & Society* 15(2), 167–82.

— (2013b) The social logics of sharing. *The Communication Review* 16(3), 113–31.

Jones, L. M., Mitchell, K. J., & Finkelhor, D. (2013) Online harassment in context: trends from three youth internet safety surveys (2000, 2005, 2010). *Psychology of Violence* 3(1), 53–69.

Jung, J., Qiu, J., & Kim, Y. C. (2001) Internet connectedness and inequality: beyond the digital divide. *Communication Research* 28(4), 507–35.

Jung, Y., Song, H., & Vorderer, P. (2012) Why do people post and read personal messages in public? The motivation of using personal blogs and its effect on users' loneliness, belonging, and well-being. *Computers in Human Behavior* 28, 1626–33.

Kapedzic, S. & Herring, S. C. (2011) Gender, communication, and self-presentation in teen chatrooms revisited: have patterns changed? *Journal of Computer-Mediated Communication* 17(1), 39–59.

Kasesniemi, E. & Rautiainen, P. (2002) Mobile culture of children and teenagers in Finland. In J. E. Katz & M. Aakhus (eds.) *Perpetual Contact: Mobile Communication, Private Talk, Public Performance*. Cambridge: Cambridge University Press, pp. 170–92.

Katz, J. E. & Aakhus, M. (2002) Introduction: framing the issues. In J. E. Katz & M. Aakhus (eds.) *Perpetual Contact: Mobile Communication, Private Talk, Public Performance*. Cambridge: Cambridge University Press, pp. 1–13.

Katz, J. E. & Aspden, P. (1997) A nation of strangers? *Communications of the ACM* 40(12, December), 81–6.

Katz, J. E. & Rice, R. E. (2002) Project Syntopia: social consequences of internet use. *IT & Society* 1(1), 166–79.

Kendall, L. (2002) *Hanging out in the Virtual Pub: Masculinities and Relationships Online*. Berkeley, CA: University of California Press.

Kibby, M. (2010) The gendered practice of fandom online. In R. Lind (ed.) *Race/Gender/Media: Considering Diversity across Audiences, Content and Producers*, 2nd edn. Chicago: AB-Longman, pp. 237–44.

Kiesler, S., Siegel, J., & McGuire, T. W. (1984) Social psychological aspect of computer-mediated communication. *American Psychologist* 39, 1123–34.

Kim, K.-H. & Yun, H. (2007) Cying for me, cying for us: relational dialectics in a Korean social network site. *Journal of Computer- Mediated Communication* 13(1). (Online) Available at http://onlinelibrary.wiley.com/doi/10.1111/j.1083-6101.2007.00397.x/full.

Kirkpatrick, D. (2010) *The Facebook Effect: The Inside Story of the Company that is Connecting the World*. New York: Simon & Schuster.

Knapp, M. L. (1983) Dyadic relationship development. In J. M. Wiemann &

R. P. Harrison (eds.) *Nonverbal Interaction*. Beverly Hills, CA: Sage, pp. 179–207.

Kollock, P. (1999) The economies of online cooperation: gifts and public goods in cyberspace. In M. Smith & P. Kollock (eds.) *Communities in Cyberspace*. New York: Routledge, pp. 220–42.

Koutsogiannis, D. & Mitsikopoulou, B. (2003) Greek and Greeklish: trends and discourses of "glocalness". *Journal of Computer-Mediated Communication* 9(1). (Online) Available at http://onlinelibrary.wiley.com/doi/10.1111/j.1083-6101.2003.tb00358.x/full.

Kramer, A. D., Guillory, J. E., & Hancock, J. (2014) Experimental evidence of massive-scale emotional contagion through social networks. *Proceedings of the National Academy of Sciences of the United States of America* 111(24), 8788–90.

Kraut, R., Mukhopadhyay, T., Szczypula, J., Kiesler, S., & Scherlis, B. (2000) Information and communication: alternative uses of the internet in households. *Information Systems Research* 10, 287–303.

Kunkel, A. W. & Burleson, B. R. (1999) Assessing explanations for sex differences in emotional support: a test of the different cultures and skill specialization accounts. *Human Communication Research* 25, 307–40.

Lampe, C., Ellison, N., & Steinfeld, C. (2007) A familiar Face(book): profile elements as signals in an online social network. In *Proceedings of Conference on Human Factors in Computing Systems*. New York: ACM Press, pp. 435–44.

Languages (n.d.). NITLE Blog Census. (Online) Available at www.hirank.com/semantic-indexing-project/census/lang.html.

Larsen, M. C. (2007) Understanding social networking: on young people's construction and co-construction of identity online. Paper presented at Internet Research 8.0 conference. Vancouver, BC, October.

Larson, K. A. (2003) The influence of gender and topic on nonverbal communication in online discussion boards. Unpublished undergraduate honors thesis, Department of Communication Studies, University of Kansas, Lawrence, KS.

— (2010) Negotiating romantic and sexual relationships: patterns and meanings of mediated interaction. (Dissertation) Department of Communication Studies, University of Kansas, Lawrence, KS. (Online) Available at http://hdl.handle.net/1808/7828.

Lave, J. & Wenger, E. (1991) *Situated Learning: Legitimate Peripheral Participation*. New York: Cambridge University Press.

Lea, M., O'Shea, T., Fung, P., & Spears, R. (1992) "Flaming" in computer-mediated communication: observations, explanations, implications. In

M. Lea (ed.) *Contexts of Computer-Mediated Communication*. London: Harvester Wheatsheaf, pp. 89–112.

Lea, M. & Spears, R. (1991) Computer-mediated communication, de-individuation and group decision-making. *International Journal of Man–Machine Studies Special Issue: Computer-Supported Cooperative Work and Groupware* 34, 283–301.

Ledbetter, A. M. (2009a) Measuring online communication attitude: instrument development and validation. *Communication Monographs* 76(4), 463–86.

— (2009b) Patterns of media use and multiplexity: associations with sex, geographic distance and friendship interdependence. *New Media & Society* 11(7), 1187–208.

Ledbetter, A. M., Broeckelman-Post, M. A., & Krawsczyn, A. M. (2011) Modeling everyday talk: differences across communication media and sex composition of friendship dyads. *Journal of Social and Personal Relationships* 28, 223–41.

Ledbetter, A. M. & Kuznekoff, J. H. (2011) More than a game: friendship relational maintenance and attitudes toward Xbox LIVE communication. *Communication Research* 39(2), 269–90.

Lee, J. R., Moore, D. C., Park, E., & Park, S. G. (2012) Who wants to be "friend-rich?" Social compensatory friending on Facebook and the moderating role of public self-consciousness. *Communication Research* 21(4), 460–87.

Lefler, J. (2011) I can has thesis? A linguistic analysis of lolspeak (Dissertation). Available at http://etd.lsu.edu/docs/available/etd-11112011-100404/unrestricted/Lefler_thesis.pdf.

Lenhart, A. & Madden, M. (2007) Teens, privacy, & online social networks (April 18). *Pew Internet and American Life Project*. (Online) Available at www.pewinternet.org/Reports/2007/Teens-Privacy-and-Online-Social-Networks.aspx?r=.

Leonard, L. G. & Toller, P. (2012) Speaking ill of the dead: anonymity and communication about suicide on mydeathspace.com. *Communication Studies* 63(4), 387–404.

Licoppe, C. & Heurtin, J. P. (2002) France: preserving the image. In J. E. Katz & M. Aakhus (eds.) *Perpetual Contact: Mobile Communication, Private Talk, Public Performance*. Cambridge: Cambridge University Press, pp. 94–109.

Licoppe, C. & Legout, M.-C. (2014) Living inside mobile social information: the pragmatics of Foursquare notifications". In J. Katz (ed.) *Living Inside Mobile Information*. Dayton, OH: Greyden Press, pp. 109–30.

Lievrouw, L. A. (2006) New media design and development: diffusion of innovations v. social shaping of technology. In L. A. Lievrouw & S. Livingston (eds.) *The Handbook of New Media, Updated Student Edition*. London: Sage, pp. 246–65.

—(2011) *Alternative and Activist New Media*. Malden, MA: Polity.

Lim, M. (2012) Clicks, cabs, and coffee houses: social media and oppositional movements in Egypt, 2004–2011. *Journal of Communication* 62, 231–48.

Lim, S., Vadrevu, S., Chan, Y., & Basnyat, I. (2012) Facework on Facebook: the online publicness of juvenile delinquents and youths-at-risk. *Journal of Broadcasting & Electronic Media* 56(3), 346–61.

Ling, R. (2004) *The Mobile Connection: The Cell Phone's Impact on Society*. San Francisco: Elsevier.

—(2005) The socio-linguistics of SMS: an analysis of SMS use by a random sample of Norwegians. In R. Ling & P. Pederson (eds.) *Mobile Communications: Renegotiations of the Social Sphere*. London: Springer, pp. 335–49.

—(2010) Texting as a life phase medium. *Journal of Computer-Mediated Communication* 15(2), 277–92.

—(2012) *Taken For Grantedness*. Cambridge, MA: MIT Press.

Ling, R. & Yttri, B. (2002) Hyper-coordination via mobile phones in Norway. In J. E. Katz & M. Aakhus (eds.) *Perpetual Contact: Mobile Communication, Private Talk, Public Performance*. Cambridge: Cambridge University Press, pp. 139–69.

Lingel, J. (2013) Information practices and urban spaces. (Dissertation) Available at https://rucore.libraries.rutgers.edu/rutgers-lib/41833.

Lingel, J. & boyd, d. (2013) "Keep it secret, keep it safe": information poverty, information norms, and stigma. *International Journal on Semantic Web and Information Systems* 2(1), 42–71.

Lister, M., Dovey, J., Giddings, S., Grant, I., & Kelly, K. (2003) *New Media: A Cultural Introduction*. London: Routledge.

Litt, E. (2012) Knock, knock. Who's there? The imagined audience. *Journal of Broadcasting & Electronic Media* 56(3), 330–45.

Liu, H. (2007) Social network profiles as taste performances. *Journal of Computer-Mediated Communication* 13(1). (Online) Available at http://onlinelibrary.wiley.com/doi/10.1111/j.1083-6101.2007.00395.x/full.

Liu, H., Maes, P., & Davenport, G. (2006) Unraveling the taste fabric of social networks. *International Journal on Semantic Web and Information Systems* 2(1), 42–71.

Livingstone, S. (2005) Mediating the public/private boundary at home: children's use of the internet for privacy and participation. *Journal of Media Practice* 6(1), 41–51.

—(2008) Internet literacy: young people's negotiation of new online opportunities. In T. McPherson (ed.) *Digital Youth, Innovation, and the Unexpected.* The MacArthur Foundation Series on Digital Media and Learning. Cambridge, MA: MIT Press, pp. 101–21.

Livingstone, S., Haddon, L., & Görzig, A. (2012) *Children, Risk and Safety on the Internet: Research and Policy Changes in Comparative Perspective.* Bristol: Policy Press.

Livingstone, S. & Helsper, E. (2013) Children, internet and risk in comparative perspective. *Journal of Children and Media* 7(1), 1–8.

Livingstone, S. & Smith, P. (2014) Annual research review: harms experienced by child users of online and mobile technologies: the nature, prevalence and management of sexual and aggressive risks in the digital age. *Journal of Child Psychology and Psychiatry* 55(6), 635–54.

Lockard, J. (1997) Progressive politics, electronic individualism and the myth of virtual community. In D. Porter (ed.) *Internet Culture.* New York: Routledge, pp. 219–32.

MacKenzie, D. & Wajcman, J. (1985/1999) *The Social Shaping of Technology.* Buckingham: Open University Press.

Madden, M., Lenhart, A., Cortesi, S., et al. (2013) Teens, social media, and privacy. *Pew Internet & American Life Project.* (Online) Available at www.pewinternet.org/2013/05/21/teens-social-media-and-privacy.

Madianou, M. & Miller, D. (2012a) *Migration and New Media: Transnational Families and Polymedia.* New York: Routledge.

— (2012b) Polymedia: towards a new theory of digital media in interpersonal communication. *International Journal of Cultural Studies* 16(2), 169–87.

Mankoff, R. (ed.) (2004) *The Complete Cartoons of the New Yorker.* New York: Black Dog and Leventhal Publishers.

Markus, L. (1994) Finding the happy medium: explaining the negative effects of electronic communication on social life at work. *ACM Transactions on Information Systems* 12, 119–49.

Marvin, C. (1988) *When Old Technologies Were New.* New York: Oxford University Press.

— (2004) Peaceable kingdoms and new information technology: prospects for the nation-state. In M. Sturken, D. Thomas, & S. J. Ball-Rokeach (eds.) *Technological Visions: The Hopes and Fears that Shape New Technologies.* Philadelphia, PA: Temple University Press, pp. 240–54.

Marwick, A. (2012) The public domain: surveillance in everyday life. *Surveillance & Society* 9(4), 378–93.

— (2013) *Status Update: Celebrity, Publicity and Branding in the Social Media Age.* New Haven, CT: Yale University Press.

— (in press) Instafame: luxury selfies in the attention economy. *Public Culture.*

Marwick, A. & boyd, d. (2010) I tweet honestly, I tweet passionately: Twitter users, context collapse and the imagined audience. *New Media & Society* 13(1), 114–33.
— (2014) Theorizing networked privacy. *New Media & Society*. (Online) Available at http://nms.sagepub.com/content/early/2014/07/19/146144 4814543995.abstract.
Marwick, A. & Ellison, N. (2012) "There isn't wifi in heaven!" Negotiating visibility on Facebook memorial pages. *Journal of Broadcasting and Electronic Media* 56(3), 378–400.
Matei, S. & Ball-Rokeach, S. (2002) Belonging in geographic, ethnic, and internet spaces. In B. Wellman & C. Haythornthwaite (eds.) *The Internet in Everyday Life*. Malden, MA: Blackwell, pp. 404–30.
Matzat, U. (2004) Cooperation and community on the internet: past issues and present perspectives for theoretical–empirical internet research. *Analyse & Kritik* 26(1), 63–90.
Mayer, A. & Puller, S. L. (2007) The old boy (and girl) network: social network formation on university campuses. *Journal of Public Economics* 92, 329–47.
McKenna, K. Y. A. & Bargh, J. A. (1998) Coming out in the age of the internet: identity "demarginalization" from virtual group participation. *Journal of Personality & Social Psychology* 74, 681–94.
McKenna, K. Y. A., Green, A. S., & Gleason, M. E. J. (2002) Relationship formation on the internet: what's the big attraction? *Journal of Social Issues* 58(1), 9–31.
McLaughlin, M. L., Osborne, K. K., & Smith, C. B. (1995) Standards of conduct on Usenet. In S. Jones (ed.) *Cybersociety: Computer-Mediated Communication and Community*. Thousand Oaks, CA: Sage, pp. 90–111.
McLaughlin, C. & Vitak, J. (2012) Norm evolution and violation on Facebook. *New Media & Society* 14, 299–315.
Mehrabian, A. (1971) *Silent Messages*. Belmont, CA: Wadsworth.
Mesch, G. (2012) Minority status and the use of computer-mediated communication: a test of the social diversification hypothesis. *Communication Research* 39(3), 317–37.
Mesch, G. and Levanon, Y. (2003) Community networking and locally based social ties in two suburban localities. *City and Community* 2, 335–51.
Mesch, G. and Talmud, I. (2006) The quality of online and offline relationships. *The Information Society* 22, 137–48.
Meyrowitz, J. (1985) *No Sense of Place: The Impact of Electronic Media on Social Behavior*. New York: Oxford University Press.
Miller, D. & Slater, D. (2000) *The Internet: An Ethnographic Approach*. Oxford: Berg.

Milner, R. (2012) The world made meme: discourse and identity in participatory media. (Dissertation) Available at http://kuscholarworks. ku.edu/dspace/handle/1808/10256.

Miltner, K. M. (2014) "There's no place for lulz on LOLCats": the role of genre, gender, and group identity in the interpretation and enjoyment of an internet meme. *First Monday* 19(8). (Online) Available at http:// firstmonday.org/ojs/index.php/fm/article/view/5391/4103.

Miniwatts Marketing Group (2013) World internet penetration rates by geographic regions. (Online) Available at www.internetworldstats.com/ stats.htm.

Mitra, A. (1997) Virtual commonality: looking for India on the internet. In S. Jones (ed.) *Virtual Culture*. Newbury Park, CA: Sage, pp. 55–79.

Monroy-Hernández, A., boyd, d., Kiciman, E., De Choudhury, M., & Counts, S. (2013) The new war correspondents: the rise of civic media curation in urban warfare. In *Proceedings of the 16th ACM Conference on Computer Supported Cooperative Work and Social Computing*. San Antonio, TX, pp. 1443–52.

Morozov, E. (2009) The brave new world of slacktivism. *Foreign Policy*. (Online) Available at http://neteffect.foreignpolicy.com/ posts/2009/05/19/the_brave_new_world_of_slacktivism.

Muscanell, N. L. & Guadagno, R. E. (2012) Make new friends or keep the old: gender and personality differences in social networking use. *Computers in Human Behavior* 28(1), 107–12.

Myers, D. (1987a) A new environment for communication play: online play. In G. A. Fine (ed.) *Meaningful Play, Playful Meaning*. Champaign, IL: Human Kinetics Publishers, pp. 231–45.

—(1987b) "Anonymity is part of the magic": individual manipulation of computer-mediated communication contexts. *Qualitative Sociology* 19(3), 251–66.

Nakamura, L. (2002) *Cybertypes: Race, Ethnicity, and Identity on the Internet*. New York: Routledge.

Nardi, B. (2010) *My Life as a Night Elf Priest: An Anthropological Account of World of Warcraft*. Ann Arbor, MI: University of Michigan Press.

Neustaedter, C. & Greenberg, S. (2012) Intimacy in long-distance relationships over video chat. In *Proceedings of the Conference on Human Factors in Computing Systems*. New York: ACM Press, pp. 753–62.

Nie, N. H., Hillygus, D. S., & Erbring, L. (2002) Internet use, interpersonal relations and sociability: a time diary study. In B. Wellman & C. Haythornthwaite (eds.) *The Internet in Everyday Life*. Malden, MA: Blackwell, pp. 215–43.

Nissenbaum, H. (2010) *Privacy in Context: Technology, Policy, and the Integrity of Social Life*. Stanford, CA: Stanford University Press.

Norman, D. (1988) *The Design of Everyday Things*. New York: Basic Books.

Norris, P. (2001) *Digital Divide: Civic Engagement, Information Poverty and the Internet*. Cambridge: Cambridge University Press.

Nye, D. E. (1997) *Narratives and Spaces: Technology and the Construction of American Culture*. New York: Columbia University Press.

—(2004) Technological prediction. In M. Sturken, D. Thomas, & S. J. Ball-Rokeach (eds.) *Technological Visions: The Hopes and Fears that Shape New Technologies*. Philadelphia, PA: Temple University Press, pp. 159–76.

O'Hara, K., Massimi, M., Harper, R., Rubens, S., & Morris, J. (2014) Everyday dwelling with WhatsApp. In *Proceedings of the 17th ACM Conference on Computer Supported Cooperative Work & Social Computing*. Baltimore, MD, pp. 1131–43.

O'Sullivan, P. B. (2000) What you don't know won't hurt ME: impression management functions of communication channels in relationships. *Human Communication Research* 26(3), 403–31.

O'Sullivan, P. B., Hunt, S., & Lippert, L. (2004) Mediated immediacy: a language of affiliation in a technological age. *Journal of Language and Social Psychology* 23, 464–90.

Oksman, V. & Turtiainen, J. (2004) Mobile communication as a social stage: meanings of mobile communication in everyday life among teenagers in Finland. *New Media & Society* 6, 319–39.

Oldenburg, R. (1989) *The Great Good Place: Cafes, Coffee Shops, Community Centers, Beauty Parlors, General Stores, Bars, Hangouts, and How They Get You Through the Day*. New York: Paragon House.

Ong, W. J. (1982) *Orality and Literacy: The Technologizing of the World*. New York: Routledge.

Orleans, M. & Laney, M. C. (2000) Children's computer use in the home: isolation or sociation? *Social Science Computer Review* 18(1), 56–72.

Ottoni, R., Las Casas, D., Pesce, J. P., et al. (2014) Of pins and tweets: investigating how users behave across image- and text-based social networks. In *Proceedings of the International AAAI Conference on Weblogs and Social Media*. (Online) Available at www.aaai.org/ocs/index.php/ICWSM/ICWSM14/paper/view/8059/8139.

Papacharissi, Z. (2002) The presentation of self in virtual life: characteristics of personal home pages. *Journalism and Mass Communication Quarterly* 79(3), 643–60.

Papacharissi, Z. & Oliveira, M. (2012) Affective news and networked publics: the rhythms of news storytelling in #Egypt. *Journal of Communication* 62(2), 266–82.

Pariser, E. (2011) *The Filter Bubble: How the New Personalized Web is Changing What We Read and How We Think*. New York: The Penguin Press.

Parks, M. (2006) *Personal Relationships and Personal Networks*. Mahwah, NJ: Lawrence Erlbaum.

—(2011) Boundary conditions for the application of three theories of computer-mediated communication to MySpace. *Journal of Communication* 61(4), 557–74.

Parks, M. R. & Floyd, K. (1996) Making friends in cyberspace. *Journal of Communication* 46(1), 80–97.

Parks, M. R. & Roberts, L. D. (1998) "Making MOOsic": the development of personal relationships online and a comparison to their offline counterparts. *Journal of Social and Personal Relationships* 15(4), 517–37.

Pascoe, C. J. (2010) "You have another world to create": teens and online hangouts. In M. Ito et al. (eds.) *Hanging Out, Messing Around, and Geeking Out: Kids Living and Learning with New Media*. Cambridge, MA: MIT Press, pp. 50–3.

Pearce, K. E. and Kendzior, S. (2012) Networked authoritarianism and social media in Azerbaijan. *Journal of Communication* 62, 283–98.

Pentzold, C. (2011) Imagining the Wikipedia community. What do Wikipedia authors mean when they write about their community? *New Media & Society* 13(5), 704–21.

Philipsen, G. (1992) *Speaking Culturally: Explorations in Social Communication*. Albany, NY: SUNY Press.

Plato (2008 [360 BCE]) *Phaedrus*. Charleston, SC: Forgotten Books.

Postmes, T. & Baym, N. K. (2005) Intergroup dimensions of the internet. In J. Harwood & H. Giles (eds.) *Intergroup Communication: Multiple Perspectives*. New York: Peter Lang, pp. 213–38.

Potts, L. (2014) *Social Media in Disaster Response: How Experience Architects Can Build for Participation*. New York: Routledge.

Powers, W. (2010) *Hamlet's Blackberry: Building a Good Life in the Digital Age*. New York: HarperCollins.

Preece, J. & Ghozati, K. (1998) In search of empathy online: a review of 100 online communities. In *Proceedings of the 1998 Association for Information Systems Americas Conference*. Baltimore, MD: Association for Information Systems, pp. 92–4.

Preece, J. & Maloney-Krichmar, D. (2003) Online communities. In J. Jacko & A. Sears (eds.) *Handbook of Human–Computer Interaction*. Mahwah, NJ: Lawrence Erlbaum, pp. 596–620.

Preece, J., Nonnecke, B., & Andrews, D. (2004) The top 5 reasons for lurking: improving community experiences for everyone. *Computers in Human Behavior* 20(2), 201–23.

Purcell, K., Buchanan, J., & Friedrich, L. (2013) The impact of digital tools on student writing and how writing is taught in schools. *Pew Internet & American Life Project*. (Online) Available at www.pewinternet.org/Reports/2013/Teachers-technology-and-writing.aspx.

Puro, J.-P. (2002) Finland: a mobile culture. In J. E. Katz & M. Aakhus (eds.) *Perpetual Contact: Mobile Communication, Private Talk, Public Performance*. Cambridge: Cambridge University Press, pp. 19–29.

Putnam, R. (1995) Bowling alone: America's declining social capital. *Journal of Democracy* 6(1), 65–78.

—(2000) *Bowling Alone: The Collapse and Revival of American Community*. New York: Simon & Schuster.

Quan-Haase, A., Wellman, B., Witte, J., & Hampton, K. N. (2002) Capitalizing on the net: social contact, civic engagement, and sense of community. In B. Wellman & C. Haythornthwaite (eds.) *The Internet in Everyday Life*. Malden, MA: Blackwell, pp. 291–324.

Rabby, M. (2007) Relational maintenance and the influence of commitment in online and offline relationships. *Communication Studies* 58(3), 315–37.

Rafaeli, S. & Sudweeks, F. (1997) Networked interactivity. *Journal of Computer-Mediated Communication* 2(4). (Online) Available at http://onlinelibrary.wiley.com/doi/10.1111/j.1083-6101.1997.tb00201.x/full.

Rainie, L., Lenhart, A., Fox, S., Spooner, T., & Horrigan, J. (2000) Tracking online life: how women use the internet to cultivate relationships with family and friends. *Pew Internet & American Life Project*. (Online) Available at www.pewinternet.org/Reports/2000/Tracking-Online-Life.aspx.

Rainie, L. & Smith, A. (2012) Politics on social networking sites. *Pew Internet & American Life Project*. (Online) Available at www.pewinternet.org/2012/09/04/main-findings-8.

Rakow, L. (1992) *Gender on the Line: Women, the Telephone and Community Life*. Chicago, IL: University of Illinois Press.

Rawlins, W. K. (1992) *Friendship Matters: Communication, Dialectics and the Life Course*. New York: Aldine de Gruyter.

Rheingold, H. (1993) *The Virtual Community: Homesteading on the Electronic Frontier*. Reading, MA: Addison-Wesley.

Rice, R. E. (1984) Mediated group communication. In R. E. Rice and associates (eds.) *The New Media: Communication, Research, and Technology*. Beverly Hills, CA: Sage, pp. 129–56.

—(1989) Issues and concepts in research on computer-mediated communication systems. In J. A. Anderson (ed.) *Communication Yearbook*, Volume XII. Newbury Park, CA: Sage, pp. 436–76.

Rice, R. E. & Love, G. (1987) Electronic emotion: socioemotional content in a computer-mediated communication network. *Communication Research* 14(1), 85–108.

Robinson, J. P., Kestnbaum, M., Neustadtl, A., & Alvarez, A. S. (2002) The internet and other uses of time. In B. Wellman & C. Haythornthwaite (eds.) *The Internet in Everyday Life*. Malden, MA: Blackwell, pp. 244–62.

Rudder, C. (2014) We experiment on human beings! (Online) Available at http://blog.okcupid.com/index.php/we-experiment-on-human-beings.

Rutter, J. & Smith, G. W. H. (1999) Presenting the offline self in an everyday online environment. Paper presented at Identities in Action Conference. University of Wales, December.

Ryan, T. & Xenos, S. (2011) Who uses Facebook? An investigation into the relationship between the Big Five, shyness, narcissism, loneliness, and Facebook usage. *Computers in Human Behavior* 27(5), 1658–64.

Sarch, A. (1993) Making the connection: single women's use of the telephone in dating relationships with men. *Journal of Communication* 42, 128–44.

Savicki, V., Lingenfelter, D., & Kelley, M. (1996) Gender language style and group composition in internet discussion groups. *Journal of Computer-Mediated Communication* 2(3). (Online) Available at http://onlinelibrary.wiley.com/doi/10.1111/j.1083-6101.1996.tb00191.x/full.

Schegloff, E. (2002) Beginnings in the telephone. In J. E. Katz & M. Aakhus (eds.) *Perpetual Contact: Mobile Communication, Private Talk, Public Performance*. Cambridge: Cambridge University Press, pp. 284–300.

Schuler, D. (1996) *New Community Networks: Wired for Change*. Reading, MA: Addison-Wesley.

Senft, T. (2008) *Camgirls: Celebrity & Community in the Age of Social Networks*. New York: Peter Lang.

Shea, V. (n.d.). Netiquette: flame wars. (Online) Available at www.albion.com/bookNetiquette/0963702513p73.html.

Sheer, V. C. (2011) Teenagers' use of MSN features, discussion topics, and online friendship development: the impact of media richness and communication control. *Communication Quarterly* 59(1), 82–103.

Shifman, L. (2013) *Memes in Digital Culture*. Cambridge, MA: MIT Press.

Shklovski, I. & Valtysson, B. (2012) Secretly political: civic engagement in online publics in Kazakhstan. *Journal of Broadcasting & Electronic Media* 56(3), 417–33.

Short, J., Williams, E., & Christie, B. (1976) *The Social Psychology of Telecommunications*. Chichester: Wiley.

Silver, D. (2000) Margins in the wires: looking for race, gender and sexuality in the Blacksburg Electronic Village. In B. Kolko, L. Nakamura, & G. B. Rodman (eds.) *Race in Cyberspace*. New York: Routledge, pp. 133–50.

Silverstone, R., Hirsch, E., & Morley, D. (1992) Information and communication technologies and the moral economy of the household. In R. Silverstone & E. Hirsch (eds.) *Consuming Technologies: Media and Information in Domestic Spaces*. London: Routledge, pp. 9–17.

Smith, A. & Dugan, M. (2013) Online dating & relationships. *Pew Internet & American Life Project*. (Online) Available at www.pewinternet. org/2013/10/21/online-dating-relationships.

Smith, A., Schlozman, K. L., Verba, S., & Brady, H. (2009) The internet and civic engagement. *Pew Internet and American Life Project*. (Online) Available at www.pewinternet.org/Reports/2009/15--The Internet-and-Civic-Engagement.aspx.

Snyder, J., Carpenter, D., & Slauson, G. J. (2006) MySpace.com: a social networking site and social contract theory. In *Proceedings of ISECON 2006*. (Online) Available at http://isedj.org/5/2.

Solove, D. J. (2007) *The Future of Reputation: Gossip, Rumor, and Privacy on the Internet*. New Haven, CT: Yale University Press.

Sorbring, E. & Lundin, L. (2012) Mothers' and fathers' insights into teenagers' use of the internet. *New Media & Society* 14(7), 1181–97.

Sparta Networks (n.d.) Lincoln uses Sparta social networks to help make dreams come true. (Online) Available at www.spartasocialnetworks. com/clients/case-studies/case-study-lincoln.

Spears, R. & Lea, M. (1992) Social influence and the influence of the "social" in computer-mediated communication. In M. Lea (ed.) *Contexts of Computer-Mediated Communication*. Hemel Hempstead: Harvester Wheatsheaf, pp. 30–65.

Spigel, L. (1992) *Make Room for TV: Television and the Family Ideal in Postwar America*. Chicago, IL: University of Chicago Press.

—(2004) Portable TV: studies in domestic space travels. In M. Sturken, D. Thomas, & S. J. Ball-Rokeach (eds.) *Technological Visions: The Hopes and Fears that Shape New Technologies*. Philadelphia, PA: Temple University Press, pp. 110–44.

Sproull, L. & Kiesler, S. (1991) *Connections: New Ways of Working in the Networked Organization*. Cambridge, MA: MIT Press.

Stafford, L., Kline, S. L., & Dimmick, J. (1999) Home e-mail: relational maintenance and gratification opportunities. *Journal of Broadcasting & Electronic Media* 43(4), 659–69.

Standage, T. (1998) *The Victorian Internet*. New York: Berkley.

—(2013) *Writing on the Wall: Social Media – The First 2,000 Years*. New York: Bloomsbury USA.

Steinkuehler, C. A. & Williams, D. (2006) Where everybody knows your (screen) name: online games as "third places." *Journal of*

Computer-Mediated Communication 11(4). (Online) Available at http://onlinelibrary.wiley.com/doi/10.1111/j.1083-6101.2006.00300.x/full.

Stephenson, N. (1992) *Snow Crash.* New York: Spectra.

Stivale, C. (1997) Spam: heteroglossia and harassment in cyberspace. In D. Porter (ed.) *Internet Culture.* New York: Routledge, pp. 133–44.

Stoll, C. (1995) *Silicon Snake Oil: Second Thoughts on the Information Highway.* New York: Doubleday.

Stone, A. R. (1995) *The War of Desire and Technology at the Close of the Mechanical Age.* Cambridge, MA: MIT Press.

Stross, C. (2007) *Halting State.* New York: Berkley Publishing Group.

Sturken, M. & Thomas, D. (2004) Introduction: technological visions and the rhetoric of the new. In M. Sturken, D. Thomas, & S. J. Ball-Rokeach (eds.) *Technological Visions: The Hopes and Fears that Shape New Technologies.* Philadelphia, PA: Temple University Press, pp. 1–18.

Stutzman, F., Gross, R., & Acquisti, A. (2012) Silent listeners: the evolution of privacy and disclosure on Facebook. *Journal of Privacy and Confidentiality* 4(2), 7–41.

Stutzman, F. & Hartzog, W. (2013) Boundary regulation in social media: online dating & relationships. In *Proceedings of the ACM Conference on Computer Supported Cooperative Work.* Seattle, WA, pp. 769–78.

Tajfel, H. & Turner, J. C. (1986) The social identity theory of intergroup behavior. In S. Worchel & W. G. Austin (eds.) *The Psychology of Intergroup Relations.* Chicago, IL: Nelson-Hall, pp. 7–24.

Tang, G. & Lee, F. L. F. (2013) Facebook use and political participation: the impact of exposure to shared political information, connections with public political actors and network structural heterogeneity. *Social Science Computer Review* 31(6), 763–73.

Thomas, D. (2004) Rethinking the cyberbody: hackers, viruses, and cultural anxiety. In M. Sturken, D. Thomas, & S. J. Ball-Rokeach (eds.) *Technological Visions: The Hopes and Fears that Shape New Technologies.* Philadelphia, PA: Temple University Press, pp. 219–39.

Thurlow, C., Lengel, L., & Tomic, A. (2004) *Computer-Mediated Communication: Social Interaction and the Internet.* Los Angeles: Sage.

Tiidenberg, K. (2014) Bringing sexy back: reclaiming the body aesthetic via self-shooting. *Cyberpsychology: Journal of Psychosocial Research on Cyberspace* 8(1), article 3.

Toma, C. L. & Hancock, J. T. (2010) Looks and lies: the role of physical attractiveness in online dating self-presentation and deception. *Communication Research* 37(3), 335–51.

Tosun, L. P. (2012) Motives for Facebook use and expressing the "true self" on the internet. *Computers in Human Behavior* 28(4), 1510–17.

Translate to Success (2009) Internet language use statistics. (Online) Available at www.translate-to-success.com/internet-language-use.html.

Tufekci, Z. and Wilson, C. (2012) Social media and the decision to participate in political protest: observations from Tahrir Square. *Journal of Communication* 62, 363–79.

Turkle, S. (1996) *Life on the Screen: Identity in the Age of the Internet*. New York: Simon & Schuster.

—(1997) Constructions and reconstructions of self in virtual reality: playing in the MUDs. In S. Kiesler (ed.) *Culture of the Internet*. Mahwah, NJ: Lawrence Erlbaum, pp. 143–55.

—(2004) "Spinning" technology: what we are not thinking about when we are thinking about computers. In M. Sturken, D. Thomas, & S. J. Ball-Rokeach (eds.) *Technological Visions: The Hopes and Fears that Shape New Technologies*. Philadelphia, PA: Temple University Press, pp. 19–33.

—(2011) *Alone Together: Why We Expect More from Technology and Less from Each Other*. New York: Basic Books.

Tuszynski, S. (dir.) (2007) *IRL: In Real Life*. (Film) DL Films.

Twitter tweets are 40% "babble" (2009). *BBC News*, August 19. (Online) Available at http://news.bbc.co.uk/2/hi/technology/8204842.stm.

Uimonen, P. (2013) Visual identity in Facebook. *Visual Studies* 28(2), 122–35.

Ullman, E. (1997) *Close to the Machine: Technophilia and its Discontents*. San Francisco: City Lights Books.

UN (2001) Human Development Report. *Making New Technologies Work for Human Development*. (Online) Available at http://hdr.undp.org/en/reports/global/hdr2001.

Utz, S. (2010) Show me your friends and I will tell you what type of person you are: how one's profile, number of friends, and type of friends influence impression formation. *Journal of Computer-Mediated Communication* 15(2), 314–35.

Valenzuela, S., Arriagada, A., & Scherman, A. (2012) The social media basis of youth protest behavior: the case of Chile. *Journal of Communication*, 62, 299–314.

Van der Heide, B., D'Angelo, J. D., & Shumaker, E. M. (2012) The effects of verbal versus photographic self-presentation on impression formation in Facebook. *Journal of Communication* 62, 98–116.

van Dijck, J. (2013) *The Culture of Connectivity: A Critical History of Social Media*. New York: Oxford University Press.

Van House, N. (2011) Personal photography, digital technologies, and uses of the visual. *Visual Studies* 25(1), 125–34.

Walker, R. (2008) *Buying In: The Secret Dialogue between What We Buy and Who We Are*. New York: Random House.

Walther, J. B. (1992) Interpersonal effects in computer-mediated interaction. *Communication Research* 19(1), 52–90.

—(1994) Anticipated ongoing interaction versus channel effects on relational communication in computer-mediated interaction. *Human Communication Research* 20(4), 473–501.

—(1996) Computer-mediated communication: impersonal, interpersonal and hyperpersonal interaction. *Communication Research* 23(1), 3–43.

—(2011) Theories of computer mediated communication and interpersonal relations. In M. Knapp & J. Daly (eds.) *The SAGE Handbook of Interpersonal Communication*, 4th edn. Thousand Oaks, CA: Sage, pp. 443–80.

Walther, J. B., Anderson, J. F., & Park, D. (1994) Interpersonal effects in computer-mediated interaction: a meta-analysis of social and anti social communication. *Communication Research* 21(4), 460–87.

Walther, J. B. & Boyd, S. (2002) Attraction to computer-mediated social support. In C. Lin & D. Atkin (eds.) *Communication Technology and Society: Audience Adoption and Uses*. Cresskill, NJ: Hampton Press, pp. 153–88.

Walther, J. B. & Burgoon, J. K. (1992) Relational communication in computer-mediated interaction. *Human Communication Research* 18(1), 50–88.

Walther, J. B., Liang, Y., DeAndrea, D. C., Tong, S. T., Spottswood, E. L., & Amichai-Hamburger, Y. (2011) The effect of feedback on identity shift in computer-mediated communication. *Media Psychology* 14(1), 1–26.

Walther, J. B., Van der Heide, B., Kim, S. Y., & Westerman, D. (2008) The role of friends' appearance and behavior on evaluations of individuals on Facebook: are we known by the company we keep? *Human Communication Research* 34, 28–49.

Warschauer, M. (2004) *Technology and Social Inclusion: Rethinking the Digital Divide*. Cambridge, MA: MIT Press.

Watzlawick, P., Beavin, J. B., & Jackson, D. J. (1967) *Pragmatics of Human Communication: A Study of Interactional Patterns, Pathologies and Paradoxes*. New York: W. W. Norton.

Wellman, B. (1988) Networks as personal communities. In B. Wellman & S. D. Berkowitz (eds.) *Social Structures: A Network Analysis*. Cambridge: Cambridge University Press, pp. 130–84.

Wellman, B. & Gulia, M. (1999) Virtual communities as communities: net surfers don't ride alone. In M. Smith & P. Kollock (eds.) *Communities in Cyberspace*. New York: Routledge, pp. 167–94.

Wellman, B., Quan-Haase, A. Q., Boase, J., Chen, W., Hampton, K., & de Diaz, I. I. (2003) The social affordances of the internet for networked individualism. *Journal of Computer-Mediated Communication* 8(3). (Online) Available at http://onlinelibrary.wiley.com/ doi/10.1111/j.1083-6101.2003.tb00216.x/full.

Welser, H. T., Gleave, E., Fischer, D., & Smith, M. (2007) Visualizing the signatures of social roles in online discussion groups. *The Journal of Social Structure* 8(2). (Online) Available at www.cmu.edu/joss/content/articles/volume8/Welser.

Whitty, M. & Gavin, J. (2001) Age/sex/location: uncovering the social cues in the development of online relationships. *Cyberpsychology and Behavior* 4(5), 623–30.

Who's Online (2014) *Pew Internet & American Life Project*, April. (Online) Available at www.pewinternet.org/Static-Pages/Trend-Data/Whos-Online.aspx.

Wiemann, J. M. & Knapp, M. L. (1975) Turn-taking in conversations. *Journal of Communication* 25, 75–92.

Wolak, J. & Finkelhor, D. (2013) Are crimes by online predators different from crimes by sex offenders who know youth in-person? *Journal of Adolescent Health* 53, 1–6.

WordPress.com (2014) A live look at activity across WordPress.com. (Online) Available at http://en.wordpress.com/stats.

Wright, K. B., Rains, S., & Banas, J. (2010) Weak-tie support network preference and perceived life stress among participants in health-related, computer-mediated support groups. *Journal of Computer-Mediated Communication* 15, 606–24.

Wynn, E. & Katz, J. E. (1998) Hyperbole over cyberspace: self-presentation and social boundaries in internet home pages and discourse. *The Information Society* 13(4), 297–328.

Index of names

Aakhus, M. 4, 51
Abbate, J. 14
Ackerman, M. 89
Acquisti, A. 122, 124, 125, 136
Adelman, M. 114
Ahlstrom, M. 167–8
Ahuvia, A. 114
Albanesius, G. 105
Albury, K. 50
Alloway, T. 27–8, 32
Alper, M. 74
Altman, I. 148
Alvarez, A. S. 166
Andersen, P. 60
Anderson, J. F. 61
Anderson, J. Q. 33, 40, 43
Andrews, D. 98
Antheunis, M. L. 134
Arriagada, A. 107
Aspden, P. 104

Baek, K. 153
Bailard, C. S. 108
Baker, A. 115, 146
Ball-Rokeach, S. 166
Banas, J. 92
Banet-Weiser, S. 50, 123, 140
Bargh, J. A. 3, 8, 94, 115, 139
Baron, N. S. 3–4, 8, 61, 71, 72–3, 75,
    124–5, 152, 153, 154, 161
Bartle, R. 16
Basnyat, I. 123
Baxter, L. 178
Baym, N. K. 52, 66, 69, 71, 86, 97, 98,
    101, 102, 117, 121, 122, 123, 126, 127,
    133, 137, 143, 152, 155, 156, 157, 162,
    163, 165 169
Bazarova, N. N. 148

Beavin, J. B. 145
Benjamin, W. 34
Berners-Lee, T. 17
Berscheid, E. 116
Bevan, J. L. 160
Bijker, W. E. 44
Bilton, N. 160
Bird, C. 155
Boase, J. 100, 162
Boddy, W. 33
Bonatsos, A. 130
Bordbar, F. 75
Boulianne, S. 103, 107
Bourdieu, P. 132
boyd, d. 18, 89, 95, 100, 106, 121–2,
    123, 130, 133, 137, 143, 151, 152, 170
Boyd, S. 92
Brand, R. J. 130
Brenner, J. 107
Briggs, A. 13
Brock, A. 69, 87, 131
Brunner, H. 71
Buchanan, J. 73
Burgess, J. 52, 70, 83
Burgoon, J. K. 141
Burke, P. 13
Burleson, B. R. 75, 92
Burnett, R. 97
Byrne, D. N. 131
Byron, P. 50

Campbell, S. 47, 102, 104, 107, 109
Campbell, W. K. 128
Carnevale, P. 8, 10
Carpenter, D. 171
Carr, N. 27, 32, 33
Cassell, J. 48, 51
Cassidy, E. M. 94, 105, 114, 137, 138, 139

Caughlin, J. P. 153, 157, 164
Chan, D. K. S. 150
Chan, Y. 123
Chayko, M. 83–4
Chen, G. M. 139
Chen, W. 100, 162, 163
Cheng, G. H. L. 150
Cherny, L. 10
Choi, J. H. 152
Christensen, H. S. 106, 108
Christie, B. 59
Citron, D. K. 65
Clark, L. S. 117
Cockroft, L. 27
Cohen, S. 49
Cole, J. 104, 143, 162, 165, 167
Coleman, J. S. 91
Collins, Jarvis L. 60, 61
Copher, J. I. 166
Cortese, J. 62
Cottingham, R. 39
Counts, S. 106
Cover, R. 131, 134, 137, 139
Craig, E. 152
Cramer, M. 48, 51
Crawford, K. 50, 97
Criado-Perez, C. 65–6
Culnan, N. J. 10
Cutrona, C. E. 85, 93, 94, 96

Daft, R. L. 59, 60–1
Dahlgren, P. 103
Danet, B. 8, 69, 70, 71, 78
D'Angelo, J. D. 135
Davenport, G. 128
Davis, K. 123
DeAndrea, D. C. 123
De Choudhury, M. 106
de Diaz, I. I. 100
Dertouzos 40
DeShong, H. 130
de Sola Pool, I. 41
Dijck, J. van 18
Dimmick, J. 29, 151, 157, 162, 163
Dion, K. 116
Donath, J. 89, 126, 132, 170
D'Orazio, R. 130
Douglas, S. 32, 40, 51
Dovey, J. 46
Driscoll, K. 14, 20

Dugan, M. 115
Dundes, A. 86
Duran, R. L. 155, 168

Eggett, D. 167
Ellison, N. 18, 91, 100, 114, 125, 128–9,
    130, 135, 137, 138, 143, 151, 152, 153,
    154, 160
Engels, R. C. M. E. 119
Erbing, L. 165
Eslami, M. 138
Eynon, R. 23

Facer, K. 48, 50
Fahlman, S. E. 68
Fang, I. 48
Feaster, J. C. 29
Ferrara, K. 71
Finkelhor, D. 48, 49
Finkenauer, C. 119–20
Fiore, A. T. 126
Fischer, C. S. 28–9, 41, 46, 48
Fischer, D. 96
Flanagan, A. J. 157
Florini, S. 69, 87, 131
Floyd, K. 114, 148
Fono, D. 89, 133, 170
Fornas, J. 5, 7
Fortunati, L. 6
Fox, S. 128
Fragoso, S. 132
Freeman, E. C. 128
Friedrich, L. 73
Fulk, J. 47, 60, 61
Fung, P. 63

Gavin, J. 128, 130
Gentile, B. 128
Gergen, K. 3, 5, 82, 102, 109
Gershon, I. 20, 51, 159, 160
Ghozati, K. 66, 94
Gibbs, J. 128–9, 130
Gibson, J. J. 51
Gibson, W. 19, 26, 84, 175
Giddens, A. 117
Giddings, S. 46
Gilbert, E. 153
Gil de Zúñiga, H. 103, 104, 109–10
Gilding, M. 127, 141, 146
Gillespie, T. 18

Gleason, M. E. J. 3
Gleave, E. 96
Goffman, E. 119, 124, 130, 167, 172
Golder, S. A. 91, 153
Görzig, A. 51
Granovetter, M. S. 145
Grant, Y. 46
Gray, K. 76
Gray, R. 152
Green, A. S. 3
Green, J. 83
Greenberg, S. 155, 158
Green-Hamann, S. 147
Gross, R. 122, 124, 125, 136
Guadagno, R. E. 161, 165
Guerrero, L. 60
Guillory, J. E. 138
Gulia, M. 93
Gurak, L. L. 7, 11

Haas, S. M. 92, 94, 95
Haddon, L. 51, 52, 53
Hall, J. A. 125, 128, 135, 136, 155,
    169
Hamilton, K. 138
Hampton, K. 100, 102, 103, 103–4,
    105, 109, 110, 162, 166
Hancock, J. T. 129, 136, 137, 138, 148
Hansen, D. 89, 97
Haraway, D. 3
Hård af Segerstad, Y. 69, 71, 161
Hargittai, E. 22–3, 24, 130
Harper, R. 155
Hartelius, E. 103
Hartzog, W. 123
Hatfield, E. 116
Haythornthwaite, C. 5, 114, 145, 153
Heer, J. 123, 170
Heino, R. 128–9, 130
Helsper, E. 23, 51
Henderson, S. 127, 141, 146
Her, E. J. 102, 103, 104, 109, 110,
    166
Herring, S. 71, 74, 75, 78, 126
Heurtin, J. P. 154
Hijazi-Omari, H. 47, 164
Hillygus, D. S. 165
Hiltz, S. R. 63
Hinnant, A. 20, 22
Hirsch, E. 53

Hochman, N. 91
Horrigan, J. 22, 128
Horst, H. A. 155, 167
Houser, M. L. 163
Howard, P. N. 108
Huberman, B. A. 91
Hughes, T. P. 44
Humphreys, L. 6, 89, 153, 154, 167
Hunt, S. 88

Irr, M. E. 92
Ishii, K. 161, 166
Ito, M. 51, 124, 159

Jackson, D. J. 145
Jenkins, H. 93
Jennings, N. A. 92
Jiang, L. C. 148
John, N. A. 153
Jones, L. M. 49
Jung, J. 22
Jung, Y. 139

Kanfer, A. G. 166
Kapedzic, S. 75, 126
Karahalios, K. 138, 153
Kasesniemi, E. 75, 162
Katz, J. E. 4, 51, 53, 103, 104, 107, 131,
    165
Kelley, M. 67
Kelly, K. 46
Kendall, L. 170
Kendall, M. 75
Kendzior, S. 109
Kestnbaum, M. 166
Kibby, M. 93
Kiciman, E. 106
Kiesler, S. 15, 61, 62
Kim, K.-H. 125, 153, 170
Kim, S. Y. 91
Kim, Y. C. 22
King, M. L., Jr. 39
Kirkpatrick, D. 124
Klein, K. 5
Klietz, A. 16
Kline, S. L. 151, 157
Knapp, M. L. 59, 116
Kollock, P. 96
Koutsogiannis, D. 78
Kramer, A. D. 138

Kraut, R. 15
Kunkel, A. 75, 156
Kuznekoff, J. H. 161
Kwak, N. 102, 104, 107, 109

Ladendorf, J. 5
Lampe, C. 91, 125, 152
Laney, M. C. 167
Larsen, M. C. 153
Larson, K. A. 75, 159, 163–4
Lave, J. 86
Law, J. 44
Lea, M. 63, 66, 132
Ledbetter, A. 117, 126, 152, 156, 157, 161, 163, 165, 166
Lee, C.-J. 102, 103, 104, 109, 110
Lee, F. L. F 107
Lee, J. R. 135
Lefler, J. 70
Legout, M.-C. 154
Lengel, L. 59
Lengel, R. H. 59, 60–1
Lenhart, A. 128
Leonard, L. G. 160
Leuders, A. 135
Levanon, Y. 103
Licoppe, C. 154
Lievrouw, L. A. 52, 108
Lim, S. 123
Lin, M. 156
Lindsay, G. B. 167
Ling, R. 5, 6, 11, 47, 52, 53, 69, 71, 72, 75, 153, 154, 162, 164
Lingel, J. 67, 95
Lingenfelter, D. 67
Lippert, L. 8
Lister, M. 46
Litt, E. 121
Liu, H. 126, 128, 132
Livingstone, S. 5, 49–50, 51
Livio, O. 105
Lockard, J. 82
Love, G. 63, 66
Lundberg, N. R. 167

MacGeorge, E. L. 92
McGuire, T. W. 61
McKenna, K. Y. A. 3, 8, 94, 115, 127, 139, 146, 149, 150, 161
MacKenzie, D. 51, 52

McLaughlin, C. 87, 89
McLaughlin, M. L. 88
McLuhan, M. 28
Madden, M. 122, 123, 152
Madianou, M. 19, 67, 155, 158–9
Maes, P. 128
Maloney-Krichmar, D. 83, 90
Mankoff, R. 38
Manovich, L. 91
Markus, L. 32
Markus, M. L. 10
Marvin, C. 2, 28, 39, 41, 48, 50
Marwick, A. 5, 74, 90, 121–2, 123, 137, 140, 160
Massimi, M. 155
Matei, S. 166
Mathews, B. 50
Matzat, U. 96
Mayer, S. 152
Meeus, W. 119
Mesch, G. 103, 117, 150
Metzger, M. J. 157
Meyrowitz, J. 29, 102
Miller, D. 19, 67, 76, 131, 155, 158–9
Milner, R. 70, 87, 108
Miltner, K. M. 70, 87, 169
Mitchell, K. J. 49
Mitra, A. 76
Mitsikopoulou, B. 78
Monroy-Hernández, A. 106
Montgomery, B. 178
Moore, D. C. 135
Morley, D. 53
Morozov, E. 106
Morris, J. 155
Mukhopadhyay, T. 15
Munroe, R. 32, 44
Munson, S. 89
Murphy, B. 155
Muscanell, N. L. 161, 165
Myers, D. 69, 139

Nakamura, L. 77, 131
Nardi, B. 51, 85
Neustadtl, A. 166
Neustaedter, C. 155, 158
Nie, N. H. 165
Nissenbaum, H. 121
Nonnecke, B. 98
Norman, D. 19, 51

Norton, H. 65
Nye, D. 32–3

O'Hara, K. 153, 155, 158
Oksman, V. 69
Oldenburg, R. 85
Oliveira, M. 108, 110
Oosterwegel, A. 119
Orff, J. 144
Orleans, M. 167
Osborne, K. K. 88
O'Shea, T. 63
O'Sullivan, P. B. 8, 69
Ottoni, R. 137

Palfrey, J. 130
Palmer, A. 96
Paolillo, J. C. 78
Papacharissi, Z. 108, 110, 126
Pariser, E. 40
Park, D. 61
Park, E. 135
Park, S. G. 135
Parks, M. R. 108, 114, 117, 126, 148, 150, 170
Pascoe, C. J. 159, 164
Pearce, K. E. 109
Pennington, N. 125, 128, 135, 136
Pentzold, C. 88
Pinch, T. J. 44
Plato 28
Popcorn, F. 43
Postman, N. 43
Postmes, T. 133
Powers, W. 13
Preece, J. 66, 83, 90, 94, 98
Probst, T. M. 8, 10
Puller, S. L. 152
Purcell, K. 73
Puro, J.-P. 5
Putnam, R. 82, 92, 104

Qiu, J. 22
Quan-Haase, A. 100, 162, 163

Rabby, M. 150–1
Rafaeli, S. 7, 62, 69
Rahaniemi, H. 26
Rainie, L. 22, 110, 128
Rains, S. 92

Rakow, L. 47
Ramirez, A., Jr. 29
Ramos-Vielba, I. 78
Rautianinen, P. 75, 162
Rawlins, W. K. 170
Raynes-Goldie, K. 89, 133, 170
Resnick, P. 89
Rheingold, H. 81, 84–5, 100
Ribak, R. 47, 164
Rice, R. E. 53, 62, 63, 66, 103, 104, 107, 165
Ritchie, T. 136
Roberts, L. D. 114, 117, 150
Robinson, J. P. 166
Rubens, S. 155
Rudder, C. 139
Russell, D.W. 93, 94, 95, 96
Russo, R. 47
Ryan, T. 161

Sandvig, C. 138, 153
Sarch, A. 163, 164
Savicki, V. 67, 75
Schegloff, E. 12
Scherlis, B. 15
Scherman, A. 107
Schouten, A. P. 134
Schuler, D. 84, 85
Schultz, J. 130
Schwartz, R. 91
Senft, T. 122–3
Seo, M. 62
Sessions, L. 105, 166
Sessions-Goulet, L. 105
Sharabi, L. L. 153, 157, 164
Shea, V. 65
Sheer, V. C. 170
Shifman, L. 70, 87
Shklovski, I. 106
Short, J. 59, 60
Shumaker, E. M. 135
Siegel, J. 61
Silver, D. 77
Silverstone, R. 53
Slater, D. 67, 76, 131
Slauson, G. J. 171
Smith, A. 107, 110, 115
Smith, C. B. 88
Smith, M. 96
Smith, P. 49–50

Snyder, J. 171
Sobule, J. 96
Solove, D. J. 121, 122, 134
Song, H. 139
Spears, R. 63, 132
Spigel, L. 28, 39, 41
Spohr, H. 93
Spooner, T. 128
Sproull, L. 62
Stafford, L. 151, 157
Standage, T. 13, 38–9, 113, 117, 120
Steiner, P. 37–8
Steinfeld, C. 91, 125, 152
Steinkuehler, C. A. 85, 92
Stephenson, N. 26
Stivale, C. 90
Stoll, C. 34–5, 82
Stone, A. R. 118, 120, 135
Stross, C. 120–1
Sturken, M. 5, 25, 34, 48
Stutzman, F. 122, 123, 136
Sudweeks, F. 7, 62, 69
Sundén, J. 5
Sveningsson, M. 5
Szcypula, J. 15

Tajfel, H. 98
Talmud, I. 117, 150
Tang, G. 107
Taylor, D. A. 148
Thomas, D. 5, 25, 34, 48
Thom-Santelli, J. 136
Thurlow, C. 59
Tiidenberg, K. 87
Toller, P. 160
Toma, C. L. 129, 137
Tomic, A. 59
Tönnies, F. 83
Tosun, L. P. 128
Trubshaw, R. 16
Tufekci, Z. 109
Turkle, S. 3, 32, 119–20, 139, 165
Turner, J. C. 98
Turoff, M. 63
Turtiainen, J. 69
Tuszynsku, S. 85
Twenge, J. M. 128

Uimonen, P. 76, 126, 132
Ullman, E. 147
Utz, S. 134

Vadrevu, S. 123
Valenzuela, S. 103, 104, 107, 109–10
Valtysson, B. 106
Van der Heide, B. 91, 135
van Dijck, J. 52
Vitak, J. 87, 89, 152
Vorderer, P. 139

Wagner, L. M. 92
Wajcman, J. 51, 52
Walker, M. B. 166
Walker, R. 5
Walster, G. W. 116
Walther, J. B. 10, 61, 63, 64, 91, 92, 115, 116, 123, 133, 141, 145, 146, 147
Watzlawick, P. 145
Wellman, B. 5, 91, 93, 100, 103, 162
Welser, H. T. 96, 97
Wenger, E. 86
Westerman, D. 91
Whittemore, G. 71
Whitty, M. 128, 130
Whyte, W. H. 105
Wiemann, J. M. 59
Wilkinson, D. 91
Williams, D. 85, 92
Williams, E. 59
Williams, R. 46
Wilson, C. 109
Witte, J. 162
Wolak, J. 48
Wright, K. B. 92, 152
Wynn, E. 131

Xenos, S. 161

Yang, J. 73
Yttri, B. 154
Yun, H. 125, 153, 170

Zabriskie, R. 167
Zhang, Y. B. 156
Zimmerman, T. 155
Zuckerberg, M. 124

General index

4Chan 87

acronyms 68–9, 86, 90
Active Worlds 17
addiction 53
affordances 56, 136, 140, 168, 172, 175,
   178
   and disembodied identities 118
   and hyperpersonal communication
      146
   and social identity 132
age
   cross-age friendships 117–18
   and internet use 21, 98
   and relational media use 132, 161,
      162
algorithms 138–9, 176
alphabet
   development of the alphabet 52, 78
   and Unicode 78
America Online 20, 112
"Ann Landers" 33–4, 36, 38, 42, 43,
   53–5
anonymity 34, 37–9
   and social cues 61, 62
   and social identity 132, 133
   and social support 92
appearance
   influence of others on 133–4
   matching hypothesis 116
   and online dating sites 129
   and social cues 61
Arab Spring 107, 109
ARPANET 14, 68
Arto 153
ASCII 70, 78
AsianAvenue 18
asynchronicity 8–9, 12, 13, 15–16, 172

and dating relationships 164
and group communication 8, 110
and self-disclosure 147
and social cues 60–1, 69, 79
and technological determinism
   27–8
audiences, disembodied 121–3, 171
authenticity 24, 38, 43, 82, 106, 178
avatars
   female 44–5, 76
   self-presentation 126
   stealing 120–1

BlackPlanet 18, 99, 131
Black Twitter 77
blogs 17, 95, 101
   languages of 78–9
   political 106, 108
bonding capital 92, 93
bridging capital 92, 93
broadband, access to 21–2
Bronze, The 85, 97, 98
Buffy the Vampire Slayer 85

Catfish 25, 113
chat 1, 13, 14, 15, 73
   and relational development 149
children and internet use 47–51,
   167
civic engagement 82, 84, 103–6, 111
communication imperative 64
CompuServe 20, 63
conflict
   and "friending" 170
   using the internet to handle 169
contextual influences
   on online communication 74–9
cross-age friendships 117–18, 163

cross-sex friendships 105, 117–18,
    142–3, 147–8, 149, 150, 163
cultural identity 76–9
    and relational media use 161–2
cultural influences 172–3
cyberaffairs 42, 120
cyberbullying 49
cyperspace 26, 84
    myth of 174–9
Cyworld 18, 125, 170

Daily Kos 95
dating sites 114–15, 126, 129
    norms 137–8, 139
"Dear Abby" 33–4, 38, 43, 53, 54, 55
deception 34
    and disembodied identities 118–20
digital divide 20–1
disembodied audiences 121–3, 171
disembodied identities 118–21
domestication of technology 26–7,
    52–6, 111
dystopian perspective 32–3, 41–3, 51,
    52, 53–4, 103, 172

electricity 2
emails 1, 4, 7, 13, 15, 71, 73, 136
    and friendships 149, 163, 169
emojis 68, 78
emoticons 68, 72, 116
emotional support 93–4, 95
esteem support 94
ethnicity
    and cultural identity 76–7
    and social networking sites 56

face-to-face communication (F+F) 1,
    11, 12, 72
    and honesty 140–1
    and internet use 166
    and mediated communication 57,
        58, 59, 61, 63–4, 71, 175, 177
    presence of communication
        technologies during 167, 168,
        169
    and relational intimacy 163
    and social norms 62
Facebook 4, 8, 18, 26, 87
    antagonism on 66
    and disembodied audiences 123

ending relationships on 159, 160
    friendships 153
    groups 85, 86
    honesty on 130
    latent ties 114
    lens model analysis of profiles 135–6
    and political engagement 107, 109,
        110
    privacy settings/policies 122, 136–7
    and relational development 115, 121
    self-presentation on 124–5, 126–7
    and the social construction of
        technology 46
    and social cues 67
    and social identity 99, 131
    social norms 89, 91
    social support 94
    and storage 12
    and technological determinism 27,
        40
    Timeline 137
families
    effects of internet use on 24, 41–2,
        165, 167, 174
FanNation 99
fans 143, 170
    communities of 8, 90, 97, 101
FAQs (Frequently Asked Questions)
    files 89–90
Farside MUD 124
flaming 58, 64–7, 72, 88, 99
Flickr 18
FourSquare (now Swarm) 4, 18, 105
friending norms 89
friendships 36, 99–100, 143–51, 168
    cross-sex friendships 105, 117–18,
        142–3, 147–8, 149, 150, 163
    and mediated relational
        maintenance 151–68
    online and face-to-face 143–5, 150
    relational development 147–51
    same-sex 150
    unfriending 160
Friendster 56, 89, 125

games/gaming 1, 4, 81
    and families 167
    MUD games 16
    role-playing 17, 76, 85, 120–1, 124,
        167–8

Gaydar 139–40
gender 74–6, 177
    cross-sex friendships 105
    female avatars 44–5, 76
    and flaming 65–6, 67
    and internet use 22, 98
    and media choice 161, 164–5
    and online communities 83
    and relational development online
        128, 130
    and the social construction of
        technology 47
    and social cues 61
Google 16, 18, 26, 132
    Google+ 66, 125
    and the "Right to be Forgotten" law
        134–5
    and technological determinism 27,
        38, 40
Grindr 94, 105

hashtags 106
Her 25
honesty 34, 63, 124, 127–30, 140–1,
    176
    influence of platforms on 136–9
humor 68–70, 87, 90, 125, 136
hyperpersonal communication
    145–7

identities 80, 177
    authenticity of 24, 38, 43
    cultural 76–9
    gender 74–6
    groups 101–2, 177
    identity demarginalization 94
    multiple 5
    personal 61, 118
    and relational development online
        113, 118–23
    shared 96–9
    social 58, 98, 99, 118, 130–3
    and social cues 9–10, 10, 12, 57–8,
        61–2
imgur 87
immediacy 69, 70, 71–2, 73
Indie-Go-Go 95
informational support 94–5
Instagram 18, 67, 74, 87, 90, 123
    self-presentation 125

Instant Messaging (IM) 1, 7, 8, 10, 13,
    15, 166
    and friendships 169
    and gender 75
    and language 72, 73
    and technological determinism 29
    and writing 71
interactivity 7, 176
Internet Connectedness Index 22
Internet Relay Chat 15
intimacy
    critical intimacy cues 12
    and self-disclosure 148
It's a Trap! 97

Kickstarter 95, 96
knowledge communities 93

LambdaMOO 16, 74, 90
language 68–70
    cultural identity and language
        78–9
    and gender 74–6
    influence of platforms on 137
    as a mixed modality 71–4
    and online groups 84–5
    and relational development online
        116
    and shared practices 86–7
Last.fm 117, 119, 131, 165–6
    and relational development 149,
        154, 163
    self-presentation 125, 126
latent ties 114
LiveJournal 18, 78, 89
locative media 18, 105
Lolspeak 86
LunarStorm 18
lurkers 97–8

mailing lists 13, 15, 18
marginalized identities 94, 95
marriage 36
    and the cyberaffair 42, 120
    effects of gaming on 168
    and relational development online
        117, 120
    and the social shaping of technology
        54–5
matching hypothesis 116

media choice
    and technological determinism
    29–32
media ideologies 159
media multiplicity
    and relationships 159, 160–5
Media Richness Theory 59, 60–1
Meme 67, 70, 87, 108
metadata 97
micro-celebrities 122–3
MiGente 18
MMORPGs 17, 85
mobile phones 1, 7, 19, 172
    and civic engagement 104
    domestication of 53
    and humor 69
    and locative media 18
    and mobility 11–12, 13
    percentage of mobile phone use
        21–2
    and privacy 5
    public conversations 171–2
    and relationship norms 167, 168,
        169
    and the social construction of
        technology 46–7
    and surveillance 4
    and technological determinism 35
    see also text messaging (texting)
mobility of media 11–12, 13, 110–11, 176
    and cultural anxieties 24–5
MOOs 16, 114, 118–19
moral panic 47–51
MUCKs 16
MUDs (Multi-User Domains) 16, 76,
    118–19, 124
MySpace 18, 89, 125, 126, 131, 153
    "Top 8" feature 170

nationality 177
    and relational development 131–2
Net, The 25
netiquette 65
network support 93, 100–2
networked collectivism 101–2
networked individualism 100
Neuromancer 26
New Yorker, The
    cartoons 33, 35, 37–8, 41–2, 44, 45,
        55

norms
    development of 178–9
    enforcers of 134
    and flaming 66–7
    influences of platforms on 137–8
    and media choice 172–3
    and relational development online
        117
    shared practices 86–91, 101
    and social cues 62, 63
    uncertain 168–72

Occupy 107, 108
Oprah 83, 94
Orkut 56, 126, 132
oversharing 171–2

peer groups 161–2
PEN 84
Pepper Spray Cop 108
Pinterest 137
The Pirate Bay 86–7, 90
PLATO 14
play 69, 70, 74
political engagement 20, 82, 106–10
polymedia 19, 172
postal mail
    and relational development 149
privacy 5, 25, 121–3, 136–7, 171
prodigy 20
protest movements 86, 107, 109
public identities 122–3
punctuation 67, 68, 72, 116

race
    and cultural identity 76–7
    and gaming 76
    and internet use 21, 38–9
    and relational development online
        117, 131, 132
    and social cues 61
radio 40, 46
Ravelry 99
reach of digital media 11, 13, 176
Rec.arts.startrek.current 64–5
Rec.arts.tv.soaps (r.a.t.s.) 86, 88, 90,
    96–7, 98–9, 114, 127
Reddit 67, 87
reflective messages about technology
    25

replicability 10, 24, 140, 176
  and social support 110
role-playing games 17, 76, 85, 120–1,
  124, 167–8
romanticism 114
Runescape 124

Second Life 17, 124, 147
self, the 3
  and disembodied identities 118–21
  and social cues 61
self-branding 122–3
self-disclosure 63, 125, 127, 146–7,
  147–8, 149, 152
selfies 5, 50, 67, 74, 90
self-perception 139–40
self-presentation 124–33, 140, 176
sexism 112
sexting 49, 50
sexual predation 48–9
shared identities 96–9
shared practice 86–81
sharing
  and social network sites (SNSs)
  153–4
Sina Weibo 18
SixDegrees.com 18
Skype 10, 12, 41, 67
SMS see text messaging (texting)
Snapchat 10
SNSs see social network sites (SNSs)
soc.culture.indian 76
social capital 91–2
  see also bonding capital; bridging
  capital
social construction of technology
  (SCOT) 11, 26, 44–51, 51
social cues 9–10, 12, 24, 79, 172, 176
  putting into digital communication
  67–71
  reduced 58–64, 146, 151
  and relational development 150
  and technological determinism
  34–5, 38, 40, 57–8
social identities 58, 98, 99, 118, 130–3
Social Identity Theory of
  Deindividuation effects (SIDE)
  132–3
social influences 172–3
Social Information Processing (SIP)

and relational development online
  115, 116–17, 141
social integration 93
social isolation 43
social network sites (SNSs) 1, 8, 13, 17,
  18, 81, 100–1
  ending/aftermath of relationships
  on 159, 160
  "friending" in 168, 170
  and mediated relational
  maintenance 151–4
  and personality traits 161
  and political engagement 107,
  109–10
  and relational development 114, 115,
  172
  self-presentation 125–6
  and social identities 99
  social norms 89, 91
  social support 92
  user names 124–8
social penetration 148
Social Presence Theory 59–60
social shaping perspective 26, 51–2,
  54–6, 111
social status
  erasure of information about 40,
  44
social support 24, 62, 91, 92–6, 103
socioemotional communication 62,
  63, 116–17
Socrates 28, 32, 33, 34, 78
space, sense of 84–6, 101
spam 16, 90
Sparta Networks 83
speech
  communities 86–7
  and online language 71–2
spelling 69, 70, 72, 116
Spotify 18, 119, 136
storage 10, 12–13, 140, 176
  and cultural anxieties 24
subcultural capital 93
support groups 8
surveillance 4, 50
Survivor 93
Swarm (FourSquare) 4, 18, 105
Swedish independent music 86, 101,
  142–3
synchronicity 8, 12, 13, 16

and group communication 8, 110
and honesty 136
and self-disclosure 147
and social cues 59, 69
and technological determinism
   27–8

Talk 15
tangible aid 95–6
tastes 126, 132
technological determinism 26, 27–44,
   51, 79, 111, 174–6
teenagers 48–9, 50
   and honesty online 130
   and privacy 121–2
telegraph 1, 2–3, 26, 46
telephones 2, 11, 13
   and communication 57, 58–9
   and dating relationships 162–3,
      163–4
   domestication of 52, 54
   and internet use 166
   and relational development 149, 159
   and technological determinism 29,
      34, 40–1
   see also mobile phones
television 41–2, 74
   and online groups 85, 88
temporal structure 8–9
text messaging (texting) 1, 4, 71, 166,
   172
   and gender 75
   and language 72
   and relational development 149,
      159, 162
   social construction of 46–7
   and social cues 67–8
   temporal structure 8
trolling 65–6, 67
Tumblr 18, 87, 125
Twitter 5, 50, 67
   attacks on women 65–6, 76
   Black Twitter 77
   groups 86

hashtags 106
language of profiles on 137
and political engagement 110
and privacy 122
and relational development 121, 123
shared practices on 86–7
and the social construction of
   technology 46
and social cues 69
and the social shaping of technology
   52
and technological determinism
   27–8, 35
temporal structure of 8

unfriending 160
Unicode 78
Usenet groups 16, 17, 18, 64, 76, 81
   honesty on 127–8
   and personal relationships 114
   shared identities 97
   shared practices 88
   social support 92, 94
user names 124–5
utopian perspectives 32, 33, 40–1, 51,
   52, 172
   and online relationships 112–13

web boards 1, 17
websites 13
Well, The 81
Wifi 104–5
Wikipedia 17, 88
Wikis 17–18, 89–90
Wordpress.com 79
World of Warcraft 16, 17
writing 2, 58, 71–4, 149

Xbox Live 161

Yahoo! 18, 73, 77, 103
YouTube 4, 7, 18, 65, 67, 101, 123, 171
   and community 82, 83
You've Got Mail 25, 147